Making Movies with Your PC

Other Prima Computer Books

Available Now!

1-2-3 for Windows: The Visual Learning Guide
WINDOWS Magazine Presents: Access from the Ground Up
Adventures in Windows
CompuServe Information Manager for Windows:
   The Complete Membership Kit & Handbook (with two 3 $1/2$" disks)
CorelDRAW! 4 Revealed!
Create Wealth with Quicken
WINDOWS Magazine Presents: Encyclopedia for Windows
Excel 4 for Windows: The Visual Learning Guide
Excel 5 for Windows: The Visual Learning Guide
Free Electronic Networks
WINDOWS Magazine Presents:
   Freelance Graphics for Windows: The Art of Presentation
Harvard Graphics for Windows: The Art of Presentation
Improv 2.1 Revealed! (with 3 $1/2$" disk)
Lotus Notes 3 Revealed!
Microsoft Works for Windows By Example
PageMaker 5 for Windows: Everything You Need to Know
Quicken 3 for Windows: The Visual Learning Guide
Smalltalk Programming for Windows (with 3 $1/2$" disk)
Superbase Revealed!
Windows 3.1: The Visual Learning Guide
Windows for Teens
Word for Windows 2: The Visual Learning Guide
Word for Windows 2 Desktop Publishing By Example
Word for Windows 6: The Visual Learning Guide
WordPerfect 5.1 for Windows Desktop Publishing By Example
WordPerfect 6 for Windows: The Visual Learning Guide
Your FoxPro for Windows Consultant (with 3 $1/2$" disk)

Upcoming Books

WinFax PRO 4: The Visual Learning Guide
Microsoft Office in Concert
Visual Basic for Applications Revealed!

How to Order:

Individual orders and quantity discounts are available from the publisher, Prima Publishing, P.O. Box 1260BK, Rocklin, CA 95677-1260; (916) 786-0426. For quantity orders, include information on your letterhead concerning the intended use of the books and the number of books you wish to purchase. For individual orders, turn to the back of the book for more information.

Making Movies with
Your PC

Robert Hone
and
Margy Kuntz

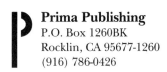

Prima Publishing
P.O. Box 1260BK
Rocklin, CA 95677-1260
(916) 786-0426

Prima Computer Books is an imprint of Prima Publishing, Rocklin, California 95677

Executive Editor: Roger Stewart
Managing Editor: Neweleen A. Trebnik
Acquistions Editor: Sherri Morningstar
Project Editor: Stefan Grünwedel
Technical Reviewers: Fred Gault, San Francisco Canyon Co.;
                    Joyce Chung and Nicholas Schlott, Adobe Systems Inc.
Storyboard Illustrator: John Kirkpatrick
Production: Blue Moon Design
Cover Production Coordinator: Kim Bartusch
Indexer: Brown Editorial Service
Cover Artist: Ocean Quigley
Cover Designer: Page Design, Inc.

ISBN: 1-55958-389-4

Library of Congress Card Number: 93-85019

Printed in the United States of America

94 95 96 97 RRD 10 9 8 7 6 5 4 3 2 1

CONTENTS

FOREWORD

The appearance of digital video is an important event for those of us who believe our desktop computers have more value to offer us than we have yet realized. Regardless of our jobs or the applications we use, the real value of computers is that they help us communicate—far more quickly, efficiently, and persuasively than we could a decade ago. The communicative abilities of computers have steadily improved, making high-quality digital typefaces and extraordinary graphics available to everyone.

But computer access to motion and sound has been slower to arrive. Without them, the computer's promise has only been partially fulfilled. We live in an age dominated by television, and there can be do doubt that video is the most persuasive of all communication technologies. Microsoft's Video for Windows and Apple's QuickTime for Windows at last give us a solid platform for computer-based video.

Anyone interested in exploring this exciting new technology, beginner or professional, should find Robert Hone's and Margy Kuntz's *Making Movies with Your PC* a superb resource. The novice will appreciate the authors' lucid explication of the principles of digital video and video editing, as well as his evaluations of available hardware and software. Especially helpful is the book's step-by-step guidance through the many steps involved in creating digital movies with Adobe Premiere for Windows.

Experienced video professionals will also find many stimulating ideas here, ranging from advice on technical topics (such as the use of special effects, music, and audio mixing) to useful suggestions on planning, shooting, and recording source video, as well as assembling specific features such as group discussions and product demonstrations. Common sense and experience are evident on every page.

And therein lies the true value of this book. In the next few years, as faster boards and more powerful application software appear, we will still need to ask the right questions and make the right decisions to create compelling results. Bob Hone's and Margy Kuntz' goal is to teach us more than how to make movies; they want us to make movies that people will respond to. A successful documentary filmmaker, Bob Hone knows that technology is the means to an end, and that end is communication.

John Warnock
Chairman and Chief Executive Officer
Adobe Systems Incorporated

ACKNOWLEDGMENTS

We would like to thank the folks at Prima Publishing—among them, Roger Stewart and Stefan Grünwedel—for their patience, encouragement, and enthusiasm. And we'd like to thank John Kirkpatrick for his clear and helpful illustrations throughout the book.

Many thanks to Matt Wagner, our agent at Waterside Productions, for pulling the deal together and getting Prima involved in the project.

A special thank-you goes out to the programmers at Microsoft, Adobe Systems, and HSC for creating some dazzling programs. We would also like to thank Creative Labs and Truevision for allowing us to review their products.

Many thanks to Steven Kirsh and Stacy Russell for taking part in the video production for this book and for lending their images to the project.

Special thanks to the video producers, directors, cameramen, writers, and most of all, the editors we've had the good fortune to work with over the years: Paul Shain, Herb Ferrette, John Nutt, Georgia Smith, Ray Telles, Joey Kwong, John Claiborne, Greg King, Brad Cochrane, Michael Chin, Michelle Riddle, Jennifer Gilbert, John Andretti, Laurie Simms, Bill Swan, Helen Silvani, Joan Saffa, Michael Tobias, Ken Ellis, Michael Schwarz, Spencer Michels, Robert Hillman, Tom Levenson, Michael Katz, and Michal Conford. All that we know about the video business we've learned from you.

Finally, we would like to thank our families—Tack and Ann Kuntz, and Jack, John, and Rich Hone—for their encouragement and support. You have been a source of never-ending strength.

INTRODUCTION

We are witnessing the convergence to two influential technologies: computers and video. Powerful and increasingly inexpensive semiconductor chips have made it possible to capture and manipulate video images on a PC.

It is as if it's 1986 and desktop publishing has just gotten off the ground. So many tools to work and play with! But while the tools are new, the craft of communicating with moving images has a tradition stretching back 80 years. The language of the moving image, the language of film and television, has its own rules, its own grammar. The goal of this book is to give you a sense of that grammar and how to use the power of the video medium to communicate your ideas and concepts.

This book consists of 14 chapters organized into three main parts. After an introductory chapter, Part I provides a basic overview of video, Microsoft Video for Windows, and Adobe Premiere for Windows—a digital video editing program. Part II, consisting of Chapters 6–10, delves more deeply into the craft of video editing. Advanced topics in video production and editing are covered in Part III, Chapters 11–14.

The chapters break down as follows:

Chapter 1, "Working in the Visual World," provides an overview of the craft of video editing and the impact of digital video.

Chapter 2, "Getting Started with Digital Video," covers the basics of working with Video for Windows.

Chapter 3, "The Picture Tells the Story," discusses the various types of shots used in video production to give a sense of the video lingo.

Chapter 4, "Editing Your Movies," explains how to use Adobe Premiere for Windows to edit digital videos.

Chapter 5, "Beyond the Basics," covers intermediate editing techniques in Adobe Premiere for Windows.

Chapter 6, "The Grammar of Visual Storytelling," explores the world of visual storytelling and the language of film.

Chapter 7, "Tricks of the Trade I: Editing a Group Discussion," is a step-by-step explanation of how to edit a digital movie of a group discussion.

Chapter 8, "Tricks of the Trade II: Producing a Short Product Demonstration," provides a detailed explanation of how to produce a short digital movie that incorporates video, music, and graphics.

Chapter 9, "Montages and Mixed Formats," explores the use of impressionistic editing techniques to produce evocative video segments.

Chapter 10, "Special Effects Wizardry," covers the bewildering array of visual special effects possible with Adobe Premiere and Digital Morph.

Chapter 11, "Advanced Audio Editing Techniques," explains how to edit an elaborate soundtrack to complement a video segment.

Chapter 12, "Getting Good Stuff to Work With," is an extensive primer of basic video production techniques.

Chapter 13, "Working with Digital Video: Compression, Input, and Final Format," provides a detailed look at how to work with digital video.

Chapter 14, "Video and Interactive Multimedia," explores the use of digital movies in interactive multimedia.

Finally, a list of suggested reading material and company information, and a glossary round out the book.

These chapters can be read in sequential order or at random. You may want to have the manuals for specific software products nearby because not all features of these products are covered in full detail.

PART I

VIDEO-EDITING BASICS

To get started making digital videos, you should know three basic things: (1) what digital video is, (2) what kind of shots you can take with a camera, and (3) how to edit those shots together with a digital video-editing program. This part of the book starts with an overview of Microsoft Video for Windows and shows you how you can use it to manipulate digital video. Chapter 3 reviews the different ways you can use a camera to capture action or a scene. Chapters 4 and 5 explain how to edit step-by-step with Adobe Premiere for Windows.

CHAPTER 1

Working in the Visual World

Welcome to the world of visual storytelling. This field, the playground of television and film professionals, used to require a lot of money (usually someone else's) and a lot of skill. But with the advent of digital video software such as Microsoft's Video for Windows or Apple Computer's QuickTime for Windows, and the introduction of low-cost video-editing programs, you can now produce your own video segments right on the computer for a lot less money.

This chapter briefly explains some of the basic elements of digital video as well as the importance of editing in the video production process.

Video Production (Before Digital Video)

The high cost of professional video equipment made it nearly impossible for the average person to learn the basics of video production. Not only were cameras expensive but so were the editing systems used to create the final programs.

Until recently, working with video meant big bucks—really big bucks. Professional video cameras cost at least $30,000. Add to that a set of lights and some sound-recording equipment, and the cost of a complete video production package goes up to $40,000 or more. Just renting this equipment for a single day can set you back $700.

Top-of-the-line camcorders, which produce pictures almost as good as professional cameras, now cost less than $2,500. Lower-end models can be bought for about $1,000. These advances have given millions of people the chance to shoot their own home videos.

But a key part of the video production process has remained difficult and expensive—editing. Standard video-editing systems, which consist of two high-end videotape machines and an edit controller, cost about $20,000. A more sophisticated editing system can run from $50,000 to $200,000.

This means that few people have had the opportunity to learn the skills of video-editing. People who work in the television industry either took classes at a college or university or picked up the necessary skills on the job. Unless you worked at a TV station or video production company (or were independently wealthy), you simply didn't have access to video-editing equipment.

The Digital Video Advantage

Digital video has changed all this. Now with a sufficiently powerful PC (386 or 486 machine), a digitizing board, and a software editing program, you have all the necessary equipment to edit video segments yourself. You can shoot scenes on an inexpensive camcorder, transfer the shots to your computer, and then edit them together. You can add dazzling special effects like the ones you see on television. You can even send your movies to your friends or business colleagues (on a couple of floppies or a removable hard disk) and they will be able to view the movies on their computers.

The type of computer you have affects how your digital videos appear on the screen: the faster the machine, the better the movies look. Therefore, a minimum of a 386 machine is recommended, though a 486 is even better. You also need a large hard drive—a *very large* hard drive. As you'll see in Chapter 13, digital video software does a clever job of reducing the amount of disk space required to store video on your hard drive; but even so, a minute of video can take up as much as 20MB of storage on your hard drive. If you are going to work with many digital videos, you'll probably need at least a 300MB hard drive. The good news is that disk space keeps getting cheaper.

The Revolution Has Started (Almost)

Unfortunately, your videos won't look like the programs you see on television, at least not for a while. There are several reasons for this. First, as you've probably seen, digital videos are still pretty small. This will change as video hardware boards that can produce full-screen movies get more powerful and less expensive. The second reason is a little less obvious and has to do with the nature of the video medium itself.

Although digital video software allows you to cut and paste video clips with ease, having this ability doesn't make you an expert video editor anymore than having a menu of fonts makes you a graphic designer. Working with moving images is unlike anything you've done before. A video editor is a storyteller who weaves his or her tale with pictures—and not just any pictures. The editor must choose among hundreds, sometimes thousands of different video clips. The choices he or she makes determine whether the final production is a finely crafted program or looks like the highlight reel from someone's home video collection.

The Role of Editing

It's not uncommon for filmmakers or video producers to shoot 10 or 20 times more material than they need. This gives video editors lots of options once they start editing the material. The editor filters out the boring or slow-moving portions of a scene and focuses on the key elements that tell the essence of the story. This is called *editing for peak effect.*

One reason why someone else's home videos are often so boring is that they are unedited: you get to see all the mistakes and have to sit through boring scenes that seem to last forever. Viewers have grown accustomed to videos that move quickly from one action to another. They are not used to seeing an event last as long on television as it does in real life.

Removing Dead Time

Many events that take place in real life actually consist of a lot of *dead time.* Consider this situation: A car drives up to a house; the driver parks the car, turns off the ignition, gets out, closes the car door, walks up the front walk, and rings the doorbell. In real time, these actions would take about a minute. But an edited version of the situation could go like this:

Shot of the car driving up (five seconds)

Shot of the car door closing (three seconds)

Shot of the person's finger pressing the button of the doorbell (three seconds)

With these three shots, the editor conveys the key elements of the scene. The viewer fills in the rest of the action (the dead time). This *conceptual compression* is one of the main ways editors make video segments move along quickly. In this case, an action lasting 60 seconds is compressed to 11 seconds.

Here's another example: A woman walks into the ground floor of a skyscraper, waits for the elevator, goes up to the 25th floor, walks down a long hall, and then enters her office. You could shorten this scene a number of ways. Here's one option:

Shot 1: Woman walks into the building (four seconds).

Shot 2: Woman walks out of the elevator on the 25th floor (three seconds).

Shot 3: Woman strolls into her office (three seconds).

In this case, an event that could take three minutes or more (depending on how long she has to wait for the elevator) is shortened to just 10 seconds. The edited segment is almost 20 times shorter than the real situation, but again, the key ideas are conveyed. In fact, the edited version is more interesting because all the slow, unnecessary parts have been removed.

Manipulating Time

If you've ever watched baseball on television, you know how slow the action can be. Everybody waits around for 20 or 30 seconds until the pitcher hurls the ball to the plate. The following example shows how editing can both compress and expand time. The batter has just swung and missed; it's now bases loaded, three balls, two strikes, two out in the bottom of the ninth:

Shot 1: Pitcher gets the ball back from the catcher (two seconds).

Shot 2: Batter kicks the dirt out of his shoes (two seconds).

Shot 3: First baseman yells encouragement to the pitcher (three seconds).

Shot 4: Pitcher raises his arms over his head to start his windup (two seconds).

These four shots condense the slow part of the game. Now comes the key moment—the pitch—and the style of editing changes to expand time and heighten the drama:

Shot 5: The batter wiggles his bat waiting for the pitch (two seconds).

Shot 6: The pitcher continues his windup (one second).

Shot 7: The first baseman crouches down, ready to field a ball hit his way (one second).

Shot 8: The batter steadies his bat (one second).

Shot 9: The pitcher completes his windup and throws the ball (one second).

Shot 10: Close shot is given of a tense expression on the first baseman's face (one second).

Shot 11: Batter swings and hits the ball (one second).

Shot 12: Pitcher's head turns as the ball flies toward first base (one second).

Shot 13: First baseman leaps up and catches the ball (two seconds).

Shots 5 to 13 take 11 seconds to show an action that lasts less than 6 seconds. All together, the edited sequence (shots 1 to 13) lasts about as long as the actual event, but the emphasis is shifted—away from the slow parts and onto the peak moment of the confrontation between the pitcher and the batter.

This is one of the main elements of effective video editing—emphasizing the key aspects of your story and removing or de-emphasizing the nonessential parts. When you think about it, this process is not all that different from writing, where you have to choose the words and phrases that stress the important part of your message. The analogy goes even further. To communicate well with words, you need to present your ideas in a way that other people can understand. That is, you follow the rules of punctuation and grammar, such as using periods, giving each sentence a subject and verb, and not switching tenses in the middle of a paragraph.

Over the last 80 years, the film industry and, more recently, the video industry, have developed their own *grammar*—a set of conventions that both editors and viewers understand.

The Grammar of Video Editing

The language of visual storytelling, the language of video and film, is a fairly recent invention. Until motion pictures were invented near the turn of the century, the world consisted of continuous images. That is, there were never any abrupt changes in what a person saw from one moment to the next.

But once events could be recorded on film and then put together with other images, a new reality emerged, one where the rules of cause and effect no longer held. A person could be in one place and then a split second later be somewhere else.

When silent films using the newly discovered technique of editing first appeared back in the early 1900s, it took awhile for audiences to get the hang of this new reality with all its jumps and abrupt changes in background. But over the last 80 years, viewers have become increasingly sophisticated. Let's go back to the example of the car and the house. People watching the edited segment wouldn't wonder how the driver got out of the car or how he moved to the front door. The fact that these details don't even enter their minds shows that viewers have learned to accept certain conventions or visual shortcuts.

There are many different styles of editing, each with its own slightly different grammar. Continuity-based editing attempts to create (or fabricate) an illusion of reality. The scenes described earlier of the baseball game and the woman in a building are examples of this style of editing. Chapter 6 delves more deeply into the subtle ways you can create a realistic video segment.

Montage editing and mixed format editing work on a more impressionistic level. They involve the combination and juxtaposition of unconnected images to produce a message or an effect. Commercials and music videos are examples of these types of editing. These editing styles are discussed in detail in Chapter 9.

No one convention or editing style applies to every situation. But the grammar of video editing provides a set of guidelines that editors follow as they build their video segments. Underlying the grammar are two basic tenets:

- **Have a message.** Don't just throw any images together. Have a clear goal in mind and choose the shots that fit that goal. This also applies to any special effects you choose to use—they should support your message, not distract the viewer.

- **Avoid confusing the audience.** Whether you are creating an illusion of reality (as in continuity editing) or conveying an idea (as in montage editing), you should avoid making any edits that break the illusion or detract from the message.

Beyond these two general rules, there are a number of other guidelines that can help you make transparent edits and produce coherent video segments. These guidelines deal with the kinds of shortcuts and visual tricks you can use in telling a particular story or conveying a certain message. There's nothing special or concrete about these rules or conventions. In fact, no one ever sat down and said, "This is the way it will be done." Instead, the rules of video grammar are the end result of years of experimentation by editors in film and television. This book, therefore, won't tell you the "right way" to edit any specific scene. The goal, instead, is to give you some guidelines that can help you produce interesting video segments on your PC. With a firm understanding of the basic rules, you'll have a solid background to begin your own experimentation.

Wrap-Up

This chapter has discussed how the advent of digital video has given you access to one of the most powerful and influential techniques known—video editing. With this technology in the hands of perhaps millions of people, who knows what will be created and what new forms of communication will arise? One thing is for sure, many people are going to have a lot of fun trying to find out.

CHAPTER 2

Getting Started with Digital Video

The introduction of digital video standards, like Microsoft's Video for Windows and Apple's QuickTime for Windows, has opened the door to inexpensive desktop video. Digital video lets you create, display, and manipulate video images in real time on your computer. This chapter provides an overview of Video for Windows, describes how it works, and demonstrates how you can use its tools to manipulate video segments on your computer. It also contains a brief discussion of QuickTime for Windows.

The first thing to realize about Video for Windows (VfW) is that it isn't a single application program like Aldus Persuasion or Microsoft Word. Rather, Video for Windows is a set of programs, including:

- VidCap (a video capture program)
- VidEdit (a basic video editing program)
- PalEdit (a color-palette editor, for adjusting the color of your video clips)
- BitEdit (a simple bitmap editor, for enhancing still images, or single frames in your video sequences)
- WaveEdit (a sound editor, for digitizing and editing audio and for creating basic special effects)

- Media Browser (a utility for viewing the clips on Video for Windows' enclosed CD-ROM)
- Video for Windows Converter (a utility for converting movies from Apple's QuickTime format).

The Video for Windows package also includes an updated version of Windows 3.1's Media Player program. Media Player lets you view digital movies, or embed them in files of other application programs, such as word processors or spreadsheets. (Perhaps you've been wondering, like many Windows 3.1 users, why Windows installed that "Media Player" icon in your Accessories group. Now you know!)

Despite this wealth of features, Video for Windows' most important characteristics are not found in any icon. They are found behind the scenes, where Video for Windows provides a file format and a communications standard that let different kinds of hardware and software work together. The goal: bringing video and sound alive on your computer.

System Requirements

To work with Video for Windows, you need a PC-compatible computer system that meets or exceeds the following requirements:

- A 80386SX or higher central processing unit (CPU), with a clock speed of at least 16 megahertz (MHz)
- At least 4 megabytes (MB) of random-access memory (RAM)
- A hard drive with at least 40MB of free space
- A VGA video display board and monitor that can reproduce at least 256 colors at 640 × 480 resolution
- An 8-bit audio board and speakers meeting Multimedia PC (MPC) specifications
- MS-DOS 3.3 or higher operating system
- Windows 3.1 software
- A video capture or digitizing board (if you wish to capture video)

This is the minimum you need. To do serious work with digital video, including capturing video, you should have a faster, "true 32-bit" microprocessor, such as an 80386/33 MHz, 80486, or Pentium, without the *SX* designation. In addition, you should have at least 4MB of RAM, and some video capture boards require at least 8MB. (There is, however, actually an upper limit here: several video boards use compression methods that limit you to no more than 14 or 15MB of RAM. Also be aware that some boards require you to run a higher version of MS-DOS.)

If you will be capturing video, you will want lots of space on your hard disk. A 300MB hard drive just to store digital movies is not out of the question. A gigabyte optical drive is not a bad idea either. The simple fact is that even with Video for Windows' built-in compression standards, video is a memory hog. A one-minute segment of digitized video can take up 20MB of disk space or more.

Finally, you might want to equip your PC with a more sophisticated video display board (such as one that can display between 256 and 16 million colors); a 16-bit sound board, for better quality sound; and perhaps a CD-ROM (Compact Disk–Read-Only Memory) drive for acquiring large video movie files.

Acquiring and Installing Video for Windows

You can buy Video for Windows software as an independent product through retail software outlets. However, many vendors of video capture boards include a free copy of Video for Windows in their packages, so you might want to look at capture boards first. In addition, if you're buying a "multimedia PC" package from scratch, you might find a copy of Video for Windows included in many packages.

Video for Windows installs like any other Windows package:

1. Place the Setup disk in your floppy disk drive.

2. Select the Run command from the Program Manager File menu.

3. In the Run dialog box, type **a:/setup**, substituting your drive letter for the *a*, and press Enter.

4. The setup program will display instructions that guide you through the rest of the installation process.

If you are installing a video capture board, you will probably need to install a "driver" file that lets Windows communicate with the board. You may also need to install configuration or compression software provided with the board. Check the video board's documentation to see what is required. If your board does not come with its own driver file, you may be able to use the driver from your original Windows 3.1 distribution disks.

In either case, install the driver as follows:

1. Open the Main group in the Program Manager window.
2. Double-click the Control Panel icon to open the Control Panel.
3. Double-click the Drivers icon to bring up the Drivers dialog box.
4. Click the Add button and choose the appropriate driver from the list.

These installation routines will normally offer to modify your system software, so that digital video features will automatically become available whenever you restart your computer. In fact, you shouldn't have to worry about any of this software after installing it, unless you want to upgrade to newer versions.

An Inside Look at Digital Video

Although you can use Video for Windows without knowing how it does its job, an overview of the way Video for Windows works can help you understand how to use video on your PC.

The main job of a digital video standard is to coordinate the playback of video and audio on your computer. Video and audio must be kept synchronous, or *in synch*; otherwise, the video will be a jumbled mess of sounds and images, like a badly dubbed foreign film in which the actor's mouth keeps moving after the lines have been spoken.

Keeping video and audio in synch is difficult because today's computers aren't really fast or powerful enough to display video and sound in real time. Video for Windows gets around this problem by handling video in a number of clever ways. To appreciate these digital video tricks, let's first take a look at what makes up a video image.

The Video Image

At its most basic level, video is a series of still images, or frames. Each frame is displayed for just $1/30$ second, but by showing 30 frames each second, video produces the illusion of a continuous image.

To make matters more complex, each frame of video is made up of two fields. An image on a television screen is created by a stream of electrons (produced by the picture tube) that race along the 525 horizontal lines that make up the screen. For a variety of reasons (none of which concern us here), the electron beam traces the odd-numbered lines first (creating the odd field). Once the beam gets to the bottom of the screen, it goes back to the top and traces the even-numbered lines (the even field). This constant switching between the odd lines and even lines is called *interlacing* and is invisible to the viewer. But because of it, each frame of video contains one odd field and one even field.

On a computer screen, however, the entire screen is redrawn, or refreshed, from top to bottom, roughly every $1/60$ second. When you want to show video on a computer screen, your computer has to convert the interlaced video images into noninterlaced images that the computer can understand.

In addition, before an analog video signal can be processed by a computer, it has to be *digitized*—that is, broken up into a collection of individual pixels. A frame of video, when converted to digital data, consists of 480 lines with each line consisting of 640 pixels. If you are working in 8-bit color, then the computer assigns one byte (8 bits) of information for each pixel. This means that to display just one frame of raw video (that is, without any compression), the computer would have to process 307,200 bytes of information. Thirty frames of raw video (one second's worth) amount to about 9.2MB of data, and 10 seconds of video amount to 92.2MB. It adds up awfully fast. If you are working with 24-bit color, then multiply all the previous numbers by three, because it takes three bytes to describe each pixel on the computer screen (instead of one byte per pixel in 8-bit color mode).

Besides eating up every last byte on your hard disk, raw video puts a tremendous strain on your computer. Every second, the computer would have to process and display more than 9MB of data. This is way beyond the capacity of any of today's personal computers.

Video Compression

Computer designers and computer chip makers have been aware of this problem for a long time, so they've developed a solution known as *compression,* which reduces the amount of information needed to show a frame of video. Whereas a second of raw video would take up 9.2MB, a compressed version of the same one second of video might take up only 500K or less. When it comes time to show the compressed images on the computer screen, the images are decompressed before they are sent to the monitor.

There are number of different ways of compressing and decompressing video. Microsoft Video for Windows offers several different compression-decompression schemes (many produced by third-party developers), and many video capture boards employ their own additional, hardware-based methods. For your purposes, Microsoft's video compression methods will meet most of your needs. A detailed discussion of video compression can be found in Chapter 13.

Video for Windows uses several other methods to reduce the size of digital video files. One method decreases your computer's workload by reducing the size of the video that appears on the screen. Typically when you view a digital movie, you see the video in a small window measuring 160 by 120 pixels (about 2.5 inches by 2 inches), which is roughly $1/16$ the full screen on a 13-inch monitor. Some movies will be 240 by 180 pixels (roughly $1/9$ the full screen). If you enlarge the size of the video window, you'll notice that the quality of the picture is reduced.

Even with the small window size, most computers still aren't able to show every frame in a second of full-motion video (which is 30 frames per second). Instead, it shows you only every other frame, or every third frame—depending on the speed of your computer.

Generally speaking, on a reasonably fast 386 or 486, every other frame is displayed. If the frames of the compressed video were each numbered (1, 2, 3, etc.), then only the odd frames (1, 3, 5, 7, etc.) would be shown in the digital movie. A slower machine, such as a 386SX, might only display every third frame, or every fourth frame. To process and display full-motion video, you'll need a relatively powerful video board that provides hardware compression.

Although this might seem like a complicated way of showing video, it is actually one of the more brilliant aspects of digital video. It means that digital movies can be played on any PC-compatible machine that can run Video for Windows. It doesn't matter if you created your movie on a 486DX2/66, it will still run on a 386/25, or even a 386SX/16, albeit at a lower quality in terms of the number of frames that are displayed per second.

Playing Digital Movies: Media Player

The Media Player lets you open digital movies in a window and play them. Through Windows' Object Linking and Embedding (OLE) facility, the Media Player can also play back digital movies inside other applications, like presentations or word-processing documents.

 Media Player and QuickTime for Windows' Movie Player are very similar. Both let you view digital movies and embed them in other applications. However, at the time of this writing, Media Player can play .AVI movies and .MOV movies, while Movie Player can play only .MOV movies. So if you get an error message when trying to open a file, double-check the file type to make sure you're opening an appropriate file format for your player.

You'll find an updated copy of Media Player with the Video for Windows software. Otherwise you can use the copy that Windows 3.1 installed in your Accessories group.

1. Launch the Media Player from the Program Manager by double-clicking its icon.

2. Once the Media Player's window appears on-screen, you can open a digital movie by pulling down the File menu and selecting Open. An Open dialog box appears that lists the digital movies stored on your hard disk. If no movies are listed in the File Name scroll box, use the Directories scroll box to switch to the directory that contains your digital movies.

3. Highlight the name of the movie you want to play and click the OK button. A small movie window will appear, displaying the first frame of the digital movie.

4. Click on the Play button (the small triangular icon located at the bottom-left corner of the Media Player control window) to play the movie.

 You can also launch Media Player by double-clicking the icon for any movie that is an .AVI file (such as the sample Windsurf Clip provided with Video for Windows). If you do this, you will see only a small movie window with no menu bar, and the movie will play automatically. The window closes once the clip has finished. To display the Media Player controls press the Stop button (the button with the small square icon) and double-click the title bar of the window.

Media Player Controls

The Media Player's controls are designed to resemble familiar objects: the pull-down menus and dialog boxes work like those in all Windows programs, while the control-panel buttons are designed to resemble the buttons on a VCR (see Figure 2-1).

Track Bar

The Track Bar runs along the middle of the Media Player control panel. You can use the slider to move through different parts of the movie. By dragging the slider bar to the right, you move to a later point in the movie (time advances from left to right). Drag the slider bar to the left, and you move backward through the movie. You can also use the small arrows to the right of the Track Bar to move through the movie one frame at a time. The button with the triangle facing

Figure 2-1. The Media Player control panel

right moves the movie forward one frame, while the button with the triangle facing left moves the movie backward one frame. These controls are more accurate than the Track Bar and are useful for finding a particular spot in a movie.

Play/Pause Button

The small triangle on the bottom-left side of the window is used to start the movie. Once the movie is playing, this icon switches to an icon showing two vertical lines. Clicking this icon pauses the movie.

Stop Button

The square icon beside the Play/Pause button is the Stop Button. It duplicates the pause function of the Play/Pause Button.

Page Left/Page Right Buttons

The center buttons with two triangles let you step through the movie in approximately 10-percent increments. The button with two triangles facing left moves the movie backward, and the one with triangles facing right moves it forward.

Previous Mark/Next Mark Buttons

The two buttons with an arrow and a vertical line, on either side of the Page Left/Page Right Buttons, are the Previous Mark and Next Mark Buttons. If marks have been set (see the Mark In/Mark Out Buttons description next), these buttons let you jump backward or forward to the nearest mark. If no marks are set, clicking the Previous Mark button will move the Track Bar slider to the first frame of the movie, and clicking the Next Mark button will move the slider to the last frame.

 You can use the Previous Mark and Next Mark Buttons in Media Player to select portions of the video by holding down the ⌈Shift⌋ key when you click on one of the buttons.

Mark In/Mark Out Buttons

The last two buttons along the bottom of the window, which look like half arrows, let you set, or *mark*, new beginning and end points for the movie clip so you can play back an abbreviated version of the movie.

Use the Mark In button to choose a new starting point, called an *In point*, and use the Mark Out button to set a new end point, called an *Out point*.

Other Media Player Features

There are a few other tricks you can do with the Media Player. The following is only a partial list. For more details check the Media Player section in your Video for Windows manual.

- **Resizing the Movie Window:** You can manually resize the movie window by dragging any corner of it. Be careful, though: enlarging or distorting the window often reduces the picture quality of the movie. The frame rate may also decrease, because the computer has to work harder to display a movie in a larger window. To resize a movie without distorting its dimensions, pull down the Media Player's Device menu, choose Configure, and experiment with different combinations of the Full Screen button and the Zoom by 2 check box.

- **Looping and Rewinding Movies:** You can set the movie to play over and over again: Pull down the Edit menu, choose Options, and check the Auto Repeat box. The movie will "loop," or keep repeating, until you click the Pause or Stop button. This option will remain in effect for this and all other digital movies you load, until you clear the check box. You can also have the movie automatically rewind when it gets to the end by selecting the Auto Rewind check box in the Video Playback Options dialog box.

- **Prioritizing Audio and Video Continuity:** In this same Video Playback Options dialog box, try giving priority to video continuity instead of audio continuity: Remove the check mark beside "Skip video frames if behind," click OK, and replay the movie. The Media Player will pause the audio track, if needed, in order to play every video frame. This option will also remain in effect until you recheck this box.

- **Placing a Movie Clip in Another Document:** You can run movies in documents created by other applications. To do this, open the file you want to use, select the Edit Menu, and choose Copy Object. Then select the document in which you want to place the clip, and choose the Paste command from the Edit menu.

Manipulating Digital Movies: VidEdit

So far, you've gotten to play digital movies with Media Player. Now the fun begins. With Video for Windows' VidEdit, you can combine and recombine individual scenes from a movie to create a whole new clip. You can also move portions of the audio around to match the video, crop and resize clips, and compress and resave previously recorded material. We'll first look at the basics of editing—selecting, copying, cutting, and pasting—with VidEdit.

First open up VidEdit by double-clicking on its icon. You'll see that the VidEdit window has some features in common with the Media Player window (see Figure 2-2).

The Playback buttons, Mark Buttons, and Track Bar perform the same functions in both Media Player and VidEdit. The Tool Bar gives you instant access to frequently used VidEdit commands, while the Data Track buttons let you pick the tracks you want to edit. The Status Bar displays information about the video sequence or selected command.

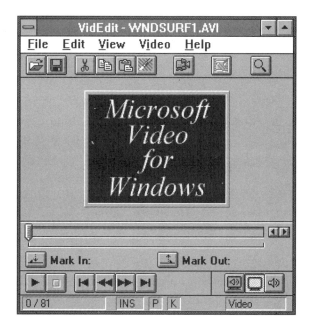

Figure 2-2.   The VidEdit screen

Next, open up a video to work with. In the following examples we'll use the Windsurf clip that comes with Video for Windows. Select Open from the File Menu, then choose Windsurf.avi from the list of files shown in the Open Video dialog box.

Selecting a Portion of the Movie

To start the editing process you need to select a portion of the movie to work with. You can select the entire movie by choosing the Set Selection option from the Edit menu, and then clicking on All in the Set Selection dialog box. But more than likely, you'll want to work with just a portion of the movie. Here's how to do this:

1. Position the slider at the beginning of the portion you want to select, for example Frame 25 of the clip. You can use the arrows to the right of the track bar to move to the appropriate frame. Or you can use the Go To dialog box to set the frame precisely. To access the Go To dialog box, either choose Go To from the Edit menu or double-click the frame number display in the lower-left corner of the Status Bar. Type in the frame number you want and click OK.

2. Set this point as the beginning of your selection by clicking the Mark In button. A small triangle appears under the track bar when you've done this. Move to the point in the movie where you want to end, such as Frame 77, then click on the Mark Out button. Notice that another small triangle shows up marking the Out point. The portion of the slider box between the start and end point turns dark gray to show you that it has been selected:

You can also use the Set Selection option in the Edit menu to set the starting and ending frames. Just choose Set Selection and type in the appropriate frame numbers in the dialog box.

3. If you make a mistake, just move the slider to the new beginning or end point and reclick on the appropriate button. Or access the Set Selection option and type in the new frame numbers. If you want to start from scratch, choose None in the Set Selection dialog box.

4. You can check to see if you selected the right portion by holding down the [Alt] key while clicking on the Play button.

Copying, Cutting, and Pasting Frames

Now that you've selected a portion of the movie, you can move it around and change it using the Copy, Cut, and Paste options under the Edit menu. (You can also access copy, cut, and paste from the Tool bar).

Before we play with these tools, it's important to point out that VidEdit has two different ways of cutting, deleting, and pasting data: Insert mode and Overwrite mode. When you use Insert mode, the Paste command inserts frames between the frames where you're pasting the video. The Cut and Delete commands in this mode remove frames and close the gap between the starting and ending points of your selection, making the movie shorter in length. When you use Overwrite mode, the Paste command pastes the selected frames *over* the old frames, so you cover other material if you're not careful. The Cut and Delete commands in Overwrite mode remove the frames from your selection but don't close the gap. Instead, the last frame before the beginning of the deleted selection is left on the screen until the end of the deleted selection.

 You can quickly see what mode you're in by checking the second box from the left on the Status Bar. If you're in Insert mode, the letters *INS* will appear in the box. If you're in Overview mode, the letters *OVR* will show up in the box. To change between the two modes, just double-click on the letters in the Status Bar.

In the following example, we'll be using the Insert mode to demonstrate the copy, cut, and paste features:

1. Select a portion of the movie using the method described in the previous section.

2. Copy this portion by choosing the Copy option from the Edit menu (or pressing Ctrl-C) or click the Copy icon on the Tool Bar.

3. Move the slider to the far right of the Track Bar (this is the end of the movie).

4. Choose Paste from the Edit menu (Ctrl-V) or click the Paste icon on the Tool Bar. This pastes the copied portion onto the end of the movie.

5. Play the movie to see what you created. If you copied and pasted correctly, the movie will look the same as the original until you get to the end, then you'll see the portion of the movie you added.

6. Now select the portion you just pasted by position the slider bar at the point where the pasted portion begins. Click the Mark In button, then move the slider to the end of the movie and click the Mark Out button.

7. Choose Cut from the Edit Menu (Ctrl-X) or click the Cut icon on the Tool Bar.

8. Play the movie again. The pasted section is gone, and you're back to where you started.

You can also cut, copy, and paste frames from one movie into another. Just open up a movie, make your selection, and copy or cut the selection. Then open the second movie, move the slider to the point where you want to insert the frames, and choose Paste.

Note

If you're moving frames between movies that are different sizes, you will get a message asking you if you want to stretch new video to be the same size as the old video. If you choose Yes, the new video may be distorted. If you choose No, then only the portion of the new video that fits into the frame of the old video will be shown. To avoid these problems you may want to use the Crop option in the Video menu before cutting and pasting between movies.

Saving Copies and Portions of Movies

It's a good idea to make a copy of a movie before you make any major changes to it. That way, you'll be able to go back to the original in case you make a mistake and delete something you need. To make a copy, choose the Save As option under the File menu and set the drive, directory, and filename for the file. You now have a duplicate copy of the original movie, which you can cut, paste, and otherwise mangle without worrying about your original.

You'll probably notice the Save Copy box in the Save As dialog box and wonder why you can't just click on the box to save a copy of your movie. You can, but you'll have to give the movie a new name (or location) anyway. The only advantage to using the Save Copy box is that it lets you keep your current movie open while saving the copy in some safe place.

You can also create a new movie based on just a portion of your original movie. Select the portion you want, copy it, choose New from the File menu, and then paste the movie portion into the new movie. You can then store the new movie on your hard disk using the Save As option under the File menu.

Capturing Digital Movies: VidCap

So far, you've been playing with samples of digital movies created by other people. But the real adventure begins when you start working with your own material. You'll need software that let's you bring the video sequences into your computer. Luckily, Video for Windows comes with an application that allows you do this: VidCap. But you'll also need additional hardware that converts video into digital movies. A number of products, called video capture boards, digitize video segments and store them as digital movies.

The number of video boards for PCs is growing insanely fast. When Video for Windows was first released, there were only two or three boards; now there are more than a dozen—with several more on the way. The various capture boards fall into one of three categories, which we've called *Getting Started*, *On Your Way*, and *Pushing the Envelope*. We describe each group briefly here; a more complete review of hardware can be found in Chapter 13.

- **Getting Started:** If you haven't worked with video before and just want to experiment with video on your PC, then you should look at the low-cost options, such as the Video Blaster (from Creative Labs). Low-end boards are generally used to capture small-sized windows at rates up to 15 frames per second (depending on your computer). You may also need to use another board to capture sound.

- **On Your Way:** To capture larger-sized windows (320×240 pixels) at a reasonable frame rate (15 frames per second) you need a board that has some kind of hardware compression assistance. VideoSpigot for Windows (Creative Labs) and the Bravado 16 (from Truevision) are two mid-range boards that allow larger window captures. Some mid-range boards, such as the VideoSpigot, also allow you to capture sound and video at the same time.

- **Pushing the Envelope:** There are a number of boards that use sophisticated compression schemes provided by hardware boards to achieve full-frame, full-motion capture and playback. These boards usually cost at least $1,500, but provide the highest level performance.

Setting Up the Hardware

The basic setup is shown in Figure 2-3. You need a source of video, such as a VCR or a camcorder. The output from the video source is sent by a cable to the input jack of the video capture board. A standard video cable with an RCA plug is sufficient (these can be bought at any electronics supply store, such as Radio Shack). If you are using an S-video deck (Hi-8 for example) and your board allows S-video input, then you will need to use an S-video cable.

Depending on your equipment, you may need to use a separate sound-digitizing board (such as a Sound Blaster or Sound Blaster Pro board) to transfer sound from your VCR into the computer. If this is the case, you will need to connect the audio output from the VCR into the input jack for that board.

It's also handy to have a standard television hooked up to your VCR while you're digitizing (most VCRs have two output ports). This allows you to look at the video images on a full screen before you digitize them.

Each of the video-capture boards comes with its own software product that works in tandem with Video for Windows' capture facilities. Together, these programs also allow you to choose how you want to save your digital movies, and at what level of compression. Unless you are running out of room on your hard disk, it's a good idea to save them at the highest-quality setting (i.e., with the lowest possible compression) that your computer can handle (see the discussion of data-capture rates in Chapter 13). This gives you the option of using any kind of compression scheme later on, without having to go back and transfer from videotape again.

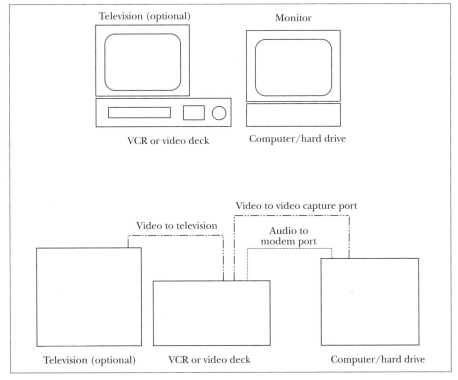

Figure 2-3.   Typical equipment layout. The basic components for working with video on your PC are the computer, a source of video (VCR), a video-digitizing board, and an audio-digitizing device. Sometimes the video- and audio-digitizing devices are contained in the same device.

Using VidCap

Now that you've got the hardware in place you're ready to start capturing some video. There are several steps to capturing a clip, which we go through briefly here. Please refer to your Video for Windows manual if you need additional information.

Setting the Capture File

Double-click on the VidCap icon to launch the program. Then before you actually capture a segment of video, you need to set up a capture file. You specify the amount of disk space that will be set aside for the capture. A typical size might be 5MB for a 15-second capture. If you decide to capture a longer segment of video, which will require more disk space, then VidCap will enlarge the file "on the fly," but you may end up losing frames during the capture. Therefore, err on the side of larger file sizes when choosing the size of the capture file.

Setting the Audio and Video Options

There are a number of different options for capturing audio and video, which are set under the Options menu:

```
┌─────────────────────┐
│ Options             │
├─────────────────────┤
│  Audio Format...    │
├─────────────────────┤
│  Video Format...    │
│  Video Source...    │
│  Video Display...   │
├─────────────────────┤
│ √ Preview Video     │
│  Overlay Video      │
└─────────────────────┘
```

The Audio Format option allows you to set the sample size of the audio capture (usually 8-bit), the number of channels (usually mono), and the frequency (usually 22 kHz). You can also use the Level button to set the volume of the incoming audio signal.

The video options are a bit more complicated but still understandable. The first thing to set is the dimension of the video image. For most of your work you will probably be using 160 × 120 pixel or 240 × 180 window.

You also need to set the number of colors used in the video image. The highest setting, 24-bit RGB, yields more than 16 million colors, but it requires three times the amount of processing and storage required by 8-bit color. The middle setting, 16-bit RGB, uses more than 65,000 colors, which is usually good enough for most video images; but even that requires two times the amount of storage and processing as 8-bit color.

The standard format for most captures is 8-bit palettized, which uses 256 colors. *Palettized* means that you create a custom set of colors, or *palette*, for the capture. A shot of a sunny beach scene will consist of mostly blue and yellow hues, so the palette for that scene will include a wide variety of different shadings for those colors. A forest scene would have mostly green and brown hues and therefore a different palette to best represent those images.

Creating a palette is done with the Palette option under the Capture menu. Choosing this option brings up a dialog box that allows you to select the method of creating a palette:

Since you are going to be working with moving video, you should use the "Start" option to create a palette from a continuous stream of images (or frames). VidCap then captures the colors from the continuous stream and create the optimal palette for that stream of frames. Therefore, it is important to play the section of tape that you actually want to capture when making the palette. After you're finished creating the palette, rewind the tape back to the point on the tape where your shot begins.

If you are capturing video for an important project that will be distributed to a large number of people (i.e., a CD-ROM) then you should try to capture at the highest quality possible (24-bit). You can convert the video clips down to 8-bit later on after you've edited them together and are transferring them to the CD. But if you start with 8-bit captures, you aren't capturing as much information, which limits your options later on when creating the final versions.

Most video decks need about five seconds to produce a stable image. It takes that long for the sensing device (the *playback head*) to achieve the proper speed. This means you should cue the tape to five or six seconds before the actual beginning point of the shot. Press the VCR first, wait five seconds, then click the Start button to create the palette. The same procedure should be followed when actually making the capture itself.

The rest of the options allow you to choose the video source type: Composite (normal) or S-Video (better, but you need an S-Video deck and a capture board that accepts this type of video). And depending on your capture board, you can also modify the video image (hue, contrast, saturation, etc.).

Whew, all those steps and we still haven't captured a frame of video! Thankfully, VidCap remembers your last settings so you generally don't have to set all these options for every capture. You will, however, want to create a new palette for each new section of video.

To sum up, for most captures, you will probably use the following settings:

Sound Format: 8-bit, 22 kHz, mono

Image Dimensions: 160×120 pixels

Image Format: 8-bit palettized

Video Source: Composite, NTSC

Capturing a Video Clip

After you've set the options and captured a palette, making the capture is fairly easy. Choosing the Video option under the Capture menu brings up a dialog box with (oh no!) more options to set:

Capture Video Sequence

Frame Rate: 15.000

☒ Enable Capture Time Limit

Seconds: 5

□ Capture Audio

Capture Method
◉ Directly to Disk
○ Capture to Memory

□ MCI control of source video

OK

Cancel

Audio...

Video...

MCI...

The frame rate is the number of frames per second contained in the digital video clip. Normal (analog) video is 30 frames per second. Unless you have one of the high-end capture boards, you will probably use a frame rate of 10 or 15 frames per second.

 The maximum frame rate you can actually capture is determined by a number of factors including the speed of your computer, the type of capture board, the number of colors you're using, and the image dimensions. A more thorough discussion of these parameters and how they affect frame rate can be found in Chapter 13.

The Enable Capture Time Limit check box allows you to constrain the length of the capture. It's generally a good idea to set this a bit larger than your intended length.

The Capture Method check box allows you choose where the massive amounts of digital video information will be stored. If you have a lot of RAM and the video clip isn't very long (and the image dimensions aren't very large) then choose the Capture to Memory option. Since storing data in RAM is very fast, this will allow you to capture at higher frame rates. Otherwise, capture directly to disk.

When you're done setting the capture options, click on the OK button. You will see one last dialog box. Now, you're finally ready to capture video. Cue the tape to five seconds before the beginning of the video you want to capture (see note on page 30), press the play button on your VCR, wait five seconds, then click on the OK button in the dialog box, and you will be capturing video.

To capture another section of video, create a new palette if the mix of colors is different, cue the tape and then capture away!

 If a message pops up like the one below, it means that your computer couldn't capture the frame rate you requested. Reset the frame rate to a lower value (i.e., 10 frames per second instead of 15 frames per second) and then capture the video again.

Setting Video Compression

If you've made a few captures then you've already seen how quickly you can fill up a hard drive with digital video files. Fortunately, with video compression you can reduce the size of these files significantly. Video for Windows comes with several different methods of compression. Choose the Compression Options item from the Video menu (within VidEdit) to bring up a dialog box that allows you to select a particular method of compression and set compression parameters:

The Target setting allows you to select the playback device for the video clip or movie. This is particularly useful when producing video clips that will be played back from a CD-ROM. Video for Windows then automatically adjusts the amount of compression needed for that playback device.

Which compression method to use depends greatly on the finality of your product. For rough versions of a movie, you might want to use Microsoft Video 1 because it is fast compression method. For final work that will be played from a CD-ROM, you should use Cinepak, which produces a very good image at fairly high levels of compressions. The drawback to Cinepak, however, is that it takes a long time to compress a movie (up to 100 minutes to compress a one minute movie.)

We've only dealt with the basics of compression here. For a slightly more detailed description, please review the Video for Windows manual. If you're still looking for more information, take a look at the compression section in Chapter 13.

Working with QuickTime for Windows

QuickTime for Windows from Apple Computer is another standard (like Video for Windows) for working with digital video information on a PC. Movies stored in the QuickTime for Windows (QTW) format have the .MOV designation as opposed to .AVI. Most full-featured editing programs (such as Adobe Premiere for Windows) allow you to store your final movie in either format. In fact, the formats are fairly similar with the following exceptions:

- QTW movies can be played on both Macintosh and PC computers. This means that you can create movies on one platform (usually the Macintosh) that can be played on both platforms.

- The playback performance for video stored in QTW format is bit better than for the same video stored in VfW format.

The only major disadvantage to QTW is that it does not come with a simple editing program (such as VidEdit). You can only cut and paste portions of clips, you can't modify the palette for an 8-bit movie, for example.

Wrap-Up

In this chapter we covered the basics of digital video, how you can use VidEdit to cut and paste digital video clips, how VidCap lets you create digital video files from videotapes, and how to compress video clips. Now, if you own a camcorder or know a friend who will lend you one, you're ready to start making your own movies. But before you set off to film your epic, you may want to take some time and learn about the various types of shots you can take with a camera, and how they might fit in your movie.

CHAPTER 3

The Picture Tells the Story

Although this book is primarily about editing, you may find yourself directing your video productions as well. Therefore, it's important that you develop a clear understanding of what types of shots you can take with a camera and how to use them in the final production.

This chapter describes the various types of shots and gives examples of when to use each one. *Static shots*, those taken without moving the camera, are described first, followed by a discussion of the different types of shots that can be taken with a moving camera.

The composition of the image is as important in a video shot as it is in a still photograph. The balance of objects on the screen, how large or small something appears, affects how the viewer perceives the image. Deciding what kinds of shots to get with the camera and which elements to include in a shot (the framing of the shot) is the role of the director, and the director's decisions ultimately determine what the editor has to work with.

There are innumerable ways of shooting a particular scene, but a few classifications have been established so that directors, camera operators, and editors can use the same language when talking about particular shots. There are three basic types of shots:

- *Static shots*, which are taken without moving the camera
- *Camera moves*, which include zooms, tilts, and pans
- *Tracking shots*, where the camera (and the tripod) is moved during the shot

Static Shots

Most of the shots you take will be static shots. This doesn't mean you're stuck with only one particular composition or framing. Almost all video cameras come with zoom lenses that allow you to frame shots in a number of ways. The various types of static shots fall into five broad categories: long, full, medium, close, and close-up. In addition to these framing classifications, there are also several terms for describing the composition of people in a frame and the angle of the camera, such as three-quarter shots, reverse shots, and two-shots. The framing terms are described first.

Long Shot

In a *long shot*, the camera is usually located far away from the subject and establishes a scene, showing how the subject fits into the surroundings. The subject appears quite small, especially in a digital video window (Figure 3-1). This type of shot is used quite a bit in feature films that are shown in theaters. Unfortunately, in the small screen size of digital video, most of the details in a long shot can't be seen. Use this shot sparingly and only in scenes that contain a lot of bold features and few details.

Full Shot

The *full shot* is also used to establish a scene, but it shows more of the subject and less of the background. Full shots of people usually show their whole body (Figure 3-2). This shot is not good for seeing facial

Figure 3-1.

A long shot is used to establish a scene or show the subject within the context of his or her surroundings.

Figure 3-2.

A full shot focuses on the subject but also shows a good portion of the surroundings.

expressions because the images are just too small. However, a full shot is useful for capturing a complete motion, such as a person walking across a room.

Because most digital videos are shown in a small window, full shots should contain only a few, clearly visible objects in the picture: for example, two or three people.

Medium Shot

Medium shots are used to show a single person with some amount of his or her surroundings, or to show relationships between people. The basic framing for a medium shot of two or three people extends from their waists to about a foot over their heads. A medium shot of a single person covers from about waist-level to a little bit above the head (Figure 3-3).

This is a good shot to capture bold gestures and expressions. For example, if you are shooting an interview with a man who talks with his hands, a medium shot will capture all his body language.

Figure 3-3.

A medium shot is used to show a group of people or capture movement within a small area. Large facial expressions can be seen but not subtle ones.

Figure 3-4.

A close shot is the standard framing for shooting a person. The viewer's attention is focused on the person's face.

Close Shot

The most common use of *close shots* is to show people's faces. The standard close shot for digital videos is a bit tighter than what you see on television; it extends from about the shoulders to just above the person's head (Figure 3-4). In a close shot, you can clearly see the person's facial expressions and, through them, her emotions.

If you are shooting this shot with a zoom lens, make sure that the camera is on a tripod; otherwise the shot will be jumpy once it is converted to digital format.

Close-Up

This kind of shot is used to show fine details, such as the time on a person's watch. The exact framing for a close-up shot varies according to the material. A close-up of a person's face would extend from just below the chin to the top of the forehead (Figure 3-5). This shot focuses the viewer's attention on the person's eyes (which often reveal the most about a person's emotions or inner feelings). Close-ups are also

Figure 3-5.

A close-up emphasizes a portion of the person's face, usually his or her eyes. It can also be used to show subtle movements, such as a hand turning a doorknob or the second hand moving on a person's watch.

good for showing subtle motions, such as a hand turning a door knob and a finger pushing a button.

Composition of Groups and Camera Angles

As with framing, there are numerous ways to shoot a group of people. Certain types of shots occur frequently and have been given specific names.

Three-Quarter Shot

When you are interviewing someone and you don't want them to talk directly into the camera, position the interviewer, the subject, and the camera as shown in Figure 3-6. This will produce the shot known as the *three-quarter shot* because it shows roughly three-quarters of the subject's face.

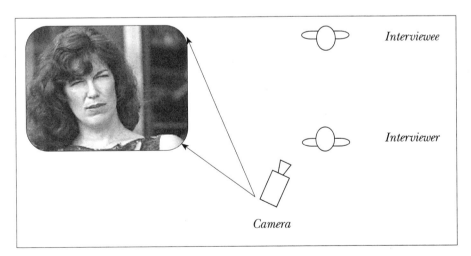

Figure 3-6.   Camera layout and framing for a three-quarter shot: This shot is standard for interviews because it shows a lot of the person's face without having him or her look directly into the camera.

Reverse Shot

The name of this shot describes the direction the camera is pointing as opposed to a particular framing. In an interview setting, the *reverse shot* shows the interviewer (the person asking the questions) instead of the person being interviewed (Figure 3-7). The camera position is reversed to show the reaction of the interviewer.

Two-Shot

The term *two-shot* simply describes a medium shot containing two people (Figure 3-8). It is often used to establish a scene where two people are talking to each other.

Camera Moves

A *camera move* is a shot in which the framing changes in the middle of the shot. For example, you could gradually zoom out from a close-up

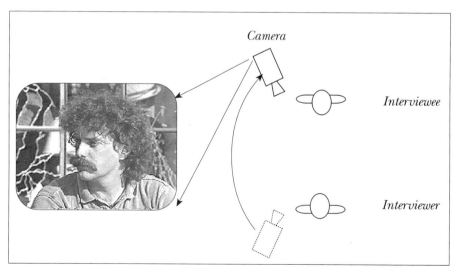

Figure 3-7.   Camera layout and framing for a reverse shot: The camera is moved next to the person being interviewed to show the reactions of the interviewer.

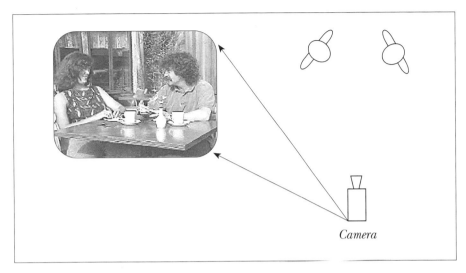

Figure 3-8.   Camera layout and framing for a two-shot: This is a medium shot that shows both parties of a conversation.

to a medium shot. The shot begins with one framing (the close-up) and ends with another (the medium shot). There are a wide variety of camera moves; the basic ones are *zooming, tilting,* and *panning.* Any camera move involves three parts: the beginning framing, the move itself, and the end framing.

 It is especially important to use a tripod for these shots if you want the shots to look smooth and not bumpy after you digitize them. (For more information about why this is important, see the section "Considering the Digital Video Disadvantage" at the end of this chapter).

Zooming

This technique involves pressing the zoom button on your camera while you take a shot. With a zoom, you can change the framing of the shot from, say, a full shot to a close shot. This allows you to focus the viewer's attention on different elements in the scene. For example, let's say you are shooting a city street in a long shot, then you zoom in to one person next to a bicycle on the side of the street (Figure 3-9). The zoom shifts the viewer's attention from the entire street to the single person.

Alternatively, if you start with a medium shot of the single person and then zoom out to show the entire street in a long shot, the focus of attention goes from the individual to the wider scene. A shot that zooms out is often called a *reveal* because it reveals the background or surroundings of the person shown at the beginning of the shot.

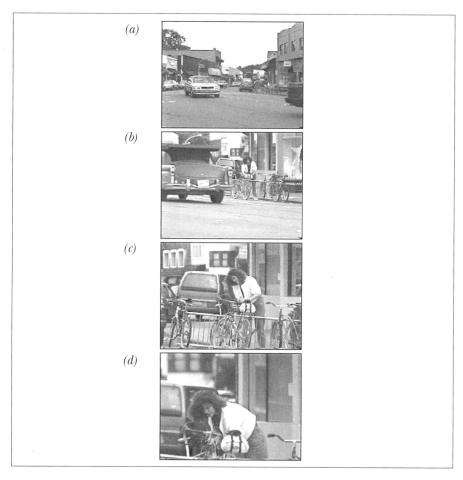

(a)

(b)

(c)

(d)

Figure 3-9. Zooming in: (a) The initial framing shows the entire street; the woman is barely noticeable. Then as you zoom in (b–d), the woman is emphasized more and more until you can't see the street anymore.

Tilting

In this type of shot, the camera is tilted up or down, as the name suggests. This is usually done to show things, such as tall buildings, that won't fit in a single static shot. Another use of this shot is to follow objects that are moving up and down, such as an elevator or machinery. You can also use tilts to shift the viewer's attention from one object to another. For example, say you are shooting two people talking: One person is standing in the street, and the other is leaning out a second-floor window. You could shoot this scene with two static shots, one of each person (Figure 3-10a), but a nice addition would be a shot that tilts up from the person on the ground to the person in the window (Figure 3-10b). This would show the gap between them (which would convey a subtle message if the people were having an argument).

Panning

In a panning shot, you rotate the camera along a level line, left to right or vice versa. These types of shots can be used in a large number of situations.

First, you can use panning shots, or *pans*, to show subjects that are too wide to fit into one shot, such as a large house or a crowd of people. Sometimes you don't have enough room between the subject and the camera to get a full shot of a scene, in which case you can use a pan to show the same thing.

A related use of a panning shot is to show a group of objects in fine detail. One example would be a long jewelry case containing priceless diamonds. To see the whole case might require a medium or maybe even a full shot, but these shots wouldn't provide enough detail of the diamonds themselves. A more attractive alternative would be to shoot a close shot of several diamonds and then pan across the case to show the whole collection.

Another use of a pan is to shift the viewer's attention from one object or person to something else. Let's say you are shooting a woman leaving on a ship as she waves good-bye to her family on the dock (Figure 3-11). By placing the camera behind the family, you can easily pan from the woman on the boat to the family, thereby showing the relationship between the two and leaving the viewer's attention on the

(a)

(b)

Figure 3-10.   (a) This scene can be shot with just two static shots—a close shot of each person. (b) By tilting the camera, you can show the physical relationship between the two people in this scene. The shot starts with a close shot of the person on the ground and tilts up to show the person in the window.

family (Figure 3-12). If you pan from the family to the woman, the viewer's attention is left on the woman.

Yet another major reason for using a panning shot is to follow motion or movement. Earlier in the chapter, the full shot was described as a good way to cover a motion, such as a person walking from left to right. However, if you want to see the person's face to catch her expressions, a full shot won't provide enough detail (Figure 3-13a). Instead, you could shoot the woman in a medium shot and then pan to the

Figure 3-11. Camera pan: The shot starts with a medium shot of the woman on board. Then as the camera pans left, we see a small section of the boat and then the family.

Figure 3-12. Camera layout for a panning shot: The camera is placed behind the woman's family on the dock. The shot starts with a medium shot of the woman on board, then pans left to show the family waving good-bye.

right as she walks (Figure 3-13b). This allows you to follow the motion but also lets the viewers see more of the woman's face than they would in the full shot.

Combining Camera Moves

Any of these three types of camera moves can be combined in a single shot (a zoom out with a pan, a tilt down with a zoom in, etc.). Sometimes a combination of moves is required when shooting a person's motion—for example a woman walking up a spiral staircase. Of course, these shots are more difficult to pull off than a shot that has only one type of move. This is particularly true if the camera moves have to start or finish at a particular point during the shot.

As an example, say you are shooting a woman walking out the bottom floor of a tall skyscraper. An interesting way to shoot this scene would be to start on a full shot looking up at the skyscraper (Figure 3-14). Then as you tilt down the building, you start to zoom in. The tilt and the zoom should be finished just as the woman walks out the door.

This shot requires three things: a smooth start and end to the tilt, a smooth start and end to the zoom, and perfect timing. If done well, this is an intriguing shot that can carry lots of messages (opening with a large foreboding building, tilting down to show how massive the building is, zooming in to focus on the solitary heroine's entrance to the street). If you are going to attempt anything this complicated, practice the shot before you actually record anything. Then, be prepared to try it again and again until you get it right.

Deciding When to Use a Camera Move

You should have a reason for using a camera move in place of two static shots. Moves without a purpose confuse the viewers, leading them down the visual equivalent of a dead end. Plan ahead: Pick a beginning framing and an end framing before you start recording. If there is no movement in the shot other than that of the camera, choose the shot and the angle so that the middle of the shot is interesting as well.

For example, in the illustration of the woman on the boat and her family, if you place the camera at position A in Figure 3-15, the middle of the shot will show just the ship; then more ship; and finally, the fam-

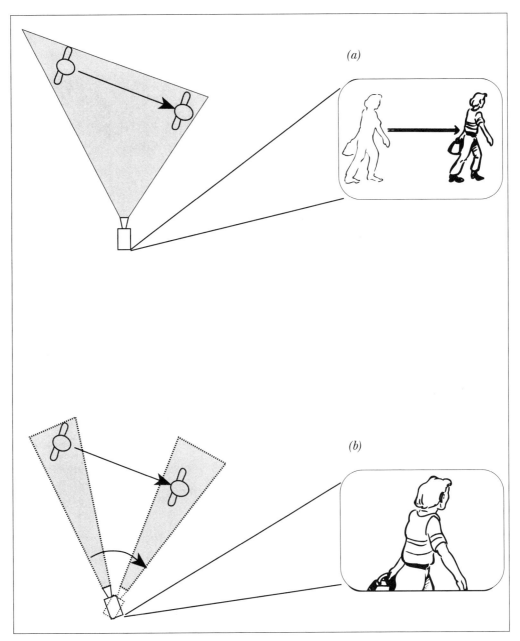

Figure 3-13. (a) Shooting someone walking with a long shot. (b) Shooting someone walking with a panning shot. The shot starts on a medium shot of the person. Then as the person walks from left to right, the camera pans to follow her.

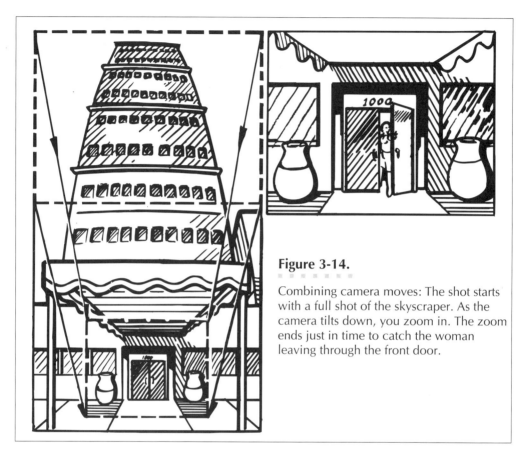

Figure 3-14.

Combining camera moves: The shot starts with a full shot of the skyscraper. As the camera tilts down, you zoom in. The zoom ends just in time to catch the woman leaving through the front door.

ily on the dock. Any connection you wanted to make between the woman and her family will be diminished by the long stretch of the ship. If, instead, you place the camera at position *B* in Figure 3-15, the shot will move quickly from the woman to the family.

When making any type of camera move (pan, tilt, zoom, or a combination), remember to *move slowly*. If you don't have much experience operating a camera, try following this simple rule: If it feels like you're zooming (or panning or tilting) at a reasonable speed, you're probably moving too fast. Slow down until it is *uncomfortably* slow.

There are two reasons for doing this: One, *you* know what you're shooting and what's coming next; the viewers don't. You have to give them a chance to stay with you. The second reason is that when you convert from videotape to digital video, all camera moves become more jumpy and jittery. A slow pan or tilt jumps less in digital video format.

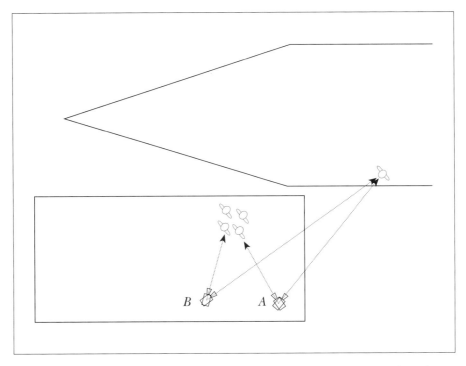

Figure 3-15.   Camera placement can affect how a panning shot looks. When the camera is placed in position *A*, a good portion of the pan shows neither the woman nor her family, just the ship. By placing the camera at position *B*, the shot moves quickly from the woman to her family.

Another general rule to follow when shooting camera moves is that you should always extend the beginning and ending shots for at least five seconds and perform the move in both directions. Here's an example that demonstrates the proper method for shooting camera moves: You are planning to zoom from a full shot of a crowd into a close shot of a woman in the center of the throng. At the beginning of the shot, you record five seconds of a static full shot of the crowd before you start to zoom in. After you zoom in (slowly) to the close shot, hold the static close shot for five seconds (with the tape still running). Then, zoom back out to the full shot and hold the full shot for yet another five seconds.

Although this might seem like a lot of work, using this method of shooting gives you many different shots to work with when you're editing the scene. You will be able to zoom in or out or use either the full shot or the close shot as a static shot. This method should be followed when doing tilting or panning shots as well.

Tracking Shots

Sometimes you need to move the camera from place to place to capture a particular motion. Let's say you're shooting a man as he walks down a corridor . You could shoot this scene by placing the camera at the end of the corridor, starting the shot on a medium shot of the man, and then gradually zooming out as he approaches you (this keeps his size within the frame constant as he approaches the camera). But you could also shoot this scene by walking backward in front of the man while framing him in a medium or close shot (Figure 3-16). A shot like this, where you physically move the camera (and yourself or the tripod), is called a *tracking shot*. There are several different types: *walking shots*, *dolly shots*, and *crane shots*.

 It is important to move slowly during a tracking shot so that the shot isn't too bumpy after you digitize it.

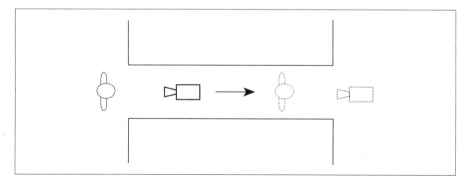

Figure 3-16.   A walking shot: The trick to making these shots work is to get very close to the subject. This allows you to use a wide-angle lens setting that minimizes the general shakiness of walking shots. You then walk backward as the subject walks forward.

Walking Shots

As the name suggests, in walking shots you walk with the camera as you're shooting. If you've already tried to do this kind of shot, you know how difficult it is to hold the camera steady as you walk. In fact, one measure of a professional camera operator is how steady his or her hand-held shot is. One way to minimize the unsteadiness is to get close to the subject and shoot him or her with the lens zoomed out to the wide position.

Because any camera movement is exaggerated when you convert to digital format, you might want to use some sort of steadying device, such as the Steadicam Jr. (by Cinema Products), which can help smooth out the bumps. Try to keep the subject in roughly the same position in the frame throughout the shot. When the image of the subject moves all around the screen, it's difficult for the viewer to follow the action.

Dolly Shots

If you want to shoot a tracking shot and it needs to be steady, then consider using some sort of moving platform, or *dolly*. There are a wide variety of dollies that vary in performance and price. At the top of the line are professional dollies that have a seat for the camera operator and a special set of wheels that turn in unison. For your work, you might consider using a *doorway dolly*, which is simply a platform on wheels that can fit through a doorway. The tripod and camera sit on top of the platform, and the camera operator stands on the platform as well. You need someone to move the doorway dolly during the shot (in the film and television business, this person is called the *grip*).

If you don't want to spend the money to rent a doorway dolly (about $75/day), try using a wheelchair. Attach a board to the armrests to get a higher vantage point for the camera operator and *voilà!* you have a makeshift dolly. You won't get as smooth a shot from a wheelchair as you would from a doorway or professional dolly, but the shot will be steadier than what you'd get from walking with the camera.

Depending on where you're shooting, there may be other ways to shoot a tracking shot. If you're in an airport, you can put the camera and tripod on a moving sidewalk and have your subject walk alongside. If you're in a hospital, try using a gurney with the camera operator sitting on top. Keep your eyes open for these possibilities because although tracking shots can be difficult to get, the movement they provide can add a lot to the final production.

Crane Shots

If you need to follow someone or something that is moving up or down, and you don't just want to tilt the camera, you need a device called a *crane*. It is unlikely that you will have the need or the budget to use a crane shot, but just in case you've got aspirations of being the Cecil B. deMille of digital video, here's some basic information.

A crane used for film or television work is like the cherry picker used by telephone repair companies to fix overhead phone lines. The camera sits in the basket of the crane and moves up and down under the control of the crane operator. If you want to move the crane to a new position, you need a crew to do so. Sound expensive? It is. Just to rent the most basic crane and hire the crew to operate it costs about $800 a day (only the major studios actually own their own cranes). If you really need a crane shot, be prepared to spend a lot of money. And if your budget is that high, plan on hiring a professional video producer or director to direct the shot.

Considering the Digital Video Disadvantage

Some of the shots described in the previous sections might not look very good when converted to digital video and shown in a small window. Most digital video windows just don't show all that much detail (at least not yet). Unless you've got the necessary hardware compression-decompression boards (see Chapter 13), which let you show digital videos on a full screen, you should concentrate on the basic shots (medium and close shots, close-ups, zooms, tilts, and pans). But try the other types of shots anyway; sooner or later full-screen technology will be less expensive, and you might as well as fool around with the various shots in the meantime.

As mentioned several times in the previous sections, if you are shooting scenes for digital videos, keep the camera steady and move the camera *very gradually* during camera moves. The reason for this is that when your computer digitizes video, it often drops intermediate frames.

For example, say you're using a 486 with a VideoSpigot for Windows board. This equipment allows you to digitize, or *capture*, video at 15 frames per second (as opposed to 30 frames per second for the original video). The digital video consists of every other frame (frames 1, 3, 5, 7, 9, etc.). The frames in between (frames 2, 4, 6, etc.) are dropped during conversion.

These intermediate frames help smooth out any motion or camera move. Without them, the digital video is jumpy. It is kind of like the herky-jerky motion of people on a dance floor bathed in strobe lights. The only way around this is to make sure that the changes between the frames that end up in the digital video (1, 3, 5, etc.) are gradual; i.e., the camera moves very slowly.

Wrap-Up

This chapter has reviewed the many different ways you can use a camera to capture a scene. It has also discussed how to compose shots specifically for digital videos. Armed with this information, you're now ready to move on to putting individual shots together in a sequence—in other words, editing.

CHAPTER 4

Editing Your Movies

Making a movie involves more than getting the right kind of shots with a camera. You need to choose which shots to use and which shots to leave on the cutting room floor. Editing also involves putting shots into a particular order so that they convey your idea.

An Overview of the Editing Process

There are many different steps to the editing process, but they can be grouped into four basic activities: collecting the video shots you want to work with; digitizing the shots to produce clips of digital video; selecting a particular cut, or portion, from each video clip; and assembling the cuts in a particular order to make a movie.

Collecting the Clips

The first step in editing is to collect all the video material and graphics you'll incorporate into a movie. This can be video you've shot yourself, videotapes from someone else, or digitized clips from a CD-ROM. The graphics can be animations or still images. You should collect more material than you need, so you won't have to spend time looking for extra material while you edit. If you're planning to include shots of nature scenes, don't just find five or six shots, find 20 or 30. You don't necessarily know what will work until you start arranging the shots into the movie.

Once you collect all your material, you should create a list of what you have and where it's located. For example, let's say you recorded shots for several scenes of two people walking and talking in a forest. You also recorded some shots of the forest itself on a different video-tape. All together, you have 60 minutes of material on two different videotapes. You need to write down which shots (the couple walking by the lake, shots of the birds, etc.) are on which tape. You also need to write down where each shot it located on each tape (how many minutes from the beginning). This way, you'll be able to find any particular shot quickly. You also need to write down where any predigitized shots, still images, and or graphics are stored on your computer (or CD-ROM).

You should then use these logs to create a list of shots to be digitized. This list won't be as long as your log, but it should include a variety of shots to give yourself some flexibility when editing. Let's say you're going to create a two-minute movie from the 60 minutes of material you shot of the nature scenes. Your digitizing list might include five minutes of material. That's a lot less than 60 minutes but still a lot more than the two minutes of the final piece.

Digitizing the Shots

After you create the digitizing list, transfer the shots to your computer using a digitizing video board. You should make sure to leave a little bit extra at the beginning and end of a shot when digitizing to gibe yourself options when editing (a detailed description of how to digitize video can be found in Chapter 13). Once a shot is digitized and stored on your computer, it is called a *clip*.

Picking the Cuts

Each clip is a segment of digitized video lasting anywhere from $1/30$ second (one frame) to several minutes. A *cut* of video can be as long as the entire video clip or as short as one frame. It depends on the situation. On MTV, the cuts generally last no longer than a second. In a documentary, a single cut might last 30 seconds or more.

In this book, the words *shot*, *clip*, and *cut* have particular meanings. A shot is a piece of videotape showing a particular scene or action. When a shot is digitized and stored on a computer (or CD-ROM), it becomes a clip. A portion of a clip that is used in a movie is called a cut.

In working with any particular clip, you probably will not want to use the entire clip in the final movie. For example, let's say you have a clip of a salesman demonstrating a new product, and the clip is 10 seconds long (Figure 4-1). And let's assume that you only want to use a three-second cut from this clip. Which three second—the first three, the last three, maybe something in the middle?

Because this situation comes up so often in editing, video editors long ago coined specific terms to describe the beginning and end of a cut. The *In point* is where the cut starts; the *Out point* is where the cut ends.

If you want to use the first three seconds of the salesman clip, you set the In point, or simply the In, at the beginning of the clip (Figure 4-2). You then set the Out at the three-second point of the clip (03:00 is the same as 3 seconds, 0 frames).

If you want to choose a cut in the middle of the clip to focus on the point where the salesman pulls out the product, set the In at the 2:15 point of the clip (2 seconds, 15 frames) and the Out at the 5:15 point (Figure 4-3). Although this cut has different In and Out points than the previous cut, the duration of the cut (how long it lasts on the screen) is still three seconds.

Figure 4-1.   Timeline view of a shot of a salesman demonstrating a product. Each box represents one second.

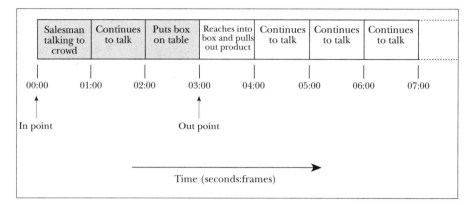

Figure 4-2.   The shaded area indicates the position of a three-second cut that starts at the beginning of the shot.

To look at this another way, imagine you're editing the following sentence with a word-processing program:

```
This is a test of the emergency video-editing system.
```

You want to pick out 15 characters from this sentence (letters and spaces). One way is to start with the word test, so you select characters starting with the *t* in *test*:

```
This is a test of the emergency video-editing system.
          test of the emerg
```

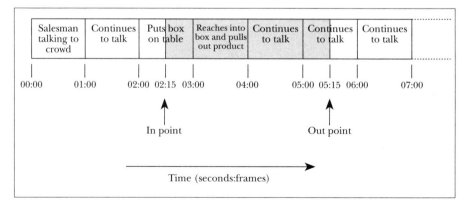

Figure 4-3.   The shaded area indicates the position of a three-second cut that starts at the middle of the shot.

In this case, the In point is the first *t* in *test*; the Out point is the *g* in *emergency*. A different way is to start the 15-character cut with the *e* in *emergency*, which gives you:

```
This is a test of the emergency video-editing system.
                      emergency video
```

Now, the In point is the first *e* of *emergency*, and the Out point is the *o* in *video*.

Of course, it doesn't make much sense to work with text this way, but it is almost exactly what you do when you select a cut from a video clip. The video clip is the whole sentence; the cut is the 15-character portion.

Assembling the Cuts into a Movie

Several software packages allow you edit video cuts on your PC. They range in price from a few hundred dollars to several thousand dollars. Most of the programs, however, use the same basic methods for editing video.

 If you're already familiar with an editing program, it might be a good idea at this point to put down the book and try setting a few In and Out points on your own video clips (it's sometimes easier to learn by doing than by reading). This is a basic part of editing, and the quicker it becomes second nature, the faster you'll move on to the fun part of editing—telling visual stories.

In many editing programs, you build your movie by manipulating icons on a timeline (Figure 4-4). The icons represent the cuts you've selected from particular clips. The length of the icon indicates the duration of the cut in the final movie. An icon may change its appearance as you lengthen or shorten the cut (by changing its In and Out points), but that's just window dressing. The important point is the length of the icon. An icon that is twice as long as another on the timeline lasts twice as long in the final movie.

The position of the icon on the timeline determines when it appears in the final movie. Time runs from left to right, with the beginning of the movie starting at the far left side and the end of the movie

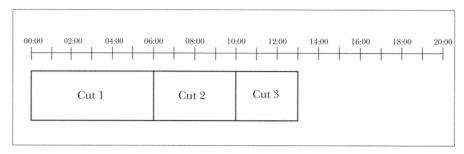

Figure 4-4.   Editing the program timeline

at the far right side; so the first cut of a movie is placed to the far left. The second cut is positioned immediately to the right of the first one, and so on.

Because you are working with digital video (as opposed to video tape; see the note on page 62), it is easy to change the order of cuts. All you have to do is change the positions of the icons on the timeline. For example, let's say you are working with the following cuts:

Cut 1: Medium shot of the audience looking bored

Cut 2: Close-up shot of salesman pulling the product out of the box

Cut 3: Medium shot of the audience looking on in anticipation

You could build the movie by positioning these cuts in order (Figure 4-4). Another way to edit these cuts together would be to show cut 3 first, then cut 2, then cut 1. To make these changes, you simply move the icon for cut 1 over to the right of cut 3 (Figure 4-5), move the icon for cut 3 all the way to the far left of the timeline (Figure 4-6), and then slide the icon for cuts 2 and 1 next to the icon for cut 3 (Figure 4-7).

Of course, this gives the scene an entirely new meaning because the audience's bored expressions now mean something completely different (i.e., the product is boring). But we're getting ahead of ourselves. The craft of visual storytelling is discussed in Chapter 6, after we cover the technical aspects of working with editing programs.

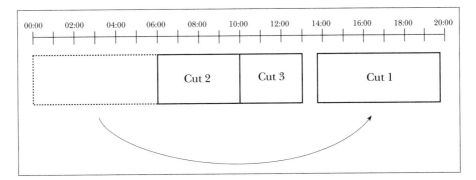

Figure 4-5.   To switch the positions of cuts 1 and 3, you first move cut 1 to the end of the segment.

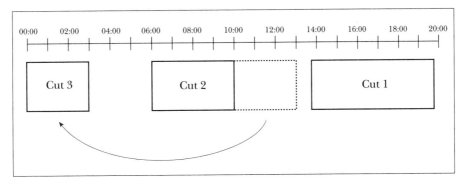

Figure 4-6.   Cut 3 is then moved to the beginning of the segment.

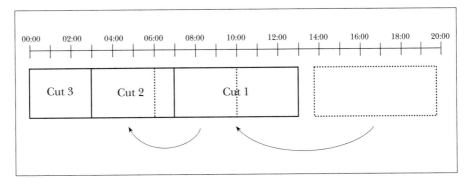

Figure 4-7.   The process is completed by sliding the cuts together to remove any gaps.

There are advantages to nonlinear editing. If you've had the opportunity to edit on a traditional, linear videotape-editing system, you'll notice that with digital editing, you don't have to set the In and Out points for the record machine. The really great thing about digital-editing systems is that they allow you to edit nonlinearly, like film. If you want to change one edit in the middle of a long sequence, all you have to do is change that edit. All the edits after that one are automatically changed. You don't have to re-edit them.

Editing Movies with Adobe Premiere

Although you can use VidEdit to do some very basic editing, if you want to create more professional pieces, it is probably best to use a full-featured editing program. Adobe Premiere was one of the first, low-cost video-editing programs for the Macintosh. It is also one of the first video-editing programs for Windows. It is not the only low-cost option, but it's a good example of a well-constructed program.

The following sections describe some of the basic features of Adobe Premiere version 1.1. If you are interested in descriptions of all the bells and whistles, please refer to the *Premiere for Windows User Guide*.

Creating Projects vs. Movies

There are two parts to making a movie with Adobe Premiere: First, you set up a *project*, then you create a *movie*. A project is a kind of working area where you make all your decisions (which clips to use, how long the cuts should be, what order do they go in, etc.) All these instructions are stored in the project file. When you actually want to see what you've created, you tell Premiere to follow these instructions and make a movie.

The project file doesn't store the actual clips or cuts. It only stores information about which cuts are used and what their order is. This helps reduce the size of the project file. A movie, however, is made up of the actual cuts specified by the project. The project is like a recipe, and the movie is the actual cake.

Note Because a project doesn't contain the actual clips themselves (only pointers to them), you must keep the video clips on your hard drive while you're working with a particular project. If you remove the clips, the project won't have anything to point to.

You can send a copy of a movie to a friend, and he or she can view it if he or she has MediaPlayer or QuickTime for Windows. If you send a friend a project, you also need to send all the video clips that are used in it. However, if you want to modify a movie, you can do so easily by opening the project for that movie, making your changes, and then creating a new version of the movie.

Making Edits with Premiere

Premiere uses four main windows to handle the various activities discussed earlier in this chapter (Figure 4-8). The Project window holds all the clips for a particular movie. The Clip window is where you set the In and Out points for a clip. You actually design the movie in the Construction window. Then you can preview your movie using the Preview window. Two other windows, the Transition window and the Info window, are described in Chapter 5.

Unlike a word-processing program or a spreadsheet, with Premiere you typically have several windows open at once while you work on a particular project. This allows you to move quickly between windows.

To demonstrate how to make a movie with Premiere, we'll use sample video clips that are provided with the program. Each window will be explained as we go through the steps of making a movie.

The Project Window

To start working on a new movie, you must first create a project. Premiere automatically opens a new, untitled Project window when you start the program. Otherwise, all you have to do is select the New command from the File menu, and choose Project from the New submenu. Then you can start collecting the video clips for the project in the Project window.

Choose the Import File Command from the File menu (press Ctrl-I)—you'll see a dialog box with the file directories. Locate and open the samples file that comes with Premiere, and double-click on the Twirl.avi file to open it.

Figure 4-8. The windows used in Adobe Premiere for Windows.

 If you want to examine a clip before adding it to the Project window, choose Open from the File menu. When the Open dialog box appears, select the clip you want to open, and click OK. The clip appears in the Clip window: just click on the play button to watch it. If you decide to use the clip, select the Add This Clip command from the Clip menu.

When the Twirl clip is imported into the Project window, Premiere creates a *thumbnail* of the clip, which is similar to the first frame of the clip (Figure 4-9). You also see a description of the clip (movie), its duration (3:15), the size of the clip (160×120 pixels), and any comments attached to it.

Figure 4-9.

The Project window

Next import the clip called Hands.avi, following the steps just described. You should now have two clips in the Project window to work with.

The Clip Window

The Clip window is where you set the Ins and Outs for a particular clip. It's similar to the VidEdit application that comes with Video for Windows.

Open up the Clip window by double-clicking on the on the thumbnail for the Hands clip. You can use the Clip window controls (shown in Figure 4-10) to move to different parts of the clip to decide where to set the In and Out points. As you move through the clip, notice that the frame indicator changes to show your exact point within the clip. The format for the frame indicator is *hours:minutes:seconds:frames*. This is the standard format in the professional video world. Play with the various controls for a while to get the hang of them.

You may find that the Frame Forward and Frame Backward controls actually move you three frames forward or backward. That's because when the clips were digitized only every third frame was captured. If you want to see every frame, use the ⬅ and ➡ keys on the keyboard.

By default, Premiere sets the In point at the beginning of the clip and the Out point at the end. (The In point is marked by a small box labeled "In" that appears in the upper-left corner of the window. The Out point is marked by a small box label "Out" that appears in the

Jog control

Slider control

Stop   Play   Duration
of cut

Frame Backward
button

Frame Forward
button

Set
marker

Goto
marker

In button

Out button

Frame indicator

Figure 4-10.   The Clip window and its controls

upper-right corner of the window.) For this example, you're going to set your own In and Out points. Use the Clip window controls to move to the 2:05 frame of the clip (2 seconds, 4 frames) and then click the In button (Figure 4-11). Notice how that the In label now appears in the window at that frame. Next, set the Out point by moving to the 3:20 frame in the clip, and clicking the Out button (Figure 4-12). The duration counter then shows that the duration of the cut is 1:16—the amount of time between the In and Out points plus one frame (see the note on the next page).

Figure 4-11.

An In point is set by clicking the In button at the desired frame. A small In label is then placed at that frame in the Clip window.

Figure 4-12.

An Out point is set by clicking the Out button at the desired frame. A small Out label is then placed at that frame in the Clip window.

 The duration in this example is 1:16 instead of 1:15 because of the way Premiere handles In and Out points. The In point is set at the beginning of a frame, the Out point is at the end of a frame. In other words, both the 2:05 frame and the 3:20 frame are included in the duration.

That's it for the Hands clip. Now open the Twirl clip in the Clip window by double-clicking on its thumbnail in the Project window. Set the In point of the clip at the 1:00 frame and the Out point at the end.

The Construction Window

The Construction window is where your movie takes shape. Click on the Construction window to make it active. (If the Construction window isn't open, choose the Construction option from the Windows menu.) This window displays, on a timeline, all the cuts in your movie and the point at which each cut begins and ends.

The window has seven rows, or *tracks*, which hold various types of clips (Figure 4-13). There are two video tracks (A and B), three audio tracks (A, B, and C), a transitions track (T), and a superimpose track (SUPER). Because you're working with just video clips, only the video tracks matter at this time; the other tracks are discussed later in this book. Most of the time, you'll be working on video track A, the primary video track. Track B is used when you want to use transitions or perform complicated edits.

Figure 4-13.   The Construction window

Click and drag the thumbnail of the Twirl clip from the Project window into the Construction window and place it in the top row (Figure 4-14). You'll see two slightly different thumbnails of the cut and a about half a thumbnail on the right edge. Each thumbnail represents one second, and because the Twirl clip lasts 2 seconds and 15 frames, the frames are represented by the remaining thumbnail fragment.

Near the top of the window is the *time ruler*, which is the timeline for the project. The scale of the time ruler determines how much time is represented by each thumbnail. You can change the scale of the ruler by adjusting the *time-unit selector*, located in the bottom middle of the window. By default, Premiere sets the time unit to one second. Try setting the unit to two seconds by clicking to the right of the selector. Notice that the cut now appears half as long. This is because the scale

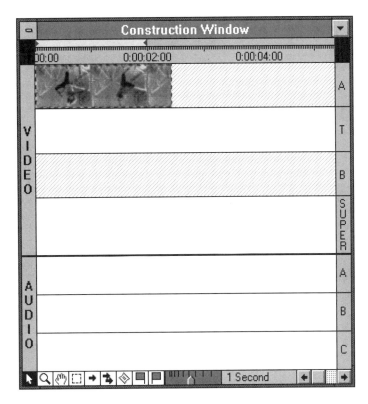

Figure 4-14.   The Twirl cut displayed in the Construction window

of the ruler is twice as large, and each thumbnail represents two seconds instead of one (Figure 4-15). If you set the time unit to shorter periods of time, the length of the cut increases accordingly (more thumbnails, each representing a shorter period of time).

You can also use the Zoom tool (it's the magnifying glass icon located in the bottom-left corner of the window) to adjust the time scale. Select the tool by clicking on the icon. Then click anywhere in the Construction window—the time unit is now shorter. To increase the time unit, hold down the ⌐Alt⌐ key while using the Zoom tool. When you're down, choose the Selection tool (the cursor arrow) from the Toolbox.

Time ruler

Zoom tool   Time-unit   Current
                   selector   time unit

Figure 4-15.   The time-unit selector is adjusted by clicking the pointer to the
                     right or left of the selector. Clicking to the left sets a smaller time
                     unit (greater resolution); clicking to the right sets a larger time
                     unit (less resolution).

Going back to the example, drag the Hands clip into the
Construction window and place it against the right edge of the Twirl cut:

Set the time unit so you can clearly see both cuts in the Construction window (either a unit of one or two seconds will work in this case). Because time moves from left to right, the Hands cut appears after the Twirl cut in the movie.

Even though it might not look like it, you've just made an edit. To actually see what the edit looks like, you need to preview the movie. Previewing puts together all the cuts that are in the *work area*, which is set by the yellow bar sitting just about the time ruler in the Construction window:

Work area

Only those cuts that lie under the yellow bar are assembled during a preview. This allows you to preview only a portion of the movie instead of the whole thing. You can drag the bar to any part of your movie; you can also increase the size of the work area by dragging the ends of the yellow bar:

Work area

To set the work area for this example, drag the right edge of the yellow bar until it reaches the right edge of the Hands cut. Now you're ready to preview your edited material.

The Preview Window

Premiere gives you a couple of different ways to preview edits. In all cases, the actual preview appears in the Preview window. Depending on your machine, the motion of the video may look a little jumpy. That's because a preview is a rough approximation of what the final movie will look like. But if you like the preview, you'll love the movie.

The most accurate method for previewing is to use the Preview command. Once the edges of the yellow bar are in the right positions, select Preview from the Project menu (or press Enter). The Building Preview dialog box appears, and gives a time estimate for building the preview. Once the preview has been built, it plays in the Preview window. You can replay the preview as many times as you want by pressing Enter when the clip is done.

You can also preview the work area by dragging the cursor along the time ruler in the Construction window. This technique, called *scrubbing*, allows you to view edits much faster than with the Preview command. However, because the speed of the scrub is set by how fast you move the mouse, scrubbing doesn't give you a good sense of the pacing in a particular potion of your movie.

Making Changes

The decision to put the Twirl cut first and the Hands cut second is just one example of how to put the two cuts together. You can easily switch the order of the cuts. Click on the Construction window to make it active. Drag the Twirl cut to any point in track A that is to the right of the Hands cut:

Then drag the Hands cut to the far left side of the track:

and put the Twirl cut against the Glider cut, like this:

Preview the movie by pressing [Enter]. You now see the Hands cut first, followed by the Twirl cut. You can add more cuts to your movie by following the steps you just took:

1. Import the video clip into the Project window with the Import command.

2. Open the clip in the Clip window and set the In and Out points.

3. Drag the clip from the Project window into the Construction window, and put it in video track A in whatever position you want.

4. Set the work area to include the new cut and preview the edits.

5. If you decide you don't want to use a clip, click on it in the Construction window and press the [Delete] key. Then move the remaining clips over so that their edges touch.

Making the Movie

Once you're satisfied with your project, you can take the next step and create an actual .AVI movie. This can be a time-consuming process, so it's a good idea to preview your project several times before you take this step.

Choose the Make Movie option from the Project menu ([Alt]-[K]). Type in the filename in the Make Movie dialog box. Try to make the name as unique as possible so that you can find it easily later on.

Next, click on the Options buttons in the bottom-left corner; the an Project Output Options dialog box appears with several different parameters you can set (Figure 4-16). Please refer to the Premiere manual for a detailed description of these parameters. The main ones that concern you are the video frame rate, audio rate, and image quality.

Generally speaking, you should try to have as high a video frame rate as possible. On many machines, you are usually limited to between 10 and 20 frames per second (fps) for a standard window size of 160×120 pixels. However, faster machines can hand between 15 and 30 fps. A larger window size reduces the frame rate.

Figure 4-16.   You set your output options in the Project Output Options dialog box.

Another way to increase the frame rate (and reduce the file size of the movie) is to reduce the quality of the image. The slider bar in the Compression box lets you set the quality of your movie (the range is from 0 to 100, with 100 being the highest quality). Make a few movies with different settings so that you get a sense of the differing qualities available.

Once you've set the appropriate options, click OK to return to the Make Movie dialog box. Then click OK again to make the movie. Your new movie will appear in the Clip window. You can view it by clicking the Play button.

Saving the Project

As mentioned earlier, you need to save projects separately from movies, if you want to make changes to them later. To save this project, choose the Save option under the File menu. Give your project a name, such as **FirstTry.ppj** (.ppj files are Premiere project files), then save it.

Wrap-Up

This chapter covered the basics of performing video edits with an editing program. But this is just the beginning. In the next chapter, you'll learn how to include audio in your movie, and how to use special effects to make smooth transitions between different cuts—as well as a few other tricks.

CHAPTER 5

Beyond the Basics

O ne of the best things about software editing programs is that they allow you to work with video in complex ways— at a fraction of what it would cost you if you were only working with videotapes. This chapter reviews some features found in most editing systems that can improve the look of your movie and increase its impact. Adobe Premiere for Windows is again used as the example, but many other editing programs have these features and some others of their own.

Clips in Motion

Chapter 4 covered the basic steps in assembling a movie:

1. Import clips into the Project window.
2. Select a cut from a video clip by setting In and Out points.
3. Position the cuts along the timeline in the Construction window.
4. Preview the edits.
5. Make the movie.

You'll continue to use those five steps for most of your editing, but at times you will want to make changes to a project. Premiere has a number of features that make it easy to manipulate cuts once they're in the Construction window.

Lengthening and Shortening a Cut

Let's build a different project to play with here. These are the steps:

1. Choose New Project from the File menu.
2. Locate the Adobe samples file and import the Closeup.avi and Fallfwd.avi clips using the Import command.
3. Open the Closeup clip in the Clip window.
4. Set the Out point at 1:23.
5. Open the Fallfwd clip in the Clip window.
6. Set the In point at 1:02 and the Out point at 3:08.
7. Click on the Construction window to make it active.
8. Drag the Closeup thumbnail from the Project window and place it on the far-left side of the Construction window.
9. Drag the Fallfwd thumbnail from the Project window and place it flush against the right edge of the Closeup cut.
10. Use the Save command in the File menu to save the project as Project2.ppj.

Set the work area by dragging the red arrow of the yellow bar until it aligns with the end of the Closeup cut. Then preview the project by pressing the [Enter] key. Let's say that you really don't like the fact that the woman is already halfway through her swing in the Fallfwd clip. You could fix this by opening the cut in the Clip window and changing the In point, but there's an easier way.

Drag the Fallfwd cut to the right so that there is a small gap between the two cuts (at least one second's worth). Then position the cursor over the left edge of the Fallfwd cut. The cursor shape changes to a *stretch pointer* (Figure 5-1). Click and drag the left edge of the cut to the left until it won't stretch any further. You've just lengthened the cut by dragging the edge of the thumbnail to extend the In point.

Double-click somewhere in the middle of the Fallfwd cut to open it in the Clip window. Go to the beginning of the cut, and you can see that the In point is now set at the beginning of the cut instead of at the 1:02 point.

Figure 5-1.   With the stretch pointer, you can increase the duration of a cut by extending the Out point.

Click on the Construction window to make it active and position the pointer over the left edge of the Closeup cut again. This time, drag it to the right. This shortens the cut by setting the In point to an later point in the clip. You can confirm this by opening the cut in the Clip window.

Sometimes when you use the Step Forward and Step Backward buttons in the Clip window you won't be able to see new In or Out points. This is because the new points may not coincide with the frames that the Step buttons jump to. For example, if every third frame of the clip is captured, then the Step buttons will move you three frames forward or backward. If your new In or Out point falls in between these three frame jumps, you won't see the label. To go exactly to the new In or Out point, use the Goto button in the Clip window and choose the In or Out option. Or you can press the left or right arrow keys (on the keyboard) to move through the clip frame by frame.

If you want to view only the cut between the In and Out points in the Clip window, hold down the [Shift] key when you click on the Play button.

You can also increase the duration of a cut by stretching the end of a cut. Position the pointer over the right edge of the Fallfwd cut. When the stretch pointer appears, drag the right edge of the Gliders cut to the right until it won't move anymore:

This lengthens the cut by setting the Out point to a later point in the clip. In this case, the cut doesn't change much because the Out point was already near the end of the clip.

 You can also change the In and Out points in the Construction window by using the In and Out point tools, which look like little flags at the bottom of the Construction window. Just click on the appropriate tool (the In point tool faces left and the Out point tool faces right) and then click on the spot on the cut where you want the new point to be. Additionally, hold down the Ctrl or Ctrl-Shift keys and click anywhere on a clip to set its In or Out point, respectively.

The advantage of changing the length of a cut in the Construction window is that it's fast—but it's not particularly accurate. However, you can use the Info window to see exactly by how much you are extending a cut. Choose the Info Window option under the Windows menu. A small window appears that indicates the duration of the cut:

Fallfwd.avi [1]
Movie
Duration: 0:00:03:23
160 x 120

Starting at: 0:00:01:24
Ending at: 0:00:05:17

Position the pointer over the left edge of the Fallfwd cut again and watch the duration indicator in the Info window as you stretch the cut.

(The duration indicator will also change as you move the In or Out point tool around the cut.) The numbers on the bottom of the Info window indicate where the cut starts on the timeline. This is particularly helpful when you are aligning cuts on different tracks (which you get to later in this chapter).

Save your project at this point with the Save command. If you haven't saved the project yet, name it **Project2.ppj**.

Splitting, Shifting, and Deleting Cuts

We'll review four other useful commands here, even though they won't become part of the final movie you're building. They are splitting a cut, copying and pasting a cut, and moving a whole group of cuts.

Splitting a Cut

In certain types of edits, you might want to split a cut into two separate cuts. This is done with the Razor Blade tool, which is the tool that looks like a small razor blade at the bottom of the Construction window. Click on the razor blade (or just press R on the keyboard), and position it over the middle of the Fallfwd cut:

Razor blade

Click the razor blade at the point where you want to split the cut, and two cuts will appear in the place of the single cut. If you look at the Project window, you can see that a new clip was added to the project (the second part of the cut).

Once you've split a cut, you can't join the pieces back together again. However, splitting a clip does not affect the actual clip—each split portion contains the whole clip. Splitting simply allows you to easily use different portions of the same clip in different places.

You might want to set the time ruler to four or eight frames to give you more resolution when splitting cuts. Unfortunately, this may move you to a different part of the timeline, so you'll have to use the slider bar at the bottom of the Construction window to find the split point again. If you use the Zoom tool, you can zoom into a particular part of the Construction window without having to scroll through to find the split point.

Copying and Pasting a Cut

At some point, you may find yourself wanting to use the same cut more than once. Luckily you can copy and paste cuts as you can copy and paste graphics or words in other software applications. To copy a cut, just click on it to select it and choose Copy from the Edit menu (or press Ctrl-C).

Pasting gives you a few more options. You'll see three Paste commands in the Edit menu: Paste, Paste to Fit, and Paste Custom. The Paste command (Ctrl-V) is straightforward—it simply pastes the copied cut into a selected area of the track. The Paste to Fit command (Ctrl-U) sets new In and Out point for your copied cut so that it fits into a selected area of the Construction window. When you choose the Paste Custom command (Ctrl-H) command, the Paste Custom Settings dialog box appears (Figure 5-2). You can use the options in

Figure 5-2.   Use the Paste Custom Settings dialog box to change the characteristics and duration of the cut you are about to paste.

this dialog box to change the characteristics and duration of the cut you are pasting. Check the Premiere user's manual for more detail about these different options.

Shifting Cuts

Say you designed a movie that has 10 cuts, and you decide that you want to insert a new cut right after the second cut of your movie. Or you want to paste a cut in between cuts 2 and 3. No problem: You simply shift cuts 3 through 10 to the right until there is enough room for your new cut:

The standard way to do this would be to move cut 10 first, then cut 9, then cut 8, etc. Fortunately, there's an easier way! You can use the Track tool (the single right-facing arrow in the Construction window) to shift a group of cuts along the timeline. Just select the Track tool, position the arrow over the earliest cut of the group you wish to move, and shift the group of cuts to a new position (right or left). All cuts to the right of the pointer will move in unison.

If you want to shift cuts in multiple tracks, say, in both the video and audio tracks, use the Multi-track tool—it look like the Track tool with a second arrow. As before, position the Multi-track Tool over a clip, and that clip and all the clips to the right of it can be moved.

Working with Place Markers

Sometimes you're not sure where you want to start or end a cut because there are several possibilities. Premiere allows you to set *place markers* at any point in a clip, which let you mark these options as possible In and Out points.

Setting Place Markers

As an example, let's say you want to mark several possible In points for the Fallfwd cut. Open the cut in the Clip window by double-clicking on the cut (in either the Project or Construction window). Using the slider bar, go to the beginning of the cut and use the Step Forward button to move forward to the 00:14 frame. Click the Mark button. A pop-up menu appears with a list of numbers, 0 to 9 (Figure 5-3). Choose 1 for this place marker.

Premiere indicates that you marked this frame by putting a bullet next to the marker number in the pop-up menu and putting a place marker with the selected number in the middle of the cut. This place marker only appears in the Clip window (and in the Construction window, but not in the final movie).

Next, use the Step Forward button to move to the 00:23 frame of the clip. Set a place marker at this point with the Mark button. This time, choose 2. Then move forward to the 1:05 frame and mark this frame with place marker 3. You now have four different options for the

Figure 5-3.

Once you decide where you want a place marker, you use the Mark button and the pop-up menu to set the place marker.

In point: the current In point at frame 1:02 and three place markers at frames 00:14, 00:23, and 1:05, respectively.

 To delete a place marker, find the frame with the marker in the Clip window, and then press ⓒ on the keyboard.

Using Place Markers

Now use the Goto button to shift between your different place markers and the In point. This lets you review the various possible In points quickly. Place markers are stored with the cut, and appear as small pointers over the cut in the Construction window (Figure 5-4). This allows you to use the stretch point to switch between different place markers.

You can also use the Clip window to switch the In point to one of the place markers. Open the cut in the Clip window, click the Goto button to move to that place marker, and set this frame as your In point with the In button.

There's another use for place markers besides keeping track of possible In and Out points. As you'll see in the next section on working

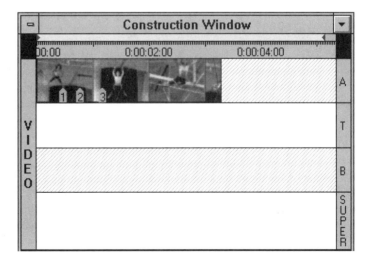

Figure 5-4.   Place markers appear as small pointers over the cut.

with audio, you'll often want to change the level of an audio track in the middle of a cut. Where you want that change to occur is often determined by what is happening in the video cut.

For example, let's say you have a video clip of a door slamming, but for some reason you don't have the audio for that piece of video. You can fix this by adding an audio clip of a door slamming at precisely the moment when the door closes. A place marker at that point in the video makes it a lot easier to synchronize the video and audio cuts at the proper point in time. Specific examples of using place markers are given in Chapter 8.

Close the project at this point and don't save the changes. Then open the Project you saved before (Project2.ppj) to continue with that example.

Adding Sound—A Crucial Step

When most people first get their hands on editing equipment, they are seduced by the visuals and don't pay enough attention to sound. But any Hollywood director will tell you that the proper soundtrack is essential for a good movie.

There are four main types of sound: voices (either dialogue or narration), background sound (also known as *ambience*), music, and sound effects. The basic steps of working with audio in Premiere for Windows are the same for all four types.

So far, we've been working with video clips that don't have audio attached to them. Unless you have a high-end digitizing board that also has sound capture capabilities, you have to have a sound board, such as the Sound Blaster board from Creative Labs, to capture audio. If you're using a digitizing board that allows audio pass-through from a sound board, then you can capture audio with your video clips. If your video board doesn't allow sound pass-through, you'll have to capture the audio separately from the video. Also, if you're working with someone else's material or with *clip media* (prepackaged sets of video clips), you might need to create your own digital audio files.

A number of products allow you to convert normal, analog audio into digital files. Techniques for digitizing audio are covered in more detail in Chapter 13. For now, the main thing to know is that Premiere can only work with digital audio files that are stored in one of two standard audio formats: AIFF and .wav.

Importing Audio Clips

Let's work with the Circus audio clip that comes with the Premiere software to see how working with audio is different than working with video. First, open the project you saved before (Project2.ppj) if you haven't already done so.

You import an audio clip in the same way that you import a video clip—with the Import command in the Project menu. Use this command to import the Circus audio clip. When the clip shows up in the Project window, notice that the thumbnail looks different for an audio clip (Figure 5-5). Instead of a picture, there's a little line called a *waveform*. Under the name of the audio clip is the duration of the clip and some technical information about how the clip is digitized (see Chapter 13 for information about digitizing audio).

When you're working with video clips that have their own audio as part of the file, Premiere imports both the audio and video portions as a *linked* clip. To change the In and Out points of the audio and video portions individually, you must break the link between the clips. To do this, import the linked clip into the Construction window and delete either the audio or video portion from the clip. Then import the clip a second time and delete which ever portion you didn't cut the first time. The two portions of the clip are now unlinked. To break an audio or video link *without* deleting the clip from the Construction window, select it and then copy and paste it into the *same* place. The source material will be unaffected, but the link will be broken.

Open the Circus audio clip in the Clip window by double-clicking on its thumbnail in the Project window. As in the Project window, there

Figure 5-5.

The appearance of an audio clip in the Project window differs from that of a video clip. The thumbnail for an audio clip is a waveform of the sound.

are some subtle differences to working with an audio clip in the Clip window compared to working with a video clip:

- The Step Forward and Step Backward buttons work the same way, except that the audio isn't broken into distinct chunks of time, or frames, as video is. To account for that, Premiere creates a thin black bar running vertically through the waveform that indicates the length of one frame.

- When you use the Play button, you'll notice that the waveform does not change as the clip is playing. To view the various portions of the clip, you need to use the Step Forward and Step Backward buttons, or use the second slider sitting above the Jog control.

- In and Out points appear as small red flags rather than square labels. The In point flag sits above the waveform and has an *I* in it, the Out point flag is below the waveform and contains an *O*. Markers also appear as small flags rather than square labels.

- With both audio clips and linked clips, a small volume control button appears next to the Goto button in the Clip window. Clicking on the button changes the *playback volume*—that is, the volume of the clip as it plays in the Clip window—but does not otherwise affect the volume of the audio. The volume button has only three settings: off, low, and high. Click on it to change the setting.

Use the slider bar to move through the clip. Notice that the clip has no sound when the waveform is flat and does have sound when there are vertical lines in the waveform.

Setting Ins and Outs

Click on the Construction window to make it active, then drag the Circus audio clip from the Project window into audio track A of the Construction window (Figure 5-6). (Because you haven't set In and Out points for this clip, Premiere automatically sets them to the beginning and end of the clip.)

Let's say we want the sound to begin at the same time the Fallfwd clip starts playing. Because the video and audio cuts are separate, you now need to synch them so that the sound starts at the same time the video starts. Change the time ruler to half-seconds so that there's greater resolution, or detail, in the timeline. Find the beginning of the Fallfwd cut, then slide the audio cut over until its left edge lines up exactly with the left edge of the Fallfwd cut. (Figure 5-7).

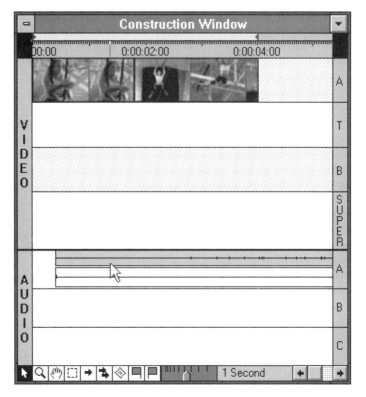

Figure 5-6.   An audio clip is moved into the Construction window the same was as a video clip, except that it is put into one of the audio tracks (A, B, or C).

Figure 5-7.   Video and audio cuts need to be synchronized so that the sound
matches the video. In this case, you line up the beginnings of
the cuts to synch them.

 **The Construction window looks a bit different in Figure 5-7 because the
Super track and audio track C were left out. To do this on your machine,
choose the Construction View option from the Project menu. A submenu
appears, listing the various combinations of tracks you can toggle on and off.**

Now the two cuts are in synch. However, the Circus audio cut provided with Premiere is a lot longer than the video cut. To fix this, first
use the scroll bar to scroll through the Construction window until you
find the end of the audio track. Then position the pointer over the
right edge of the audio cut. The stretch pointer appears. You can then
drag the right edge of the audio cut until it lines up with the right
edge of the Fallfwd video cut (Figure 5-8).

 **Stretching the audio doesn't affect the quality of the sound; it only
changes the duration of the cut.**

Figure 5-8.   By using the stretch pointer, you can adjust the length of the
audio cut to match the video cut.

Reset the time ruler to one second, so you can see all the cuts in the
Construction window, and then reset the work area to include the
audio and video cuts (Figure 5-9). Preview the work area by pressing
Enter. You should see the Closeup cut, followed by the Fallfwd cut and
hear the Circus audio while the Fallfwd cut is playing.

You may notice that you don't hear a lot of the music—that's
because the beginning of the clip contains mostly silence, with a few
"Um-dah-dahs" thrown in. To make the melody start playing when the
Fallfwd clip starts, you have to set a new In point. To do this, open the
audio cut in the Clip window by double-clicking on it. Then use the
Step Forward and Step Backward buttons (or left and right arrow keys
on the keyboard) to move to the point where the melody starts in:
around 2:23. Click In to set the new In point. Next, go back to the
Construction window and stretch the right edge of the audio clip until
it once again matches the right edge of the Fallfwd clip. Hit Enter to
preview the result.

Figure 5-9.   Resetting the work area by moving the red arrows allows you to preview only a portion of the project.

Working with More Than One Audio Clip

The first video cut now seems a bit hollow without any audio. You can fix that by adding a piece of music or sound. For the second piece of audio, let's use the "Ta-da!" sound that comes with Windows. You'll should find this file in your Windows directory. Import the Tada audio clip into the Project window. Then drag it into the Construction window and place it at the beginning of the movie in audio track B (Figure 5-10). Notice that there is a gap between where the Tada audio cut ends and the Circus audio clip begins. If you try to stretch the Tada clip to fill up the gap, it won't stretch—that's because the clip itself is too short. To fill the gap (so there isn't a block of silence), you can try several different techniques. The first is to reset the In point of the Circus clip, but this would result in the Circus audio starting before the Fallfwd clip. The second is to *loop*, or paste together, several copies or portions of the Tada clip. In normal circumstances this would be the way to go. However, in this case, hearing the Tada clip more than once sounds sort of odd.

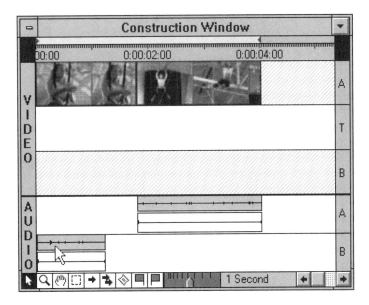

Figure 5-10.   When you are working with more than one audio cut at a
particular point in the timeline, you need to put the second
audio cut in audio track B (or C).

 You can loop together several cuts of the same section of music using the
Copy and Paste commands. First select the cut you want to loop then
choose Copy command under the Edit menu (Ctrl-C). Click on the blank
section of the audio track, then choose the Paste command from the Edit
menu (Ctrl-V).

The third technique is to shorten the Closeup video so that it is the
same length as the Tada clip. This is the choice we're going to use. To
make the Closeup and Tada cuts end at the same time, shorten the
Closeup cut using the stretch pointer. Then use the Multi-track tool to
slide the Fallfwd and Circus clips to the left until they touch the right
sides of the other cuts. Preview the work area.

Adjusting the Volume of an Audio Cut

At times you may find that you want to have two audio clips that *overlap*—that is, two cuts that are positioned in the same part of the timeline:

For example, say you're putting together a movie that has opening music followed by a narrator speaking. It might sound a bit odd if you have the music just stop and the narration begin. If you overlap the two cuts, however, Premiere will mix the sounds together so that music continues to play when the narrator starts to speak. Sometimes the cuts will sound good when mixed; at other times you'll want to change the volume of the cuts so that one sound is louder than the other.

You can adjust the volume, or *level*, of an audio cut using the *fade control*. The fade control is under the waveform for each audio cut. Position the pointer cursor over the line in the center of the fade control in the Circus audio, and a *finger cursor* will appear:

Click the mouse to create a handle, which is shown as a small black dot. By dragging the handle up and down, you can change the volume of the audio cut at that point—higher is louder, lower is quieter.

Let's change the volume on the Circus clip so that the music gradually fades out as the clip ends. Move the handle you created back onto the center line and position the pointer along the center line and underneath the 3:00 point on the timeline. (You may want to reset the time scale to see this point more clearly.) Click the mouse once to create a handle at this point, but don't move the handle. Next, move the cursor to the end of the Circus audio cut, and click and drag a handle down to the bottom of the fade control:

When you preview the work area, you'll notice that the Circus audio gradually decreases so that by the end of the cut you don't hear it at all.

You may notice that sometimes the audio and video don't stay in synch during a preview. Unfortunately, the only solution to this problem is to actually make a movie and review the movie by opening it with the Open command in the File menu. To cut down on the processing time, set the work area to cover just the part of the project you're interested in reviewing as a movie. Then choose the Make Movie option in the Project menu and click on the Options button in the Make Movie dialog box that appears. Select Work Area in the drop-down list box at the top of the second dialog box. This tells Premiere to make a movie only of the work area, not the entire project.

You can also choose the Make Work Area option in the Project menu to make a temporary movie of the work area.

You might want to play around with different levels for the Circus and Tada audio cuts. One thing to try is to gradually increase, or *fade in*, the level of Tada audio cut 1 at the beginning of the movie. Another common technique, called a *cross-fade*, is where you *fade out*, or gradually decrease, the level of one audio cut as you fade in a second audio cut.

You now have all the basic tools for working with audio in your movies. A more detailed discussion of how and when to incorporate audio can be found in Chapter 11.

Incorporating Graphics

In addition to working with video and audio, you can also insert a still image, or *graphic*, into your movies. The files you use can be in a variety of formats, including PCX (.pcx), TIFF (.tif), Targa (.tga), Adobe Photoshop (.psd), Windows bitmap (.bmp or .rle), and Macintosh PICT (.pic). The images can be of any size (although you need to have the correct aspect ratio—four units horizontal for three units vertical).

 Tip Although you can use any size graphic, it is a good idea to make the size of the graphic match the size of your movie. So if your movie is the standard size (160 by 120 pixels), then your graphics should be that size as well. The quality of the graphic is better because you aren't forcing Premiere to resize the image.

Working with Graphics

For this example, we'll use the Rings bitmap that comes with Premiere. Import the graphic using the Import command, as you would with a video or audio clip. As you can see, a small thumbnail appears in the Project window as well as some technical information about the image, such as its size and duration:

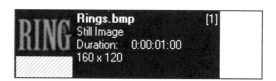

By default, a still image is assigned a duration of one second when it's imported.

Drag the thumbnail of the graphic from the Project window into the Construction window and place it in video track A next to the end of the Fallfwd video cut. Extend the Rings cut using the stretch pointer to make the cut last three seconds:

You can also change the duration of graphics in the Clip window. Double-click on the graphic to open the Clip window. You'll see that instead of the regular controls, there is only a Duration button at the bottom left. Click on the button, then type in the new duration in the Duration dialog box. You can also use the Duration command in the Clip menu.

Change the work area (by moving the red arrows) so that it covers just the Fallfwd video cut and the graphic, then preview the work area. You'll notice that the change, or *transition*, from the Fallfwd cut to the graphic seems fairly abrupt. We'll fix this problem in the next section, which covers special effects.

Creating Graphics in Premiere

In addition to importing graphics created by other programs, you can also make some useful graphics within Premiere itself.

Making a Still Image from a Video Clip

You can create a bitmap image of any specific frame in a video cut, essentially taking a snapshot of that frame, and then use that image in your movie as you would any other graphic. Open the Fallfwd video cut in the Clip window and move to the last frame of the cut. To make a bitmap image of this frame select the Export command in the File menu, and choose the Frame as Bitmap option from the Export sub-menu. Save the bitmap image as **Fall.bmp**.

Import the bitmap image you just created into the Project window with the Import command. Slide the Rings graphic to the right so that there is roughly a two-second gap between the Fallfwd cut and the Rings graphic. Drag the Fall.bmp thumbnail from the Project window and place it in the gap and against the right edge of the Fallfwd cut. Extend the right edge of the Fall.bmp graphic so that it fills the gap (using the stretch pointer):

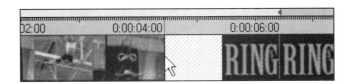

Set the work area to cover just the Fallfwd cut and the Fall.bmp graphic, and preview the work area. By making a bitmap image of the last frame of the Fallfwd cut and then tacking it on to the end of the video cut, you have created a *freeze frame*. These are particularly useful when you want to extend a cut, but the video clip isn't long enough.

Making a Colored Background

Sometimes you need to add a graphic made of a solid color. These can be used as elements or backgrounds for special effects (don't worry, we'll get to them soon). Choose the Add Color Matte option in the Project menu. A color bar appears that lets you choose the color of the graphic (Figure 5-11). For this example, let's use white. Drag the slider (located to the right of the color bar) to the top of the scroll bar. This changes the level of brightness so you can get a pure white. Then click the OK button and give the matte a name (such as **White Matte**).

A thumbnail for your new graphic shows up in the Project window. Click on the Construction window to make it active, then slide the Rings graphic to the right to create about a one-second gap between it and the Fall.bmp graphic. Drag the thumbnail of the White Matte into the Construction window, and place it in the gap you just created:

Figure 5-11. By adjusting the luminosity bar at right you can set the brightness of the matte. You can also select a particular color by clicking anywhere inside the color box or by entering precise percentages for hue (color shade), saturation (color purity), luminosity (color brightness), red, green, and blue.

Move the Rings graphic so that it sits flush against the White Matte. Set the work area to cover the Fallfwd cut, the Fall.bmp graphic, the White Matte, and the Rings graphic, and then preview the work area. What you should see is the Fallfwd clip move, then freeze, then one second of a plain white screen, then the Rings graphic.

Playing with Special Effects

Until now, you made edits by putting one cut directly against another. In film and TV parlance, this type of edit is called a *cut*. If the images aren't all that different or there is some kind of movement in the video shot, the transition between one cut and the next isn't particularly noticeable. But as you saw in the previous section, sometimes a simple edit just doesn't make it.

The term *cut* is used to mean a variety of things, depending on the situation. When referring to a particular piece of video or audio in the Construction window, a cut is a specific portion of a clip, a *clip* being an actual Windows file (either video, audio, or graphic). When talking about edits, the word *cut* describes the most basic edit, where one piece of video is placed right next to another. The word *cut* is used as a verb, as in "to cut" from the Fallfwd video to the White Matte graphic. In this case, it means to make a simple edit, i.e., a cut.

Special effects allow you to make smoother transitions from one video cut to another. A special effect is like an audio cross-fade—one video cut is fading out and another is fading in—except with special effects, you have a lot more options in how the video fades in and out.

In Premiere, special effects are called *transitions*. If you open the Transitions window by choosing that option from the Window menu, you'll see that you have a choice of 35 different special effects. Each provides a different kind of transition from one video cut to another (Figure 5-12). Use the scroll bar to scan the entire list of special effects.

Figure 5-12.

The icon for each special effect indicates the kind of transition that effect creates.

The animated icons next to the various special effects indicate what the effect looks like in the final movie. The letter *A* in the icon refers to video track A, the letter *B* to video track B.

In this example, you will use the Cross Dissolve effect as a transition from the Fall.bmp graphic to the White Matte. Click on the Construction window to make it active, then drag the White Matte graphic from video track A to video track B, and position it under the Fall.bmp graphic (Figure 5-13). Adjust the position of the White Matte graphic so that its right edge lines up with the right edge of the Fall.bmp graphic (you might want to set the time ruler to a half-second to increase the resolution of the timeline).

Click on the Cross Dissolve effect, drag it into the Construction window, and place it in the track labeled T (for Transition) between the Fall.bmp graphic and the White Matte graphic (Figure 5-14). The small arrow on the left side of the Cross Dissolve icon, called the Track

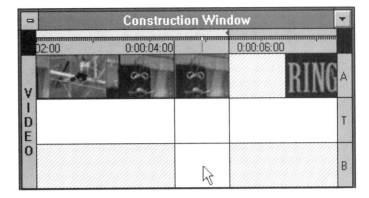

Figure 5-13.   The background matte is moved from video track A to track B.

Selector button, indicates which way the transition is going: a downward arrow means that the transition goes from the video cut in track A to the video cut in track B; an upward arrow means the opposite.

Make sure that the Cross Dissolve effect begins at the same point that the White Matte begins and ends where the Fall.bmp graphic ends (Figure 5-15) Use the stretch pointer to line up the ends of the transition with these cuts.

Set the work area so that it covers the Fall.bmp graphic and the White Matte, and preview the work area. The Fall.bmp should fade away into blank white screen.

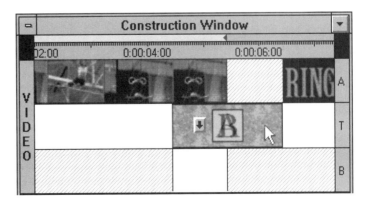

Figure 5-14.   Special effects are placed in the T track between the two video cuts you want to make a transition between.

Figure 5-15.   You need to make sure that the effect begins where the White Matte ends and ends where the Fall.bmp graphic ends.

You can also use *scrubbing*—**moving the cursor along the timeline—to preview the transition. However, this technique does not accurately reflect the speed of the transition.**

Unfortunately, a transition won't show up well in previews (unless you have a very fast machine). To see what it really looks like, you have to actually make the movie.

As with a graphic or video cut, the length of a transition icon affects how long the transition lasts. If you want a quick transition, then make the icon shorter with the stretch pointer. For a longer transition, make the icon longer. There is no correct length for a particular transition. It depends on the situation. Try out a few different transitions at different lengths and see what you like.

In general, the more complicated an effect, the longer it should last. For example, the Funnel effect is more complicated than the Cross Dissolve effect. Therefore, you might need 30 frames for the Funnel effect, but only 15 frames for the Cross Dissolve.

Back to the example: You'll now use another special effect to make a transition from the White Matte to the Rings graphic. Extend the White Matte graphic with the stretch pointer so that its duration is two seconds long (use the Info window to see the duration). Then slide the Rings graphic to the left so that it overlaps the White Matte by about 20 frames—no need to be exact at this point (Figure 5-16).

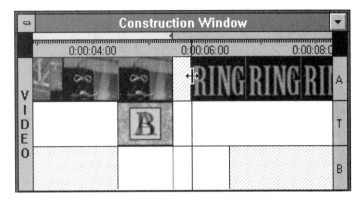

Figure 5-16.   You need to create an overlap between two video cuts to make a transition with a special effect. Here the overlap is about 20 frames.

 You can calculate the exact amount of overlap using the Info window. Essentially, you want to compare the points on the timeline where the White Matte ends and the Rings graphic begins. To calculate the ending point of the White Matte, click on the White Matte and write down the ending point that appears in the Info window. Now compare this with the starting point of the Rings graphic, as indicated in its Info window. The difference between the two numbers is the overlap.

Click on the Transitions window and scroll down the window until you see the Zoom effect. Drag the icon for the Zoom effect and place it in the Transitions (T) track between the White Matte and the Rings graphic. Line up the beginning of the effect with the beginning of the Rings graphic (Figure 5-17).

Complex transitions, such as the Zoom effect, can be modified in several ways. We're not going to review all the different modifications you can do to special effects in this book; they are handled well enough in the Premiere manual. For this example, click on the Track Selector button to make the arrow point upward and leave the other controls as they are:

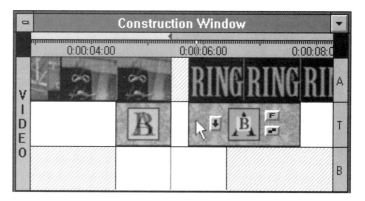

Figure 5-17. The Zoom special effect is placed between the Rings graphic and the background White Matte graphic.

Shorten the effect with the stretch pointer so that the effect ends at the end of the White Matte graphic (Figure 5-18). Set the work area to cover the Fallfwd cut, the Fall.bmp graphic, the White Matte, and the Rings graphic. This time, make a movie of the work area, so you can see the special effects in all their glory.

Once the movie has been created, use the Play button in the Clip window to review it. You should see the Fallfwd clip, watch it dissolve into a white screen, and see the Rings image zoom in. Note that the Fall.bmp image doesn't show up by itself; you immediately start to dis-

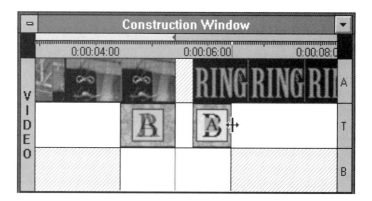

Figure 5-18. The length of the special effect should match the length of the overlap between the two video cuts.

solve to the White Matte. That's why you created the freeze frame. If you hadn't made the Fallfwd cut last longer with this freeze frame, you would have had to start the dissolve transition in the middle of the Fallfwd cut.

If you're happy with the way the transitions look, make a movie of the entire project. First reset the movie output options. Select Make Movie from the Project menu, then click on the Options button at the bottom of the dialog box (Figure 5-19).

Then select the Entire Project option in the Project Output Options dialog box (Figure 5-20) and click on the OK button. Give your movie a name, and click on OK again. When the movie has been assembled, just click on the Play button in the Clip window to review your work.

There are a number of other interesting things you can do with Adobe Premiere for Windows, such as superimpose titles and apply filters and visual effects to video cuts. These are discussed later on in the book. If you want to try them out now, please refer to the Premiere manual.

Figure 5-19.   Clicking on the Options button in the Make Movie dialog box allows you to change the parameters for making the movie.

Figure 5-20. The Project Output Options dialog box allows you to change a number of parameters for making a movie, including the frame rate, audio rate, and amount and type of compression. You can also choose to make a movie of the work area or the entire project.

Wrap-Up

This chapter introduced many new commands and tricks, so here's a quick review of what we covered.

Modifying Video Clips

- You can change the length of a cut with the stretch pointer or the In point and Out point tools.

- You can use the Info window to determine the exact length, or duration, of a cut.

- You can split a single cut into separate cuts using the Razor Blade tool.

- You copy cuts by selecting them with the pointer and selecting Copy from the Edit menu (Ctrl-C).

- You paste cuts by selecting a blank portion of a track with the pointer and selecting one of the paste commands from the Edit menu.

- You can move a whole group of cuts using the Track tools.

- You can set place markers in a cut to mark alternative In and Out points.

Working with Audio

- Audio clips can be manipulated the same way as video clips.

- You can mix two sounds by placing them on separate audio tracks.

- You can change the level of an audio cut by creating a handle in the Fade Control box and moving the handle up and down with the finger pointer.

Incorporating Stills and Graphics

- You can import graphics into your movie in a variety of formats.

- You can change the length of a graphic by using the stretch pointer or by using the duration button in the graphic's Clip window.

- You can create a bitmap image from a video clip and use it as a freeze frame.

- You can create solid-color graphics with the Make Color Matte command from the Project menu.

Special Effects

- Special effects allow you to make subtle, eye-catching transitions between two video cuts.

- You can change the length of a transition by using the stretch pointer.

- The direction of the transition is set by the Track Selector button on the transition icon.

As mentioned before, this isn't a complete list of the things you can do with Premiere, but it's enough at this point. Now you're ready to move on to the next level of editing—using pictures to convey an idea or tell a story.

PART II

INTO THE CUTTING ROOM

There are two parts to editing: the physical task of putting separate cuts of video together and the conceptual task of conveying a scene or an idea. Part I of this book dealt with the physical means of stringing several cuts into a video segment. Part II uses those same skills to explain the larger task of using images to express ideas and tell stories. Chapter 6 discusses the language of film and television. Chapters 7, 8, and 9 lead you through the processes of weaving a visual story and creating montages. Chapter 10 shows you how to add spark to your productions with special effects.

The Grammar of Visual Storytelling

L earning to edit is not unlike learning to play hockey. First, you have to learn how to skate, then you can start learning how to play the game. Likewise, you need to get comfortable with the basic steps of editing before you can begin to work on the conceptual level of telling stories.

Three Styles of Editing

All the various types of video segments fall into one of three categories: those created with *continuity editing*; those with *montage editing*; and those produced with a mixture of techniques, loosely called *mixed-format editing*. Continuity editing is used to tell visual stories, but montage editing involves the use of a collection of images to convey an emotion or idea. Mixed-format editing borrows techniques from both montage and continuity styles to convey ideas and stories.

In continuity editing, the emphasis is on telling a story that contains characters and action. There is usually a clear sense of progression—a beginning, middle, and end. The story develops through the interactions of the characters with their surroundings and each other.

As the editor, you are trying to create a reality that the audience will believe; so, special care must be taken to present scenes that are understandable and seem normal to the viewer. There are plenty of examples of continuity editing. In fact, most of the editing you see in feature films, television movies, and sitcoms is of this type because these presentations are telling a story.

In montage editing, the emphasis is on conveying an idea or concept. The images are chosen for their conceptual and emotional value, not for the way they convey a scene. There generally isn't a plot, dialog, or a storyline, although a well-edited montage builds several ideas into a larger concept.

Montage editing is the easiest kind of editing to do because you are not constrained to assemble shots into a scene, as you are in continuity editing. Any one shot can go before or after any other. But montage is the hardest type of editing to do well, because you don't have the structure provided by a storyline. You are dealing only in concepts.

Examples of montage editing are found in impressionistic television commercials and music videos and some sports segments. The appeal of montages is that they operate on an emotional level, not an intellectual one. They can also present an idea quickly. The disadvantage is that the idea can't be too complex or elaborate and still reach a large percentage of the audience.

Mixed-format editing is like montage editing in that the basic goal is to convey ideas; there's no attempt to fabricate a reality. But a mixed-format piece is less impressionistic than a montage. It can often include dialog and/or descriptive narration. Elements of a story can be included (without distinct continuity). Examples of mixed-format pieces are political commercials, most product commercials and music videos, and informational videos.

You already edited in the montage style when you edited the examples in Chapters 4 and 5 (although if you look back you will see that the cuts weren't linked by any concept); so in a sense, you already know the basics. A more involved discussion of montage and mixed-format editing is given in Chapter 9 after we cover the basics of continuity editing.

Continuity Editing—Fabricating Reality

The central goal of continuity editing is to create an artificial world in which your story takes place. This world is artificial because you, the editor, decide how the world is put together. You can have someone drive from one part of a town to another in seconds (even though in reality the locations are separated by 20 miles). You can slow down and speed up time. You can rearrange the order of cuts and completely change the meaning of a scene. You can create a scene where two people are talking to each other by telephone, yet in reality, they are in the same room. You can combine elements of the real world with animation and still make it believable.

Sound like fun? It is. But there's a catch. You have to make this world believable to the viewers. If the viewers don't buy the world you've fabricated, or they become lost and confused, then you've wasted your time (and probably a lot of money).

The easiest way to make sure your world is believable to make it exactly match reality—one to one. That is, in fact, how the first film-makers operated.

The first silent films were made by simply placing a camera at an event and then rolling the film. The camera captured the action from one perspective in its entirety (or until the film ran out). The film was a verbatim recording of the event from the viewpoint of an onlooker.

Then, around the turn of the century, a new form of film emerged that showed reality not as it was, but as the director-editor wanted to portray it. *The Great Train Robbery* (1903) by Edwin Porter was one of the first films to connect seemingly dissimilar shots into a unified story. Porter combined three scenes: a band of robbers riding away on their horses, a bound-and-gagged telegraph operator, and a group of towns-people swarming to form a posse. Without sound (these were still the days of silent films), Porter conveyed the drama and excitement of the story—a story that existed nowhere but in the final film.

D. W. Griffith took this new editing technique a step further in his film *The Birth of a Nation* (1915), which used different camera angles of the same scene (in essence, different perspectives) to heighten the drama of Lincoln's assassination. By interweaving these different perspectives, Griffith was able to manipulate time to increase the tension of the scene.

These landmark films and those that have followed in that tradition (i.e., most films and television programs) present a new reality—one created by the combination of individual, dissimilar images, a reality that is unlike anything else in the real world.

The real world around us is continuous; that is, there are no abrupt changes. Events proceed smoothly in time; people don't suddenly appear and disappear. But in the reality of film or video, the viewers are confronted with abrupt changes at every edit. The reason this style of presentation works at all is that the human brain is capable of looking past the edits (if they're done correctly) and assembling the individual cuts into a larger story.

The goal of continuity editing, therefore, is to add continuity to these discontinuous images so that the viewers can create the story in their heads. Many times, the images themselves don't tell the whole story, so the viewer fills in the gaps with his or her own experiences and knowledge of the world.

Taking Apart an Edited Scene— Car and Driver

Let's go back to one of the examples mentioned in Chapter 1 to see how a series of shots can tell a story. The scene of the man driving up to the house involved three shots:

Shot 1: Car driving up (five seconds)

Shot 2: Car door closing (three seconds)

Shot 3: Close-up of a man's finger pressing the button of the doorbell (three seconds)

When a viewer watches this scene, he or she subconsciously fills in the parts not shown (the driver turning off the ignition, opening the car door, walking up the front walk) to complete the story. Figure 6-1 shows how the real situation is compressed in the edited segment and then recreated when the viewer watches the video.

If these shots were edited in a different order—for example, the car driving up, the doorbell being pushed, then the car door closing—a different story would be told. (If the driver is already out of the car, who closed the door?) The images are the same, but the viewer fills in the gaps with other information to make sense of the shots (i.e., there was someone hiding in the back seat).

So it's not just the information in the images but their placement within a scene that creates the story. One of the most useful means for keeping the viewer in tune with your story is providing a sense of progression with the shots.

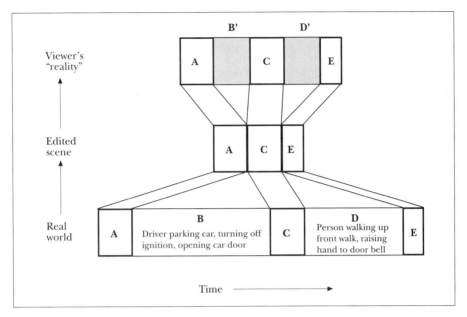

Figure 6-1.   Editing condenses a scene down to its key parts. As viewers watch the edited scene, they recreate the story in their minds.

Taking Apart an Edited Scene 2— Baseball Game

The baseball game example discussed in Chapter 1 also illustrates the use of progression, so we take another look at it here.

In this example, time is compressed in the beginning of the scene, but because the action is boring (the pitcher walking around the mound), there isn't much for the viewer to fill in. Still, each shot moves the story along so that the viewer doesn't get bored. Figure 6-2 shows the camera positions for this scene, and Figure 6-3 shows the view from each camera:

Shot 1 (camera 2): Pitcher gets the ball back from the catcher.

Shot 2 (camera 1): Batter kicks the dirt off his shoes.

Shot 3 (camera 3): First baseman yells encouragement to the pitcher.

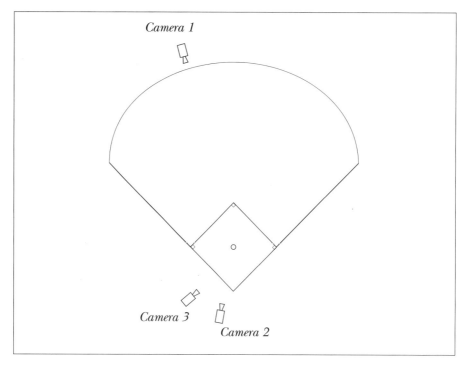

Camera 1

Camera 3

Camera 2

Figure 6-2.   Camera layout for baseball example

Shot 4 (camera 2): Pitcher raises his arms over his head to start his windup.

Now, several different perspectives of the same event (the pitch and hit) are combined to slow the action down. Even though the shots don't actually follow the real sequence (see Figure 6-4), their placement in the edited scene shows a sense of progress:

Shot 5 (camera 1-A): The batter wiggles his bat waiting for the pitch.

Shot 6 (camera 2-A): The pitcher continues his windup.

Shot 7 (camera 3-A): The first baseman crouches down ready to field a ball hit his way.

Shot 8 (camera 1-B): The batter steadies his bat.

Shot 9 (camera 2-B): The pitcher completes his windup and throws the ball.

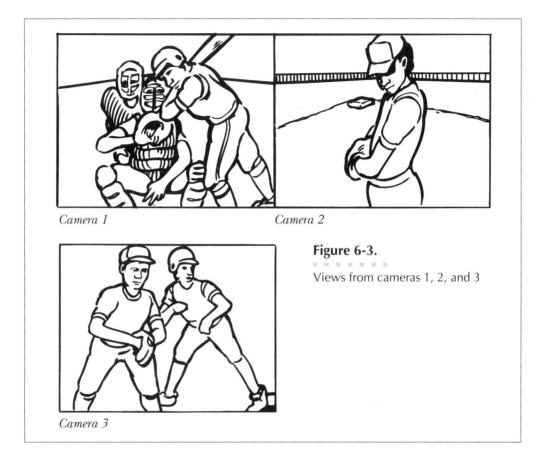

Camera 1   Camera 2

Figure 6-3.

Views from cameras 1, 2, and 3

Camera 3

Shot 10 (camera 3-B): Close shot shows the tense expression on the first baseman's face.

Shot 11 (camera 1-C): Batter swings and hits the ball.

Shot 12 (camera 2-C): Pitcher's head turns as the ball flies toward first base.

Shot 13 (camera 3-C): First baseman leaps up and catches the ball.

Compare the editing diagram of the second part of this scene (Figure 6-4) with the one for the man and car scene (Figure 6-1). In this case, several simultaneous perspectives are interwoven, or *intercut,* to produce the story.

There are several things to note in this baseball scene. Some of the shots could be deleted without ruining the story (e.g., shots 10 and 12);

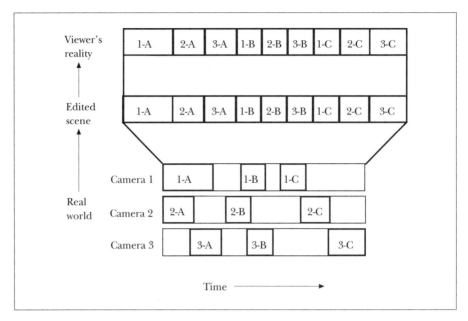

Figure 6-4.   By intercutting among three views of the same scene, the editor can expand time and increase the drama of a scene.

they merely increase the tension. Other shots could be moved into a different place (e.g., swap shots 9 and 10). The overall effect would not be all that great. These are subjective choices that each editor makes.

Another thing to notice is that the scene depends on the viewer understanding the basic layout of a baseball diamond and the respective positions of the pitcher, batter, and first baseman. If you were editing this scene for people who didn't know baseball, you would need to add a full shot of the infield to establish the scene, then show a similar example of a pitch so that the viewer understands the climax.

Creating Continuity with One Camera

Few people can afford the luxury of using several cameras to shoot a scene. The common alternative is to shoot a scene several times (several *takes*) from different camera angles. However, this introduces the problem of matching the motions or positions of people from one take to the other.

Continuity of Position

Figure 6-5 shows the layout for a scene of a man and a woman talking at a table. There are five basic shots that can be taken from the three camera positions:

Camera Position 1:
A full shot that establishes the scene (Figure 6-6a)

Camera Position 2:
A medium shot of the man showing a bit of the woman's shoulder (Figure 6-6b)
A close-up of the man (Figure 6-6c)

Camera Position 3:
A medium shot of the woman showing a bit of the man's shoulder (Figure 6-6d)
A close-up of the woman (Figure 6-6e)

Figure 6-7 shows how four of these shots might be edited together to form a scene:

Shot 1 (camera 1): Full shot of man talking and woman listening

Shot 2 (camera 2): Medium shot of man talking

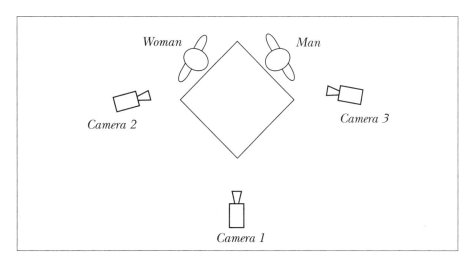

Figure 6-5.   Camera layout for conversation example

(a)

(b)

(c)

(d)

(e)

Figure 6-6.

Five shots can be taken from three camera positions: (a) two-shot of man and woman from camera 1, (b) medium shot of man from camera 2 (this shot often includes a portion of the person in the foreground, in this case, the woman), (c) close-up of man from camera 2, (d) medium shot of woman from camera 3, and (e) close-up of woman from camera 3.

Figure 6-7.

The edited scene for the man and woman conversation starts with a two-shot to establish the scene. With shots 2 and 3, the editor moves the viewer closer to the action. Shot 4 shows the man's reaction to the woman's comments.

Shot 3 (camera 3): Close-up of woman listening and then talking

Shot 4 (camera 2): Close-up of man's reaction

In the baseball scene, you were always *cutting*, or editing, from one person to a different person (i.e., pitcher to batter). In this case, you are cutting between different shots of the same person; for example, the man is seen in both shot 1 and shot 2 but from different angles.

For this edit to work, for the viewer to accept it and not get confused or distracted, the man must be in about the same position; that is, there has to be continuity of position. If he is resting his arm on the table in shot 1, then shot 2 must show the same thing.

If instead, he has raised his hand to his chin in shot 2 (Figure 6-8a), then when the shots are edited together, the man's hand suddenly jumps from the table to his chin (Figure 6-8b). This type of edit, called a *jump cut*, distracts the viewer and should be avoided in continuity editing.

The best way to avoid jump cuts is to choose shots where the position of the main character doesn't change. The positions of secondary characters don't matter as much (the position of the woman's shoulder in shots 1 and 2 isn't particularly important because she isn't the center of attention).

Note

In continuity editing, the editor is dependent on the director getting the right footage (having enough different angles, making sure people are in the same positions in different shots, etc.). If you are acting as your own director, you'll have the good fortune of suffering with all your directing mistakes as you try to edit your footage. I say "good fortune" because that's the fastest way to become a better director.

Figure 6-8. Maintain continuity of position by avoiding jump cut: (a) man changing his position by placing his hand on his chin and (b) jump cut caused by a change in the man's position.

There are a few general rules regarding which kinds of shots can be edited together. These rules have as much to do with how shots are directed as how they are edited. Here are two of the main ones.

You shouldn't cut from one shot of a person talking to a shot of the same person from the same camera position and framing (focal length). This is invariably a jump cut (people never remain in exactly the same position). This is why it's important to shoot a scene from different angles. If the shot changes enough (different angle, background, distance, etc.), the viewer won't notice subtle differences in a person's position.

Another jump cut occurs if you cut from a medium shot of a person directly to a close-up of the person taken from the same camera angle. Although this type of cut is done often in television news pieces, you should try to avoid it. Television camerapersons are under tremendous time pressures and sometimes don't have the option of shooting several takes from different angles. If you want to use a medium and close-up from the same angle, insert a shot of the same person from a different angle between the two shots.

You can cut from a long shot of a person talking to a close-up shot of him or her. The framing is different enough that the slight jump of the person's head position between the shots won't be noticed.

Continuity of Motion

When people move during a shot, maintaining continuity is a bit more difficult. However, this doesn't mean you should avoid having your characters move—far from it; video loves motion. It's one of the things this medium does better than any other. And it turns out you can use the motion to your advantage when editing.

Let's change the scene with the man and woman to introduce some action. This time, after the woman is talking for a while, the man gets up and gestures (Figure 6-9). One way of editing this scene is shown in Figure 6-10:

Shot 1 (camera 1): Full shot of man talking and woman listening

Shot 2 (camera 2): Medium shot of man talking

Shot 3 (camera 3): Close-up of woman listening and then talking

Shot 4 (camera 1): Medium shot of man starting to stand up

Shot 5 (camera 2): Close-up shot of man finishing the action and gesturing

The scene includes the additional shot from camera 1 (shot 4) to show the beginning of the man's action. The action is split up and shown in two shots because this makes the edit smoother: the motion attracts the viewer's eye and de-emphasizes the edit (Figure 6-11). In Chapter 7, we'll go into the details of how to match motion between two cuts. The main thing to realize here is that the motion must appear smooth when viewed in the edited scene.

Figure 6-9.

Frames from a medium shot of the man standing up, from camera 2's position

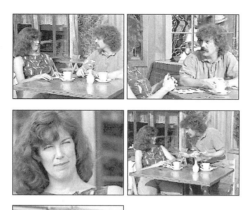

Figure 6-10.

In this edited scene, we cover the man's movement with two shots (4 and 5).

Figure 6-11.

Matching the movement of the man in shots 4 and 5 creates a smooth edit because the movement attracts the viewer's eye.

Using Cutaways

The previous two sections discussed how to maintain continuity when the same person is shown from two different angles. If for some reason you can't match a person's position or motion between two shots, then insert a shot of someone or something else to hide the problem.

In the first version of the man and woman scene (Figure 6-7), the shot of the woman (shot 3) comes between two shots of the man (shots 2 and 4). In this case, you wouldn't have to worry if the man moved his hand from the table to his chin. Because of the intervening shot of the woman, the viewer won't remember exactly what the man's position was in shot 2 and won't notice the change. This is a very common way of getting around continuity problems.

We've all seen the shot of a television news reporter listening intently to a person being interviewed. Chances are that shot is being used to hide a jump cut (like 90 percent of the time). The shot of the reporter allows the editor to connect two different quotes, or *sound bites,* **and then hide the edit with the cutaway of the reporter. These shots are so useful for editing interviews that it's standard for television producers to shoot a reporter cutaway even if they don't think they'll use it. Sometimes, these cutaways are shot without the interview subject even in the room! A production assistant substitutes for the interviewee, and the reporter looks at and listens to the assistant. The reporter can also ask questions of the speaker-assistant. When edited with the interview, the question seems natural (that is, if the reporter is any good at acting, which most of them are).**

When there is motion in the scene, and you have continuity problems in matching the motion, you can use the actions of other characters to solve the problem. To go back to the second version of the man and woman scene (Figure 6-10), let's say the woman looked up as the man stood up. This would allow us to edit the scene in the following way:

Shot 1 (camera 1): Medium shot of man talking and woman listening

Shot 2 (camera 2): Medium shot of man talking

Shot 3 (camera 3): Close-up of woman listening; then talking; and after a few seconds, looking up

Shot 4 (camera 2): Medium shot of man finishing the action of standing up

The motion of the woman's eyes and head indicates that the man stood up. This unseen but implied action is completed in shot 4. Because the motion is implied, you can make actions happen faster than they typically would. The trick is to include some part of the motion in the final shot to complete the action.

Continuity of Place

The man-and-woman scene starts off with a full shot showing both characters. This is called an *establishing shot* because it lays out, or establishes, how the characters are positioned in their surroundings and with respect to each other. This helps orient the viewer, which is why most scenes start with an establishing shot.

Once you establish the scene, you then have to stick to that layout. If the man appears on the right side of the screen and the woman on the left, as in Figure 6-6, then they have to appear that way in all the shots for that scene (or until you reestablish the scene). Notice that even though shots 2 through 5 (Figures 6-6b, c, d, and e) were taken from a different angle than shot 1, the man is still on the right and the woman is still on the left.

Defining the Line of Interest

The man and woman stay on the same side of the scene because all the different camera positions lie on the same side of the *line of interest,* an imaginary line running through the central characters in a scene (Figure 6-12). Every scene has a line of interest; once you select a camera position, all other camera positions must lie on the same side of the line. Moving the camera to the other side of the line of interest, *crossing the line,* causes the characters to switch sides (onscreen) and that confuses the viewer. For example, let's say you added another camera position (camera 4 in Figure 6-13). A shot from this angle would show the woman on the right and the man on the left:

If you were to edit this shot together with a shot from camera position 1, the man and woman's positions would suddenly flip.

Staying on the same side of the line of interest is particularly important when there's movement in the scene. Let's say you're editing a scene from a football game (the camera positions are shown in Figure 6-14). Shots from camera 1 show the red team on the right and the blue team on the left (Figure 6-15a) Shots from cameras 2 and 3 show the same orientation, but the shots from camera 4 show their positions reversed (Figure 6-15b).

Now, let's say the red team quarterback heaves a long pass. You start with a shot from camera 1, with the ball traveling from right to left. Then, you cut to a shot from camera 4. Which direction is the ball traveling? From left to right. In shot 1, it was traveling right to left. Besides violating the laws of physics, this thoroughly confuses the viewer.

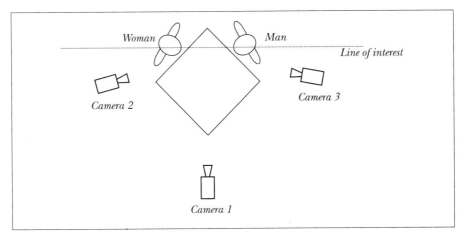

Figure 6-12. The line of interest is an imaginary line that determines the geometry of a scene. Once you've picked a camera position on one side of the line, all other camera positions must be on the same side of the line of interest.

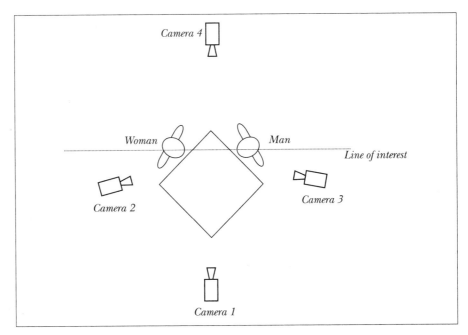

Figure 6-13. Crossing the line with camera 4 confuses the viewer because the man and woman suddenly switch positions on the screen.

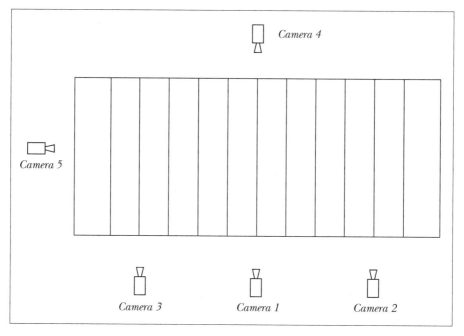

Figure 6-14.   Camera layout for the football sequence

Note   If you happen to watch football games, you've probably noticed the words *reverse angle* appearing on the screen during replays. Television directors put these words up on the screen to signal that they've crossed the line and that the directions are reversed. The reverse-angle shots are taken with a camera on the opposite side of the field, like the camera in position 4 (Figure 6-15b) in this example.

Using a Neutral Shot

Fortunately, there is a way to cross the line without confusing the viewer and that is to use a *neutral shot*, a shot that lies right along the line of interest. The shots from camera 5 (Figures 6-14 and 6-15c) are neutral in that the red team and blue team aren't on any particular side (they're on the top and bottom of the screen). This allows you to cut to any of the other cameras and reestablish the scene on the same side

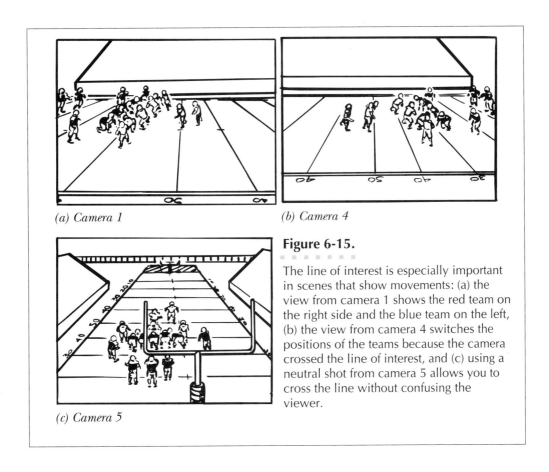

(a) Camera 1

(b) Camera 4

(c) Camera 5

Figure 6-15.

The line of interest is especially important in scenes that show movements: (a) the view from camera 1 shows the red team on the right side and the blue team on the left, (b) the view from camera 4 switches the positions of the teams because the camera crossed the line of interest, and (c) using a neutral shot from camera 5 allows you to cross the line without confusing the viewer.

of the line of interest (cameras 1, 2, or 3) or on the opposite side (camera 4). Here's how the scene might be edited:

Shot 1: Camera 1

Shot 2: Camera 3

Shot 3: Camera 5

Shot 4: Camera 4

Shot 5: Camera 5

Shot 6: Camera 2

The shots from camera 5 act as transitions between the shots on opposite sides of the line of interest.

Neutral shots are invaluable when editing material shot by a director who doesn't know about the line of interest. If you are going to be working on someone else's stuff, look for neutral shots, and remember where to find them.

Editing for Peak Effect—Choosing the Right Shots

If you follow the grammar laid out in the previous sections, your videos will be understandable and coherent to the viewer, but they won't necessarily be exciting. It's the same thing with writing—a grammatical sentence isn't enough to inspire the reader.

Creating an exciting video segment involves making lots of decisions, most of them subjective, about which pieces of video to include. The grammar of editing spells out what edits you can't make (i.e., jump cuts), but that still leaves you with a lot of options.

A general rule is that, when possible, a shot should include motion or emotion. A shot of someone talking blandly gets boring after a few seconds; a shot of a person fighting back tears holds the viewer for 20, maybe even 30 seconds. Likewise, a scenic outdoor shot, although it's interesting, holds the viewer's attention a lot longer if there is some kind of action in it.

This applies to almost all shots. If you are using a shot of a person listening to someone else, choose a cut where the person is moving his or her head (even subtly) or where he or she shows some emotion. If you using an establishing shot of people at a table, start the cut when one of the people moves in some way (raises his or her arm, leans back, etc.). Every time you have to decide which part of a shot to use, which cut to take, look for motion or emotion. The final video segment will be much more interesting.

Another way to introduce motion into an otherwise boring shot is to move the camera. This is one reason why Hollywood directors go to such lengths to make the camera move (by putting it on a car, using cranes, etc.).

Becoming a Better Editor

At this point, you're probably not an expert editor, but you are an expert watcher, and all those years of staring at the boob tube are now going to pay off. But first, you have to learn a new way of watching television (or movies for that matter).

Try the following exercise sometime while you're watching a television movie (or a sitcom):

1. Record the movie as you're watching it.

2. Get a piece of paper, a pencil, and a watch.

3. Rewind the tape to any particular section of the movie.

4. Play the movie and make a mark on the paper each time a new shot appears. Don't look at the paper while you make the marks, or you'll miss what's happening on the screen. (The marks don't have to be beautiful, only clear.) Don't try to follow the story; you're looking for edits.

5. Do this for two minutes, then count the number of marks on the paper and divide that number by two. The result is the average number of edits per minute. Depending on what you're watching, the edit rate can vary from 10 to 30 or higher.

6. Calculate how long the average cut lasts by dividing the average number of edits per minute into 60 (60 seconds per minute). If the edit rate is 30 edits per minute, then the average cut is only 2 seconds long.

You'll probably be surprised at how short an average cut lasts. That's because when you're casually watching television, you are following the story that's being created in your head, not the individual shots that help create that story.

Now rewind the tape and watch the same section again, only this time don't make any marks. Instead, try to notice each edit and try to follow the story. It's hard at first, but it gets easier with practice.

Congratulations, you're now analyzing the video instead of just watching it—one of the first steps toward becoming an expert editor! You've broken the illusion and are seeing the individual parts that make up the story.

Practice this new way of viewing television by looking for the different kinds of shots used in a scene. Try to notice the editing pattern used. Look for the establishing shot and try to pick out what the line of interest is. They're all there; they've always been there. Only now, you have the skills to pick them out.

Wrap-Up

This chapter covered some of the basic rules of video-editing grammar and showed a few short examples of how the rules are used. The next two chapters show you, step by step, how to edit several real-world situations.

CHAPTER 7

Tricks of the Trade I— Editing a Group Discussion

H ow many times have you suffered through lengthy meetings where only one or two really good points were made? Well, now you have the ability to separate the wheat from the chaff, so to speak, through editing. This chapter uses a fictitious example of a company meeting to demonstrate how this is done.

Your company is developing a new database product that incorporates digital video files. The head of the software group recently met with two outside consultants who had tried out the new package. The meeting was taped and you have been asked to produce a short digital movie of the meeting so that it can be distributed to the rest of the software team. Your boss, the head of the software group, has given you a rough idea of the parts of the meeting he wants included in the movie. There's about one hour of material on videotape, and you've got to shorten it to about four minutes. First we look at how to edit two sentences together, then we tackle the larger task of editing the two-minute segment.

The Problems with Talking Heads

This assignment involves three main tasks: picking the right sections of video to use, editing the segments together, and covering any jump cuts that arise. Because you are only working with footage of people talking (known in the TV industry as *talking heads*), you don't have many options, so you have to get fairly creative in your choice of video sections.

One of the first things you might notice when you listen closely to the tape of a person talking is that people don't talk the way they write. They pause, they insert *um*s and *ah*s, they ramble, and they often don't talk with correct grammar. For example, in the videotape of the meeting, the boss starts off with the following comments:

> *Boss:* Thank you for coming in to talk with us today about the new database software product we've developed. As you know, ah, or as you've seen, this product will allow people to add or put digital movies into any record in their databases, ah, so they can quickly access visual information tied to particular data. We've been working on this for nearly, um, nearly two years or so and um, it's been pretty challenging to stay up on the changes going on, you know, the introduction of Video for Windows *and* QuickTime for Windows, plus all the hardware advances. Well, we're pretty excited about it and wanted to get your comments.

Believe it or not, this is how most people talk! We don't notice these little imperfections in real conversation, but they stick out like sore thumbs in a video segment. With editing, you can clean up a person's speech, taking out all the *um*s and repeats.

In addition, the final digital movie is only going to be a few minutes long, so each quote, or *sound bite*, has to be succinct. Remember, time is a precious quantity in video, so you don't want to waste it on meaningless material. So how do you decide which pieces of video and audio to use—which sound bites? Answer: by focusing on the message you want to convey and remembering what your audience needs and wants.

In this example, the audience (the software team) already knows about the product, so you don't need to include the boss' description of the product in the movie. All you really want is a quick introduction, which can be achieved with the following two sound bites:

> *Boss:* Thank you for coming in to talk with us today about the new database software product we've developed. / we're pretty excited about it and wanted to get your comments.

The slash (/) indicates where the edit was made. This reminds you that there will be a jump cut when you edit these quotes together. Notice that the edited version doesn't contain all the ideas of the original quote—only the ones important to the audience.

 Short sections of speech usually work best in video; a sound bite lasting 7 to 12 seconds is fairly common. Occasionally, you have a long sound bite, but it's not a good idea to keep the same person's face on the screen too long (the viewers will get bored).

Once you decide which sound bites to use, your next goal is to make these two sentences sound like they are not separate cuts, that is, as if they were said together in the first place. The main trick is to put the correct amount of pause in between the sentences. Let's take a look at how this is done using the meeting example and Adobe Premiere. The techniques shown here can be applied to your specific situation as well.

 You can get a rough idea of how long a sound bite lasts by formatting the transcript of a person's interview in the following way: Use a monospace font (such as Courier) with a 10-point type size. Set the left margin at 3 inches and the right margin at 6 inches. With this formatting, each line represents roughly two seconds.

Editing Two Sentences Together

The first step is to digitize the boss' introductory comments and store them on your computer. Although you might be tempted to digitize the entire introduction, remember that the middle sentences won't be used; they would take up precious space on your hard drive. Instead, locate the sentences you need, in this case:

- `Thank you for coming in to talk with us today about the new database software product we've developed.`

- `. . . we're pretty excited about it and wanted to get your comments.`

Now, digitize these sentences. Before each transfer, write down where on the tape the material comes from (how far from the beginning of the tape in minutes and seconds), so you can find it if you need it again.

 Make sure to digitize at least an extra half-second of material at the beginning and end of each sentence. This gives you flexibility later on when editing. Also, digitize the material at the highest possible frame rate. This helps you find the proper In and Out points more easily.

Once the material is digitized, import both clips into the Project window of Premiere using the Import command. Then open clip 1 in the Clip window by double-clicking on the thumbnail of the clip in the Project window.

Listen to the clip several times. After you get a sense of the flow of the sentence, move to the beginning of the sentence and use the Step Forward and Step Backward buttons to find the point where the first word of the sentence starts. Then move back (earlier) five frames using the Step Backward button and set this as your In point. This sets a five-frame *pad* that prevents the sound of the boss talking from starting right at the beginning of the clip.

Now move to the end of the sentence and find the point where the last word of the sentence stops. Step forward seven frames and set this as your Out point. The pad at the end of the sentence is longer than the pad at the beginning because people tend to start sentences cleanly but often extend the last word of a sentence.

 The five-frame pad at the beginning of the clip and the seven-frame pad at the end are only initial starting points. Don't kill yourself trying to figure out exactly where the sentence starts and stops—just get close. You'll probably change the In and Out points later anyway after you preview the edit.

Open the next clip (the last sentence of the boss' introduction) and follow the same steps to set the In and Out points. Then move both cuts into the Construction window (by dragging them from the Project window). Place cut 2 directly after cut 1 as shown next:

Set the work area to include both cuts, then press the Ⓡ key to preview the edit.

This section is written as if you were actually working with the video clips from the meeting. Of course your meeting will be different. Most of the techniques demonstrated in the example, however, will apply to your particular situation.

Fixing Unnatural Pauses

If you're really lucky, the edited piece will sound perfectly fine. But most of the time the pause between the sentences won't sound natural: it will be either too short or too long.

Shortening a Long Pause

The problem here is that there is too much time (or space on the timeline) between the two sound bites (Figure 7-1). There are two possible causes: there is too much pad at the end of cut 1 or there is too much pad at the beginning of cut 2. We start by assuming that there is too much pad in cut 1. To fix this, perform the following steps:

1. Open cut 1 in the Clip window.

2. Use the Goto button to go to the Out point.

3. Step backward two frames and set this point as your new Out point.

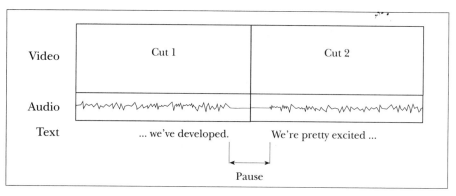

Figure 7-1. A long pause between two sentences is caused by too much pad on either the end of the first sentence or the beginning of the second sentence.

By shifting the Out point earlier, you move closer to the end of the first sentence (Figure 7-2), which reduces the pad.

Go back to the Construction window. Notice that there is a small gap between the two cuts that formed when you made cut 1 shorter. To fix this, drag cut 2 to the left to eliminate the gap.

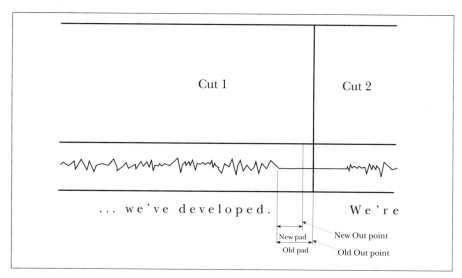

Figure 7-2. You can shorten a long pause by setting an earlier Out point for the first sentence. This decreases the amount of pad at the end of the first sentence, which reduces the duration of the pause.

Preview the edit by pressing the Ⓡ key. If the pause is still too long, try reducing the pad on cut 2 with the following steps:

1. Open cut 2 in the Clip window.

2. Use the Goto button to move the In point.

3. Step forward two frames and set this point as your new In point for cut 2.

By shifting the In point later, you move closer to the beginning of the second sentence (Figure 7-3), which decreases the pad in cut 2. Go back to the Construction window, drag cut 2 to the left to eliminate the gap, and preview the edit.

If you get tired of switching between windows, try using the stretch pointer in the Construction window to change the In and Out points for the cuts as follows:

1. Set the time ruler indicator to four frames (you need a lot of resolution because you are changing the In and Out points by at most four or five frames).

2. You might also find it helpful to open the Info window, which displays the actual timing of the In point.

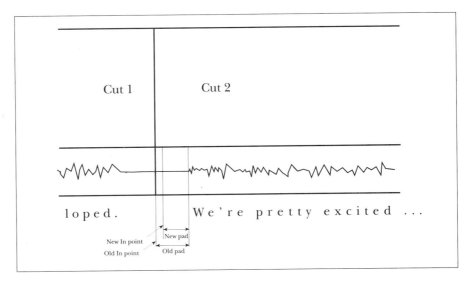

Figure 7-3. You can shorten a long pause by setting a later In point for the second sentence.

3. Find the point where the two cuts meet (the *edit point*).

4. Use the stretch pointer to move the In point of cut 2 later (to the right) or the Out point of cut 1 earlier (to the left).

5. Use the time ruler at the top of the Construction window or the Info window to see how much you are changing the In or Out point.

6. After you change the In and Out points, drag cut 2 to the left to eliminate any gaps.

Lengthening a Short Pause

In this case, the problem is that there isn't enough time (space on the timeline) between the two bites (Figure 7-4). You need to increase the time between the cuts and, as with a pause that is too long, you have two distinct options: you can increase the pad at the end of cut 1 or increase the pad to the beginning of cut 2.

 You can't solve this problem by simply moving the cuts apart. Although you can set the correct amount of pause between the two sentences, there is a disconcerting absence of sound during the gap. This is because a gap in the audio track, unlike pad, does not contain any of the ambience, or low-level background sound, that is present in almost every room.

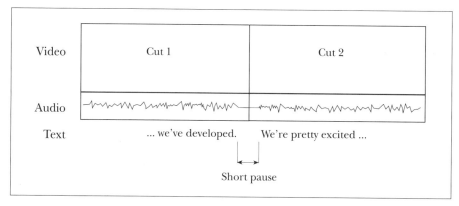

Figure 7-4. A short pause between two sentences is caused by too little pad on either the end of the first sentence or the beginning of the second sentence.

For this example, we increase the pad at the end of cut 1 with the following steps:

1. While still in the Construction window, move the cuts apart so that you can reset the In and Out points.

2. Open cut 1 in the Clip window.

3. Use the Goto button to move to the current Out point.

4. Set a marker at the current Out point so that you can find it later.

5. Step forward three frames and set this point as your new Out point.

By moving the Out point later (Figure 7-5), you moved farther away from the end of the first sentence, thereby increasing the pad.

 There is nothing special about three frames. If the pause between the two sentences is very short, you might need to add five frames, maybe even seven frames. After a while, you can tell how much pad you need to add just by listening to the edited section.

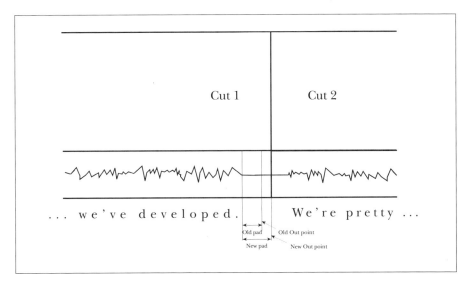

Figure 7-5.   You can lengthen a short pause by setting a later Out point for the first sentence. This increases the amount of pad at the end of that sentence, which increases the duration of the pause.

Go back to the Construction window and drag cut 2 to the left to eliminate any gap that remains. Then preview the edit. If the pause still doesn't sound natural, continue to add pad to cut 1 until the sentences seem to flow together.

If you can't seem to change an In or Out point in the Clip window, go back to the Construction window and make sure there is a gap separating the two cuts. Premiere won't let you extend a cut if there isn't room to do so.

When you keep adding pad to the end of the first cut, you'll run into the next sentence, which you don't want to use (Figure 7-6). If this happens, you need to reset the Out point of cut 1 to an earlier point (if you marked a previous Out point with a marker, then go to that marker and reset the Out there). You then increase the pad at the beginning of cut 2, as follows:

1. Open cut 2 in the Clip window.

2. Use the Goto button to move to the current In point.

3. Set a marker at the current In point, so you can find it later.

4. Step backward several frames and set this point as your new In point.

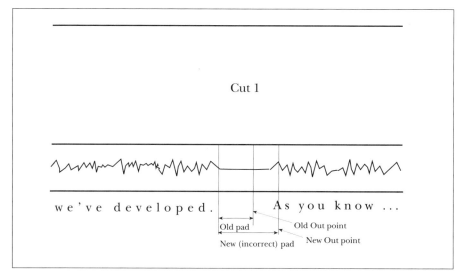

Figure 7-6. If you keep setting a later Out point for the first sentence, you will run into the next sentence on clip 1.

By moving the In point earlier, you move farther away from the beginning of the second sentence (Figure 7-7), which increases the pad.

If the two sentences you're working with don't have enough pad at the beginning and end of the sound bites, you can still lengthen the pause by moving the cuts apart on the timeline, then filling the gap you created with a short cut of ambience. Just find a small section of audio from the videotape where no one is talking. Digitize it and place it in the gap. That fixes the pause and prevents the sound from dropping out.

When you're satisfied that the two sentences sound natural, you're ready to move on to the next step—covering up the jump cut in the video.

Hiding the Edit

If you have been previewing the edits in audio-only mode, reset the preview options so you can see the video as well. Although the audio sounds correct, there is an abrupt change, or *jump cut*, in the video

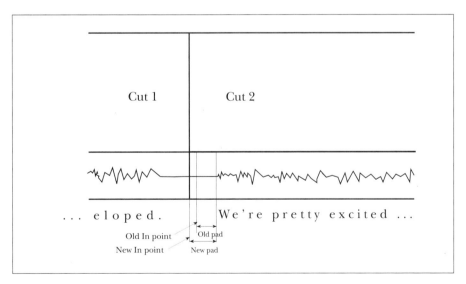

Figure 7-7.   You can lengthen a short pause by setting an earlier In point for the second sentence.

portion. You can fix this by replacing part of the video with a cutaway of someone (or something) else, which hides the jump cut.

Choosing a Cutaway

At this point, you need to go back to the videotape and look for a shot of one of the consultants listening to your boss. The main thing to look for is a shot where the consultant looks interested and shows some movement. The consultant has to be looking at the boss for the cutaway to work.

Don't choose this shot haphazardly! It can dramatically affect the message of the final piece. In a sense, you are adding an editorial comment. If the person in the cutaway looks interested, then the boss' comments are interesting. If the person in the cutaway looks bored or isn't paying attention, then you make that comment about the boss' introduction. The cutaway is a crucial element of the visual story; in some cases, it's more important than the video of the main speaker.

Adding the Cutaway to the Sequence

After selecting the shot you want to use as the cutaway, digitize it and then import the digitized clip into Premiere. Drag the clip from the Project window into the Construction window and place it in video track B (Figure 7-8). The cutaway is positioned so that it straddles the edit between cuts 1 and 2. We want the cutaway to last for two seconds, so adjust the length of the cutaway to two seconds using the stretch pointer and the Info window. If necessary, reposition the cutaway after adjusting its length.

 You don't always have to center the cutaway over the edit point, but some part of the cutaway must cover the edit point. Try moving the cutaway to different positions to see what works best.

You don't want to use the audio portion of the cutaway, only the video, so delete the audio portion by clicking on it and pressing the D key.

Now we need to tell Premiere how and when to switch from the video of the boss in video track A to the cutaway in track B. We don't

Figure 7-8. Editing together two sentences from the same person often causes a jump cut. You can hide the jump cut by adding a cutaway.

want to use a fancy transition between the two, so we just use a transition known as the Direct transition which simply swaps tracks A and B.

Open the Transitions window, scroll down, and select the Direct transition by clicking on it. Drag its icon into the Construction window, and place it in the T track so that it sits above the cutaway:

Click on the transition direction arrow so that it points up—this makes the cut in track B appear in place of the cut in track A. Adjust the length of the Direct transition using the Stretch pointer, so that it matches the length of the cutaway:

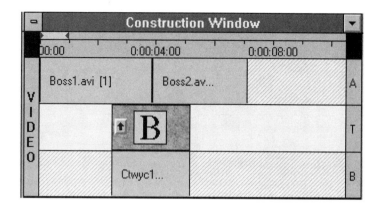

As you preview the work area, you first see and hear your boss speaking the first part of sentence 1. Then you continue to hear the boss, but you see the consultant listening. This cutaway lasts two seconds, after which you see the boss finish speaking the second sentence. The insertion of the cutaway hides the jump cut.

Adjusting the Length of a Cutaway

Sometimes, you will want to increase or decrease the duration of the cutaway—for example, to show a particular reaction from one of the listeners. Adjust the duration of the cutaway by varying the length of both the cutaway and the Direct transition in unison. Here's how you create a longer cutaway:

1. Increase the length of the cutaway in track B using the stretch pointer until its duration is three seconds (use the Info window to see its exact duration).

2. Position the cutaway so that it straddles the edit point.

3. Extend the Direct transition so that it matches the length of the cutaway and sits directly over it:

Now when you preview the work area, the cutaway lasts three seconds instead of two.

To shorten a cutaway, you need only decrease the size of the Direct transition because that determines how long the video in track A is replaced by the video in track B.

The More the Merrier—Group Discussions

Now that you've gotten the hang of cutting words together, known also as *dialog cutting*, you're ready to build a larger piece that includes several people talking. Although group discussions are trickier to edit than an individual talking, the task involves the same three steps: choosing the right sound bites and images, putting the sound bites together, and covering up the edits with cutaways.

The main difference between editing a group discussion and editing one person talking is that you want to develop a sense of flow within the edited piece. You don't want to just put several sound bites together. Real conversations don't usually occur that way. Instead, people ask questions, they pause after someone has said something interesting, and they talk over each other. The more you can introduce these elements into the edited piece, the more realistic your piece will be.

Choosing the Right Sound Bites

The best sound bites work on two levels: *what* a person says and *how* he or she says it; that is, (1) whether what the person is saying (the information) is interesting and an important part of the overall message or story, and (2) whether they say it with emotion or at least convincingly.

Unfortunately, the two don't always go hand in hand. You can have sound bites that look great in a transcript but seem flat and boring in the video. Other times, a quote that seems to make little sense in the transcript comes to life when you see how the person uses pauses and facial expressions when saying it. One way to track the quotes that fulfill both needs, the visual and the content, is to log the tape, noting the best sound bites and where they occur in the tape.

Logging the Tapes

You're not going to transfer all the material shot of the consultant's meeting, so you have to decide which sections to include. You could start at the beginning of the tape and transfer anything that looks interesting, but you might fill up your hard drive before you get through just one tape.

A better way is to *log* the entire tape, noting the parts that seem interesting and where they are located (how far from the beginning of the tape in minutes and seconds; many video cassette players have a counter that displays this). This way, you can review the log of the whole tape and then decide which parts to include before you actually do the transfers.

Although it can be tedious, it's important to write down how far into the tape a particular section resides. This allows you to find it quickly when it comes time to transfer it.

If you're not working with a transcript of the meeting, you should note good sound bites and where they occur. You can then go back and transcribe the bites after you finish logging the tape (see the discussion in the next section on why transcripts are helpful).

Using Timecode

If you are working on a large project with several videotapes, you might want to consider using a special numbering system called *timecode*, which assigns a specific number to each frame of video.

The timecode signal is placed either in one of the audio channels or as part of the video signal. Some videotape machines and most software editing programs can decipher this signal and display it.

You may hear people talk about SMPTE timecode, or just SMPTE (pronounced "simptee"). SMPTE is the acronym for the Society of Motion Picture and Television Engineers, which established the timecode system.

There are several advantages to the timecode system, but the one that interests us here is that when you log a tape, it allows you to write down the exact position of a particular shot without having to reference how far into the tape it is. When you're working with several tapes, this makes it a lot easier and faster to find the shots you want. Let's look at a typical situation and compare the benefits of timecode and non-timecode logging.

First, let's look at working without timecode. You made your log and noted that a good listening shot occurs 10 minutes and 15 seconds into the tape. The next day, you put the tape into the machine and notice that it's at the end. Now you have to rewind the tape to the beginning and then advance 10 minutes and 15 seconds to find the shot.

Let's look at the same situation using timecode. On your log, you noted that the listening shot occurs at 10:15 (10 minutes, 15 seconds). As before, when you put the tape into the machine, you notice that it's at the end. But this time, you also see the timecode for your current position, for example, 30:15 (30 minutes, 15 seconds). All you have to do is rewind 20 minutes, and you are at exactly 10:15.

The full format for timecode is *hours:minutes:seconds:frames* (e.g., 3:22:15:12). Each tape is assigned an arbitrary hour when you add timecode. For example, in this case we might have assigned the tape with the listening shot to hour 1. The full timecode for the listening shot would then be 1:10:15:00, or 1 hour, 10 minutes, 15 seconds, and 0 frames. Because the log is only intended to be a guide to the material on the tape, it's not necessary (in fact, it's quite tedious) to mark down the frame numbers for particular shots. Because the hour is set for the entire tape, it's not necessary to write down the hour either; so 1:10:15:00 becomes 10:15, as before.

Selecting the Sound Bites

If you have the luxury of having someone transcribe your tapes for you, great! Otherwise, you need to do it yourself. A transcript makes it easier to select the sound bites you want because you can read faster than you can listen. In addition, you can jump to different parts of an interview or a meeting much faster on paper than you can on video-tape. If the transcript was prepared before the log, mark on the transcript which sound bites you'd like to use and then note where these bites occur as you log the tape.

 Note   **Which sound bites to use depends on the situation and the message or story you're trying to present. If you are not using narration, then the sound bites need to fit together to create a sense of a conversation. It often helps to imagine that you're reading the script for a movie and read the sound bites aloud as you assemble them. After a while, you'll be able to just look at two sentences and tell if they fit together.**

Remember that the sound bites need to be succinct, so you should look for ways to shorten a sound bite or pull out the essential material. For instance, going back to the example of the boss' introduction, the unedited version lasts about 36 seconds. The edited version lasts only 10 seconds or so.

Making a Paper Cut

Although it's tempting to dive right in and start editing, a better and more efficient way to proceed is to first spend some time planning the video segment on paper. It's easier and quicker to change your mind on paper, which encourages you to try different options.

The standard way of planning an edited segment on paper is to create what's called a *paper cut*, which is a rough outline of the sound bites and shots you're going to use. The usual format for a paper cut is shown in Figure 7-9. Descriptions of video shots are put in the left-hand column, and audio clips are put on the right. The column margins are set so that there are about 35 characters per line for the audio, which translates to about 2 seconds per line in the edited segment (Courier font with 10-point type size, 3-inch left margin, 6-inch right margin). The tape locations (or timecode) of the video and audio clips are also noted so that you can find them later on.

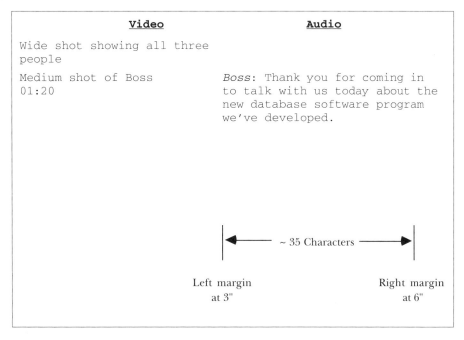

Figure 7-9.   Formatting for a paper cut, which is a rough outline of the sound bites and shots you're using

One of the main advantages of creating a paper cut is that you can review it with someone, say your boss, before you spend a lot of time transferring the video material and editing it. Also, you'll be able to spot potential problems (such as difficult jump cuts or potentially boring sections) by looking at the paper cut. This helps you prepare for problems before you start editing.

Figure 7-10 shows an example of a paper cut for the software meeting example. This isn't the complete paper cut; it only covers a little less than two minutes. The paper cut for the entire video segment, which lasts four minutes, would be nearly twice as long.

A lot of decisions went into this paper cut, so we go through it step by step. The transcript for this section is shown in Figure 7-11 for your reference.

Wide shot showing all three people	
Medium shot of Boss (01:20)	*Boss*: Thank you for coming in to talk with us today about the new database software program we've developed.
Medium shot of Boss (01:50)	*Boss*: We're pretty excited about it and wanted to get your comments.
Medium shot of Consultant 1 (02:20)	*Consultant 1*: It seems like a pretty good product, the commands seem straightforward, the organization is fairly clear, although I've got some questions about how you handled certain situations.
Close shot of Consultant 1 (03:10)	*Consultant 1*: Take, for example, after I replace a movie in a record with a newer movie, what happens to the old movie, the old version? It seems as though it just hangs around, taking up space on my hard drive.
Close shot of Boss (retake) (57:30)	*Boss:* We've wrestled with that one for a while. Did you try using the Archive command?
Close shot of Consultant 1, then a zoom out to two-shot of Boss and Consultant 1 (03:32)	Consultant 1: Yeah, I did, but it seems, well, couldn't you somehow ask the user whether or not he wanted to keep the old movie during the during the Replace procedure?
(previous shot continues) A zoom in from two-shot of Boss and Consultant 1 to medium shot of Boss (03:42)	*Boss:* We've thought about that... but we were afraid that that would make it too easy for someone to delete a file by accident.
Camera moving at the beginning of shot, then close shot of Consultant 2 (04:10)	*Consultant 2*: What if you modified the Archive command in some way ...
Close shot of Consultant 2 (04:18)	so that the user could quickly glance over a list of the old versions before deleting them.

Figure 7-10.   Paper cut for the software consultant meeting

Close shot of Consultant 2 (04:26)	Maybe you could stack them up in order, like a flip book ...
Close shot of Consultant 2 (04:32)	and then the person would simply have to choose Save or Delete.
Close shot of Boss (04:50)	*Boss:* Mmmm, sounds interesting. I'll have Cheryl, one of our programmers, look into that. Any other comments, good or bad?

Figure 7-10 (continued).   Paper cut for the software consultant meeting

Boss: Thank you for coming in to talk with us today about the new database software program we've developed. As you know, ah, or as you've seen, this product will allow people to add or put digital movies into any record in their databases, ah, so they can quickly access visual information tied to particular data. We've been working on this for nearly, um, nearly two years or so and um, it's been pretty challenging to stay up on the changes going on, you know, the introduction of Video for Windows and QuickTime for Windows, plus all the hardware advances. Well, we're pretty excited about it and wanted to get your comments.

Consultant 1: Thanks for bringing me in on this project. I think you guys should be commended for trying to get the product out so quickly, it's obvious you've put a lot of time and energy into this. It seems like a pretty good product, the commands seem straightforward, the organization is fairly clear, although I've got some questions about how you handled certain situations. Of course, I've only had a few days to look it over.

Boss: What situations did you have a problem with?

Consultant 1: Well, I wouldn't really call them problems, it's just, well, take for example, after I replace a movie in a record with a newer movie, what happens to the old movie, the old version? It seems as though it just hangs around, taking up space on my hard drive.

Boss: Yes, we've wrestled with that one for a while. Did you try using the Archive command?

Figure 7-11.   Partial transcript of the software consultant meeting

Shot 1—Wide Shot

It's important to establish the scene, so the first shot of the piece is a wide shot showing all three people. Notice that there isn't any audio planned for this video shot. You could use music here to introduce the piece. Another option (which we explore later) is to start the movie with a title that fades out over the first shot.

Shots 2 and 3—Boss Talking

These are the two clips from the boss' introduction we edited together before. Because there isn't a video shot separating them (at least not yet), there is a jump cut.

Shot 4—Consultant 1 Talking

If you refer to the transcript, you'll notice that the first part of his comments were left out. Although it's nice to get compliments, we included the important part of his first paragraph—his critique.

Shot 5—Consultant 1 Talking

Again, if you refer to the transcript, you'll see that the boss' question and the first part of the consultant's answer were left out. One reason for doing this is to save time, the other (which you can't see from the transcript, only the log) is that the camera was still moving from a shot of the boss to a shot of the consultant as the consultant responded. By losing the beginning of the consultant's response, we avoided having to use a shot where the camera is in the middle of a move.

Shot 6—Boss' Response

Notice that the tape position for this shot is 57:30. This means that it was shot after the meeting was over. What happened was that the camera operator knew that the boss' response hadn't been captured on camera (the camera was still pointing at the consultant when the boss responded.) The camera operator asked the boss to repeat his question after the meeting was over so that it could be recorded.

Shots 7 and 8—Consultant and Boss Talking

These are really two parts of the same continuous shot; they are separated here to indicate when a new person is speaking. The camera technique shown here—a close shot of one person, a zoom out to a two-shot when the first person stops talking, then a zoom in to the second person as he's talking—is a common way of shooting two people. If done correctly, it allows you to switch from one person to another without having to perform an edit.

Shots 9, 10, 11, and 12—Consultant 2 Talking

These are small chunks of consultant 2's comments, which convey a complete idea when put together. The main reason for "cutting her up" is to save time. The other reason is that by eliminating the less important words and phrases, we increase the impact of what the consultant is saying.

Making the First Cut

Now that you have a detailed paper cut, assembling the first version of the video segment, or the *rough assembly,* is fairly easy. First you transfer the footage from the videotape into digital files on your hard disk. Then you assemble the clips in the Construction window, setting In and Out points for each clip.

Transferring the Footage to Disk

Digitize the sections you want, using the time markings shown on the paper cut. Be sure to transfer a little bit of extra material at the beginning and end of each shot. This gives you more flexibility when you start editing.

Launch Adobe Premiere if it isn't already running. Create a new project using the New command in the File menu. Then import the clips into the Project window using the Import command. You can import all the clips at one time or as you go along, whichever seems easier to you.

Assembling the Cuts

Because you worked out most of the problems in the paper cut, all you need to do is simply set the proper In and Out points for each clip and lay the clips end to end. If you're not sure how to edit sound bites together, please refer to the discussion earlier in this chapter that covers this topic.

As you assemble the cuts in the Construction window keep in mind the following points:

- Each cut should be placed in video track A.

- Don't worry about jump cuts; we'll fix them later.

- If you are trying to fix the pause between two sound bites, set the Preview option so that you are only previewing the audio. Remember to click the Video Preview check box back on when you want to preview the video portion.

- There should be a slightly longer pause between sound bites from different people. For example, you might want to have a pad of about 15 frames between shot 3 (boss' sound bite) and shot 4 (consultant's sound bite).

- Reset the work area so that you only preview the portion of the movie that you're currently working on.

- If you can't seem to adjust the In and Out points for a cut in the Clip window, make sure there is a gap between that cut and other cuts in the Construction window.

- Save the project every now and then so that you won't lose what you've done if the computer goes down or locks up.

Once you place all the cuts down in the Construction window and set the In and Out points for each clip, the Construction window should resemble Figure 7-12.

 Because you are working with different clips for your example, the Construction window for your project won't be the same as Figure 7-12, but the basic features (a string of video and audio cuts laid down from beginning to end) should be the same.

Because the rough assembly won't be the final version of your movie, you should set the output options to minimize the size of the movie you create. Choose the Output Options command in the Project menu. Set the frame rate to 10 frames per second (fps). Set the quality adjustment inside the box labeled Compression to low. Adjust the

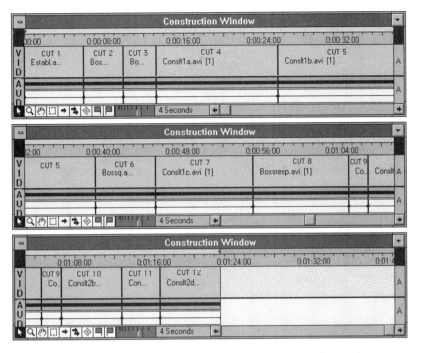

Figure 7-12.   Rough assembly for the software consultant video segment

audio rate to the lowest setting (11 kHz). Then choose the Make Movie option from the Project menu to create the rough assembly.

Brace yourself and then watch the movie. It will not be pretty—there will be lots of jump cuts. Then play the movie again with your eyes closed. Does it sound right? Does it sound like a conversation?

If it does, then you're ready to move on to the next step—fixing the video. If it doesn't sound right—if there's a pause that's a little too short—you should go back and fix that edit in the Construction window and make a new copy of the movie (you might want to give it the same name as the earlier version to same space on your hard disk).

Fixing the Video

If the audio part of the rough assembly works (sounds fine), then it's time to fix any jump cuts or video problems in the movie.

Creating a Fix List

Play the movie and keep a *fix list* of when jump cuts occur and which cuts are involved. Also, note if the camera moves during any of the sound bites. For this example, the list looks like this:

1. Jump cut, cuts 2 and 3, boss
2. Jump cut, cuts 4 and 5, consultant 1
3. Camera move, beginning of cut 9, consultant 2
4. Jump cut, cuts 9, 10, 11, and 12, consultant 2

Finding Suitable Cutaways

Go back to your tape log and find the cutaways you need to fix these problems. Use the list you just created to determine which person should be shown in the cutaway. There are a few basic rules that can help you decide which shots to use as cutaways:

- The cutaway has to show someone other than the person who's talking.

- The person shown in the cutaway should be looking at the speaker and seem interested in what the speaker is saying.

- It helps to have a little motion in the shot; i.e., the person shifts position in his or her chair, moves his or her hands, or makes a facial expression of interest (raising eyes).

- The facial expression of the person in the cutaway should match what the speaker is saying; i.e., if the speaker tells a joke, then the cutaway should show a person laughing.

- Successive cutaways should not be of the same person—alternate who is shown in a cutaway.

- Don't lose a person. If you haven't seen one of the speakers on camera in a while, show that person in a cutaway.

In this example (the meeting between the boss and the consultants), the following cutaways would be digitized and used in the movie:

Consultant 1 looking at the boss

Consultant 2 looking at consultant 1

Consultant 1 shifting his attention from the boss to consultant 2

Boss looking at consultant 2

Adding the Cutaways to Fix the Movie

We now look at how each cutaway would be used to fix the jump cuts and video problems on the fix list. Remember that cutaways are placed in video track B and their audio portions are deleted.

Fix 1—Jump Cut between Cuts 2 and 3   Insert a shot of consultant 1 looking at the first speaker:

Use the Direct transition to cut to the cutaway. You could use a shot of consultant 2 but because the viewer hears consultant 1 talk next, this cutaway helps set that person up.

Fix 2—Jump Cut between Cuts 4 and 5   Insert a shot of consultant 2 looking at consultant 1:

We haven't seen consultant 2 since the establishing shot (cut 1), so it's a good idea to remind the viewer that she's there.

Fix 3—Camera Moving at the Beginning of Cut 9   This fix is a bit more difficult to do because it takes a while for the camera to become steady. Therefore, you need to use a cutaway that lasts longer (about five seconds) and still seems interesting. The easiest way to do this is to use a shot that has a lot of movement in it.

Within this scene, however, there isn't a whole lot of movement in the first place—a few head nods, people tapping pencils, etc. That's okay. What you need is a shot that has more motion relative to the average shot for the scene. In this case, a shot of consultant 1 moving his head and shifting his attention from the boss to consultant 2 is different enough and has enough motion to keep the viewer interested.

But this shot introduces a new problem. Until now, there has been no connection between the cutaway and the audio playing underneath. However, in this case, you need to synch the movement of the consultant's head with the audio edit between the boss talking and consultant 2 talking. If consultant 1 moves his head too soon, before consultant 2 starts talking, the video and audio won't make sense together (how did he know she was going to start talking?).

The best way to synch video and audio is to use markers (remember them from Chapter 5?). In fact, synching audio and video is much easier with digital video than with traditional video because of markers. Here's how it's done in this example:

1. We open the cutaway of consultant 1 listening in the clip window and find the frame where the consultant turns his head. We set a marker at this frame:

2. We drag the cutaway of consultant 1 into the construction window and place it in video track B underneath cuts 8 and 9:

3. The small "1" marker located on the cutaway shows exactly when the consultant turns his head. Clicking on the "1," we then move the cutaway until the "1" is positioned directly under the edit between cuts 8 and 9. By clicking on the "1" marker to move the cutaway, we allow Premiere to "snap" the marker into exact alignment with the edit between cuts 8 and 9:

Place a Direct transition between the cuts in tracks A and B. Set the work area so that it includes part of cut 8, the cutaway, and part of cut 9, and preview the work area. If consultant 1 is moving his head too early with respect to the audio, drag the cutaway to the right. If consultant 1 is moving his head too late, drag the cutaway to the left. Preview the work area again. Keep adjusting the cutaway's position until the audio and video are in synch.

Because we know that there is a jump cut between cuts 9 and 10, we can eliminate the camera move problem and that jump cut by covering cut 9 completely with one cutaway. Simply extend the cutaway of consultant 1, using the stretch pointer, until the end of the cutaway lines up with the beginning of cut 10. Set the position of the Direct transition to that point as well:

Now you won't see the video portion of cut 9 in the movie, although you will hear its audio (consultant 2 talking).

Fix 4—Jump Cuts between Cuts 9, 10, 11, and 12   We've already fixed the jump cut between cuts 9 and 10. Because cut 11 is short, we can use a cutaway to cover it completely. This eliminates the jump cut between cuts 10 and 11 and the jump cut between cuts 11 and 12. We just used consultant 1 in a cutaway, so we use a shot of the boss this time:

In this example, we end cutaways at the earliest possible point (when the jump cut is eliminated). You can extend the cutaway to make the cut seem smoother.

Reviewing Your Work

Once you put in all the cutaways and fix all the jump cuts, you're ready to review your work. If you've changed the output options since you created the rough assembly, set the compression quality to low and the audio rate to the lowest setting (11 kHz). You should also set the frame rate to 15 fps. Then choose the Make Movie option and create a new version of your movie.

 If you have enough room on your hard disk, you may want to keep a copy of the rough assembly around for comparison with the new version.

If you aren't satisfied with the cutaways you added, go back and fix them before proceeding. As mentioned before, the final, edited video segment is about four minutes long. What we covered is about 1 minute and 40 seconds.

On a movie this large, you might find it useful to break it into two parts and assemble each part in a separate Premiere project. You've already completed the first part, so all you have to do is open a new project with the New command under the File menu and continue where you left off.

When you're satisfied with both parts, you can combine them by opening the project for part 1 and importing the movie for part 2. When you make a new movie, it includes both parts 1 and 2.

Adding the Finishing Touches

At this point, you've completed the assignment: you condensed a 60-minute meeting into a four-minute digital movie. But you can take it a step further and use the tools provided by Premiere (or other editing programs) to spice up the movie with some extra touches.

Adding an Opening Title

You might want to add a title to the beginning of the movie so people know what they're watching. First, you have to create the title in a paint program or in Premiere's built-in titling feature, and store it as a graphic file.

When creating a title, set the size of the title graphic to the same size you use in your digital movie (usually 160 by 120 pixels). This way, the title won't change much when you import it into Premiere. It's also a good idea to use a sans-serif font, such as Helvetica, with a fairly large type size (at least 20 point or larger) so that the title is readable. You should also make sure that there is a lot of contrast between the fore-ground (the title) and the background. Light-colored letters on a dark background work well.

Create another graphic, a *background graphic*, that contains just the background you used for the title.

Open the project for your movie and import the title and back-ground graphics using the Import command. Drag the title graphic into the Construction window, place it in video track B, and position it under the first cut in video track A:

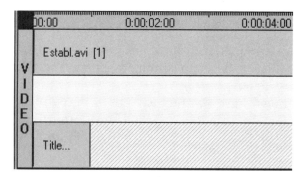

One way to use the title is to fade in the title, then cross-dissolve between the title and the establishing shot. Here's how this is accomplished with Premiere:

1. Shorten cut 1 (the establishing shot), using the stretch pointer, so that there is a three-second gap between the beginning of the movie and cut 1:

2. Lengthen the title graphic with the stretch pointer so that its duration is four seconds. You might want to use the Info window to determine when you've set the correct duration:

3. Drag the background graphic from the Project window into the Construction window and place it in the gap to the left of cut 1.

4. Extend the background graphic so that it fills the gap:

5. Open the Transitions window and select the icon for the Cross Dissolve transition. Drag the transition into the Construction window, place it in the T track, and position it at the beginning of the movie.

6. Shorten the transition with the stretch pointer until its duration is 20 frames:

7. Make a copy of the Cross Dissolve transition with the Copy and Paste commands. Position transition 2 so that it starts at the beginning of cut 1:

8. Adjust the length of transition 2 so that its right edge lines up with the right edge of the title graphic:

9. Change the direction arrow for transition 2 so that it points upward.

10. Set the work area to cover just the first eight seconds of the movie and preview the work area.

There's quite a bit going on in the first six seconds, so let's step through it. The movie starts off with the background graphic in video track A. The title graphic (in video track B) immediately starts to fade in. The title graphic runs by itself for one second. Next the establishing shot starts to fade in as the title fades out. Then there are two seconds of the establishing shot before the boss' introduction begins.

This is only one of many possible ways to use a title to introduce a movie. You can use different transitions. You can fade the title in and out over a background graphic and then fade in the first cut. Play around and see what you can come up with.

The ability to experiment with transitions is one of the truly amazing benefits of digital video editing. If you were working with videotape to experiment with transitions like there, you would have to rent what's called an online editing system. These systems rent for at least $250 an hour. With the meter ticking that loudly, it's hard to get into an experimenting mood.

Adding Ending Credits

Now let's wrap up the movie by fading out the last cut and putting up the credits. This is similar to what you did in Chapter 5, so we go through it quickly here:

1. Using a paint program or Premiere's titling feature, create a credits graphic and save it as a graphics file.

2. Create another graphic with the same background as the credits graphic, and save it as a graphics file.

3. Import the credits graphic into Adobe Premiere.

4. Go to the end of the movie in the Construction window using the slider bar at the bottom of the window.

5. Drag the background graphic into video track B in the Construction window and position it to start right after the end of the last cut:

6. Extend the right edge of the background graphic so that its duration is six seconds. You might want to use the Info window to determine the duration:

7. Open the Transitions window and select the Cross Dissolve transition. Drag its icon into the Construction window, place it in the T track, and position it after the last cut:

8. Set the duration of the transition to one second using the stretch pointer.

9. Position the transition so that its left edge lines up with the right edge of the last cut.

10. Extend the right edge of the last cut so that it lines up with the right edge of the transition:

11. Drag the credits graphic from the Project window into video track A in the Construction window and position it about 15 frames after the end of the last cut (you may want to set the time ruler indicator to half a second to increase the resolution of the Construction window):

12. Extend the right edge of the credits graphic so that its duration is four seconds.

13. Open the Transitions window and choose any transition you want. Drag the icon for that transition into the Construction window, place it in the T track, and position it so that it begins when the credit graphic begins. Set the duration of transition 2 to one second using the stretch pointer:

14. Click on the transition direction arrow to make the arrow point upward (you might have to extend the transition to see the direction arrow and then readjust its length after you set the arrow).

15. Go back to the Transitions window and choose another transition at random. Drag the icon for that transition, place it in the T track, and position it so that it ends when the credit graphic ends.

16. Set the duration of transition 3 to one second with the stretch pointer. Make sure that transition 3 ends when the credit graphic ends:

17. Set the work area to include just the last 10 seconds of the movie and preview the work area.

What you see is that the last cut fades out, leaving just the background graphic. Then the credits appear, using whichever transition you chose. The credits run for two seconds and then disappear through whichever transition you chose.

When you're satisfied with the changes you made to the beginning and end of the movie, choose the Output Options command. Set the compression quality level to normal and the audio rate to 22 kHz. Then set the frame rate to the maximum allowed by your hardware.

Choose the Make Movie option and go out and get some lunch. It might take Premiere as long as 20 minutes to compile the movie.

If you want to reduce the size of the movie file, reset the output options to reduce the frame rate or compression quality.

Wrap-Up

Although this chapter is long, it really covers only three main tasks: selecting the best sound bites, editing the sound bites so that they sound natural, and covering jump cuts with cutaways. Along the way, we covered a few skills that can help you do these tasks—namely, logging your tapes and using transcripts—and we discussed a few techniques for using cutaways.

These skills allow you to edit any scene in which people are talking. In addition to meetings, these include interviews, lectures, and dramatic pieces, such as skits and plays. The techniques covered in this chapter also come in handy when producing and editing a product demonstration tape—the subject of the next chapter.

CHAPTER 8

Tricks of the Trade II— Producing a Short Product Demonstration

I n the last chapter you worked with one type of footage—talking heads. But one of the great advantages of video is that you can incorporate many different types of imagery into the same piece. In this chapter, you learn how to combine animation, talking heads, audio voice-overs, and illustrative footage into an informative product demonstration piece. We continue the example discussed in Chapter 7, a new database program, to cover these new topics.

The new database is getting ready to be released. It's been through beta testing and most of the bugs have been worked out. Your boss raved about the piece you did on the consultants' meeting and now he wants you to create a new movie for a small conference coming up. The movie should describe and demonstrate the product and run by itself on a computer in the booth. He wants it to last about two minutes and he's given you a small budget that covers the costs of one day of shooting.

An Overview of the Phases of Production

The main problem you face when producing a piece is deciding what to do—what should be put in and what should be left out. Fortunately, you have a shooting budget, so you can plan the project out first, shoot the material you think you need, and then edit together the final piece. These tasks correspond to the three phases of production: pre-production, production, post-production.

Pre-Production

In the pre-production phase, you try to plan the project in as much detail as possible. The more time you spend researching the topic, thinking about the script, and determining what kind of footage you need to shoot, the fewer mistakes you'll make during production. Pre-production planning increases the chances that you'll have the right material when it comes time to edit the piece.

Many producers and directors use a three-step process in planning a production:

1. Create a rough outline of the project that answers a few basic questions: What are you trying to say? What are the main points you want to get across? What do you want the viewer to come away with after watching the piece? This outline, sometimes called a *treatment*, should also include rough estimates for the amount of time and money you expect to spend on research, shooting, animation or graphics, and editing. It can be as short as one page or as long as 10 pages, depending on the length and cost of the final piece.

2. Write a very rough draft of the script. This draft, often called a *shooting script*, helps you decide what footage you need to shoot. Don't spend a lot of time struggling over the script at this point, as it will probably change when you start editing. But simply going through the steps of putting words to your production forces you to think about the footage you need for particular parts of the piece.

3. Draw rough sketches, or *storyboards*, for individual scenes. If you are working on a large or complicated project, you will want to take this step, but for most of the work you do with digital movies, a detailed shooting script suffices.

Don't agonize over every line of the script or plan out every camera angle in detail. The whole point of this process, of these three steps, is to make you think out the project before you pick up a camera.

Production

The production phase can be the most exciting and the most frustrating part of making a video segment. Even armed with a good shooting script, you still have to make countless decisions. You need to discuss with the cameraperson (or decide for yourself) how to light a scene and which shots to take. If you are working with actors or interview subjects, you need to direct them (telling them where to stand or sit, what to do, and when to start). You are often on a tight schedule and sometimes have to decide, on the fly, which shots you won't get because you don't have time.

 A basic guide to lighting, shooting, and directing can be found later in the book in Chapter 12.

Directing isn't for everyone. If you're an adrenaline junkie and enjoy being under pressure, you'll love the challenge. However, if the thought of having to make 30 or 40 decisions in one day gives you nightmares, you might want to think about finding a director to handle the actual production phase.

 Given all these pressures, it's really important to have a well-thought-out shooting script to fall back on when things need to be changed.

Post-Production

Post-production is where it all comes together. In a simple project, like the one you did in Chapter 7, the main tasks are writing and editing.

But in many projects, post-production also includes a number of other tasks, such as:

- Logging the tapes
- Acquiring additional footage or stills from outside sources
- Acquiring or producing music and sound effects
- Getting clearance to use acquired material that is copyrighted (footage, stills, music, and effects)
- Creating graphics or animation
- Transferring footage from videotape to digital format
- Writing the script
- Editing a rough assembly
- Rewriting the script
- Recording narration
- Editing a rough cut
- Adding music
- Adding sound effects
- Creating the final movie

Each production includes some subset of this list. The project you'll work on in the next section covers all these steps, except acquiring footage, getting clearance, and adding sound effects (some of which are covered in Chapter 11).

Pre-Production for a Product Demonstration Movie

Now that you've got the basic idea of what's involved in producing a video piece, let's return to the software demo your boss asked you to produce. The final piece will be about two minutes long, so you don't have a lot of time to deliver your message. You could shoot one scene that lasts the entire two minutes, but a better idea might be to use several different elements to make your points.

Because you're going to be a spending a lot of time on this project (and a bit of money), you probably want to make sure your boss is going to like the project when it's finished. The easiest way to do this is to keep him informed at various stages of the development (as opposed to daily reports). The first stage is the treatment.

Writing the Treatment

Write one sentence that sums up what you are trying to say—one sentence, that's it. If you feel like you can't express your concept in one sentence, then you haven't refined the idea enough yet. For example, let's say you are trying to write the summary for the software demo piece and manage to boil it down to the following three sentences:

```
This digital video segment will start with a flashy anima-
tion to attract attention. Then it will demonstrate the
features of our product. It will end with testimonials from
current customers praising the product.
```

That's close, but it's describing what the movie will look like, not what its message will be. A better summary would be:

```
This digital video segment will show how our product com-
bines the power of digital video with advanced database
technology, producing a comprehensive database solution.
```

This sentence gives the main message: the movie will show how our product offers exciting new features. Describing how you do that comes later; you first need to have a clear idea of what your goal is.

Once you've got the central idea, you can hang all the other details—how you show the features, what images and footage to use, etc.—onto this central idea. A sample treatment for the software demo project is shown in Figure 8-1.

Note that all the various content elements fit into the central idea (you may sometimes describe particular elements in more detail). There's now a bit more shape to the project; you can even get a rough idea of how much it will cost. Try to be realistic when you estimate the costs. Better to scale back your grand ideas now rather than in the middle of production.

Software Demonstration Segment
Treatment

Summary

This digital video segment will show how VisualData combines the power of digital video with advanced database technology, producing a comprehensive database solution.

Content Elements

Salesperson introducing product on-camera

Brief demonstration of software

      Basic features

      Real-world examples

Customer testimonials (2)

      Real estate broker

      Corporate communications manager

Salesperson closing the piece

Production Elements

One day of shooting

      Salesperson intro and wrap-up

      Software demonstration

      Customer testimonials

Budget

Pre-production (three days, in-house producer)	$ 900
Production (one day, in-house producer)	$ 300
One day of shooting (Hi-8 camera package, crew)	$ 1,000
Transfer and editing (three days, in-house producer)	$ 900
Misc. (tape, crew lunch, other)	$ 100
Approximate cost	$ 3,200
Out-of-pocket costs (1 shooting day & misc.)	$1,100

Figure 8-1. Treatment for the software demonstration project. All the ideas for the movie, including the cost, are summarized at a glance.

If you're part of a committee that's developing a project like this, try to get everyone to agree on the central idea, write it down in a memo, distribute it, and try to get people to sign off on it. Then you will have something concrete to rely on when someone wants to change the production.

Writing a Shooting Script

A *shooting script* is similar to the paper cut you created in the last chapter in that it describes the video and audio parts of the piece (Figure 8-2). The main difference is that the shooting script is a plan, a blueprint for the piece. It's a way for you to think ahead about the kinds of footage you need to shoot.

Software Demonstration
Shooting Script

Opening - Special effect reveals product logo	Music
Salesperson on-camera (OC)	VisualData - A revolutionary database program that combines state-of-the-art database technology with the visual power of digital video.
Woman typing at computer	(Salesperson voice-over [VO]) Now, you can create integrated solutions ...
Shot over woman's shoulder looking at computer screen	to your most difficult data management problems.
Extreme close-up of computer screen showing menu selection	With easy-to-use commands, you can quickly add ...
Close-up of computer screen: Digital movie appears on screen	digital movies to individual records in your database.

Figure 8-2. Shooting script for the software demonstration project. Here you can see what scenes need to be shot and what the actors will say.

Close shot of woman's face	The possibilities are limited only by your imagination.
Close-ups of screen:	
Real estate example	Real Estate ...
Manufacturing example	Manufacturing ...
Corporate communications example	Corporate Communications ...
Ima Buyer, real estate agent, on-camera	Buyer - VisualData gives me a powerful edge in the competitive real estate market. When a client comes into my office, not only can I show them a list of houses they might want to buy, I can also show them what the houses really look like, inside and out. That's a tremendous benefit for them and a real advantage for me.
Les S. More, corporate communications manager, on-camera	More - I had been working with digital video for just six months and my hard drive was already littered with digital movies. I desperately needed to not only organize the movies, but also keep track of where they came from, who held the copyright, and so on. VisualData was the answer to my prayers.
Salesperson on-camera	VisualData - A power-packed database that solves your current needs and opens up new possibilities for the future.
Closing - logo dissolves on, then disappears through special effect	Music

Figure 8-2 (continued).   Shooting script for the software demonstration project

The shooting script shown in **Figure 8-2** describes one way of organizing the segment, and a fairly standard one at that. You might approach it in a different way. That's the subjective judgment each producer/director gets to make. But the sample illustrates basic techniques that apply to most shooting scripts.

Notice in the shooting script that most of the piece can be scripted; that is, because you are using an actor (or a colleague) to promote the product, you can specify exactly what he or she says. Let's step through each part of the shooting script to see how it was created.

Opening

We want to grab the viewer's attention at the beginning, so we introduce the product logo with a special effect.

Introduction

We want to say the name of the product and give a brief introduction. We could do this with some footage of the product, but the casual viewer usually pays closer attention to a talking head (at least for five or ten seconds).

Product Demonstration

If you still have the viewers' attention—if they haven't wandered off to the next booth—they're ready for some specific examples of your product. In this example, we decided to show a person using the software on a computer before focusing on specific features. A narrator describes the basics of the program. This is called a *voice-over* because the narrator's voice is heard over the pictures.

In a scene such as this where we are writing narration to match the video, we need to think about both the pictures and the words. We step through each shot in the scene to demonstrate the process:

Shot 3 (Opening shot): It's a good idea to introduce the scene with an establishing shot; in this case, a woman typing at a computer. Because we aren't showing any details of the program, the narration deals with generalities.

Shot 4 (Over the shoulder): This shot serves as a bridge between the opening shot and a shot of the computer screen. We are gradually moving the viewer's attention from the overall scene to the computer screen. We aren't showing the details of the program, so the narration is general.

Shot 5 (Close-up of the screen—Menu): Here we're matching the pictures to the words, showing the viewer what the narrator is talking about.

Shot 6 (Close-up of the screen—Digital movie): We're matching pictures to words.

Shot 7 (Close shot of woman's face): The last two shots were of the computer screen, so we want to introduce a different shot for variety's sake. Here the picture (shot of the woman) and the words (your imagination) work together to make the change.

Shots 8-10 (Series of examples): Now we go back to the computer screen to show several examples of the things a person can do with the product.

Customer Testimonials

Using customer testimonials is a tried and true way of establishing credibility for a product. Of course, because you're editing the piece, only good, positive testimonials will be shown; so, it's a kind of a contrived credibility—but it works anyway. You don't know beforehand what the person will say exactly, but for the purposes of a shooting script, you can just make it up. This also helps you guide the person during production to say something that fits into the piece.

Salesperson Wrap-Up (or Outro)

Because we used a shot of the salesperson on camera to introduce the product, we'll use a similar shot to wrap up the piece.

Close

Because this piece may run in a continuous loop, we'll close the piece by dissolving in the product logo and then making it disappear with a special effect. The final frame will match the first frame of the segment.

Production for the Demo

There are four main production elements for this piece: the salesperson's intro and outro, the product demo, and the two testimonials. We'll talk about the nitty-gritty details of production in Chapter 12, but here are some thoughts about how the elements for this piece would be shot, which may be applicable to your situation.

Salesperson Intro and Outro

The salesperson should be looking directly at the camera because you want him or her talking to the viewer. Because the salesperson has to look good—i.e., confident—and say the right words, it's a good idea for you to watch his or her delivery and have an assistant review the script as the person is talking. After each take, the assistant tells you whether the salesperson said the right words.

Product Demo

Establish a line of interest and stay on one side of it. In this case, the line of interest runs between the woman at the computer and the computer screen.

Get extra shots of the woman, such as her typing on the keyboard and glancing up and down from the keyboard to the screen, so that you have several options when you are editing. A shooting script is only a guide; you should always cover yourself with extra shots and cutaways.

Use a tripod when shooting the computer screen. Most likely you'll be zooming in to get the close-ups, and it's difficult to keep the camera steady for these shots without a tripod.

Customer Testimonials

The standard format for customer testimonials is to have the customer talk to someone off-camera—that is, someone (yourself) who is not seen. This way, they do not look directly into the camera, which helps distinguish them from the salesperson.

Because you are using two testimonials, it's a good idea to shoot the interviews so that each person appears on a different side of the screen—i.e., customer 1 is on the left side of the screen and customer 2 is on the right side. Figure 8-3 shows how these interviews would be shot.

Post-Production for the Demo

Now all you have to do is put the piece together. Of course, as you start building the piece, problems may arise, so be prepared to deviate from the shooting script. After all, what matters is not how well you follow your plans but how the final piece looks.

Preparing for the Edit

In this case, we followed the shooting script fairly closely, so a paper cut isn't necessary. This is generally true for heavily scripted productions—that is, productions where you specify beforehand what you want people to say and do.

Logging the Tapes

This production involves a variety of different elements (salesperson's intro, customer testimonials, etc.), and you need to be able to find any particular element quickly. In editing, organization is not a virtue, it's a necessity. The standard way of organizing your material is by *logging* the videotapes (logging was covered in detail in Chapter 7).

As you go through the tape of the salesperson's intro and outro, you should note the best versions, or *takes*, and where they occur on the tape. The only part that requires some tricky editing is the product demo. You should therefore write a detailed log of that footage (the woman at the computer and the screen shots), describing each shot and its location on the tape. Review the tape of the customer testimonials and note the location of the best takes.

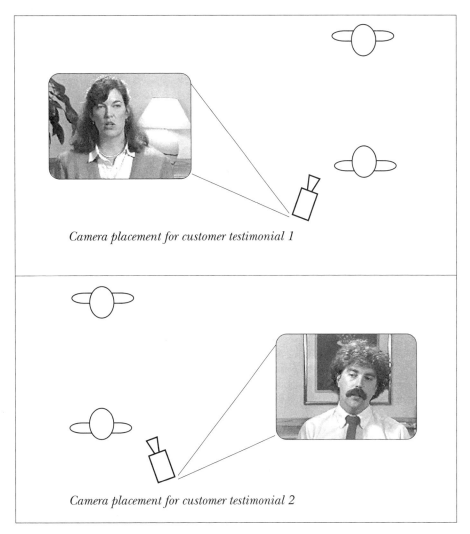

Camera placement for customer testimonial 1

Camera placement for customer testimonial 2

Figure 8-3.   When shooting two interviews that will be placed one after another in the edited video segment, it is often a good idea to shoot them so that the people face different ways.

Transferring the Material

At this point, you should have identified the key footage for the piece. Digitize the footage, making sure there is a little extra at the beginning and end of each shot. Transfer each product demo shot separately; this makes it easier to find a particular shot later on. Remember to provide descriptive titles for each shot, so you can identify the file without having to view it.

Recording the Scratch Narration

Using a sound digitizer, record the narration that will be used as voice-over material. You could record the salesperson's final voice-over now, but you would have to record it again if you change the script. A better idea is to record a *scratch narration* (or *scratch track*) of yourself reading the voice-over. This allows you to change the script and rerecord the narration easily, without having to involve another person. Then, when the piece is finished, you can record the salesperson and replace the scratch narration with the real one.

 Professional narrators usually talk more slowly than normal so that viewers can understand their words clearly. Therefore, be careful to talk slowly when recording scratch narration; otherwise, the real narration will be longer and you'll have to re-edit the movie to fit it in.

When recording the scratch narration, record each chunk of narration separately. This allows you to move small pieces of narration around to fit the pictures. A huge piece of narration can't be manipulated that way. A chunk of narration covers one idea and ends in a definite way; for example,

```
Now you can create integrated solutions
```

is not a chunk of narration because although it is a complete idea, it is leading into the next phrase. The whole chunk is

```
Now you can create integrated solutions to your most diffi-
cult data management problems.
```

In this example, there are seven different chunks of narration:

- ```
  Now you can create integrated solutions to your most dif-
  ficult data management problems.
  ```

- ```
  With easy-to-use commands, you can quickly add digital
  movies to individual records in your database.
  ```

- The possibilities are limited only by your imagination.
- Real estate ...
- Manufacturing ...
- Corporate communications ...
- VisualData—A power-packed database that solves your cur-
  rent needs and opens up new possibilities for the future.

Chunks 4, 5, and 6 consist of only one or two words, but they're still chunks because they convey an entire thought. The use of chunks will become clearer once you start editing.

Editing the Rough Cut

Now we step through the process of editing the rough cut. Because most of the piece was scripted, all we have to do is drop in the best takes of each section. The only detailed editing we do is in the product demo section.

We're using Adobe Premiere for Windows to demonstrate the process, but the basic steps would be similar in another editing program. Your particular video piece would involve different video clips and most certainly would be edited differently. But many of the techniques described in these section are applicable to your situation.

Importing the Clips

To get started, we import into Premiere all the clips we digitized. This includes the video clips and the chunks of scratch narration. The video and audio cuts used in this example are listed in Table 8-1.

Table 8-1. **Video and Audio Cuts Used in the Product Demonstration Segment**

Cut	Description
Cut 1	Product logo
Cut 2	Salesperson intro
Cut 3	Establishing shot of woman typing at computer
Cut 4	Over-the-shoulder shot of woman at computer
Cut 5	Computer screen—menu selection
Cut 6	Computer screen—digital video clip
Cut 7	Woman's face
Cut 8	Computer screen—real estate example
Cut 9	Computer screen—manufacturing example
Cut 10	Computer screen—corporate communications example
Cut 11	Customer testimonial 1
Cut 12	Customer testimonial 2
Cut 13	Salesperson outro
Cut 14	Product logo
Audio cut 1	Now you can create integrated solutions to your most difficult data management problems.
Audio cut 2	With easy-to-use commands, you can quickly add digital movies to individual records in your database.
Audio cut 3	The possibilities are limited only by your imagination.
Audio cut 4	Real estate ...
Audio cut 5	Manufacturing ...
Audio cut 6	Corporate communications ...
Audio cut 7	VisualData—A power-packed database that solves your current needs and opens up new possibilities for the future.

Adding the Opening Animation

We're going to use a special effect to introduce the product logo. We're jumping ahead a little bit (special effects are covering in detail in Chapter 10) but the one shown here is fairly straightforward.

First, we need to create the special effect. We import the product logo (made in Photoshop) and place it in track A of the Construction window. Its duration is set to two seconds with the stretch pointer. Clicking once on the clip to select it, we then choose the Filters option from the Clip menu:

A filter is a special effect that changes the look of a clip or graphic, similar to the way filters are used in Photoshop. Premiere comes with more than 30 different filters. In this example, we select the Pointillize filter from the list. You can set the amount of the effect; in this example, we use a setting of 4:

This groups individual pixels together in round clumps, kind of like an impressionist painting. With a setting of 4, the image is fairly distorted:

We now want to dissolve from the distorted logo to an undistorted logo. A second copy of the logo graphic is dragged from the project window and placed in track B and aligned with the clip in track A. We place a Cross-Dissolve transition between the two clips:

We make a movie of this effect, naming it "Logofx." By dissolving between the filtered and the unfiltered clip, we make the image become progressively clearer:

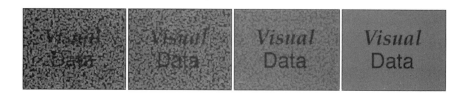

Now that we've created the special effect, we can remove the clips in track A and B and start on the piece itself. We want to dissolve in the special effect over a background. We could just dissolve in from black, but in this case we want to dissolve in from a dark blue background (it works better with the beginning of the special effect clip).

You can create a colored background by selecting Make Background Matte from the Project menu. We choose a dark blue color from the color wheel, name it "Blue Matte," and then drag it the Construction window and place it in video track A. Using the stretch pointer, we set the duration of the matte to six seconds. We import the Logofx clip and then place it track B at the beginning of the movie. We then add a Cross Dissolve transition between the two clips and set its duration to two seconds:

By dissolving from the dark blue matte to the special effect, we gradually introduce the special effect, which then reveals the product logo:

We now want to the logo to appear by itself for one second. We drag a logo graphic from the Project window and place it in track B next to the special effect clip. We then add a Direct transition so that the logo clip appears in place of the blue matte:

We're now going to use the same effect we used to introduce the logo to take it away. Another copy of the Logofx clip is dragged into track B and placed next to the logo graphic clip. Because we want to reverse the special effect (since we're making the logo go away), we apply a useful filter called Backwards that makes the video clip run backwards. We then add a Cross Dissolve transition between the second Logofx clip and the blue matte and set the track selector so that the transition is from track B to track A:

The end result is that the logo appears through a special effect, appears by itself for one second, and then disappears through a special effect, as shown in Figure 8-4.

This may seem like a lot of work for only five seconds of video, but without digital video and programs like Premiere you would have to spend nearly $100 to produce this effect on a traditional video editing system.

Figure 8-4.   The complete opening animation for the product demo piece. The logo dissolves in, appears for one second, then dissolves out.

 Note   **Filters and other special effects are covering in much greater detail in Chapter 10.**

Adding the Salesperson's Intro

As the following illustration shows, the video clip of the salesperson's intro (cut 2) is dragged into video track B of the Construction window so that we can create an overlap with the animation of 15 frames:

We open cut 2 in the Clip window and set the In and Out points with a five-frame pad at the beginning and end of the cut. The In point is then set 15 frames earlier so that the salesperson doesn't start talking until the transition between the animation and the salesperson's intro is finished.

The next step is to open the Transition window and drag the Cross Dissolve effect into the T track in the Construction window. We position the effect and modify its length with the stretch pointer so that it matches the overlap between the animation and salesperson cuts.

Editing the Product Demo Scene

Okay, now for some detailed editing. In this scene, we need to edit the shots so that they fit the words and create a sense of progression visually. The first two shots of the scene are the most difficult, so we'll look at those two in detail.

Cutting on Movement   As mentioned in Chapter 6, when editing scenes in which there is some kind of movement, it's often a good idea to put part of the movement in one shot and the rest of the movement in a second shot. The continuity of the motion across the edit attracts the viewer's eye and de-emphasizes the edit.

In this case, we want to edit the establishing shot of the woman (cut 3) and the over-the-shoulder shot (cut 4). We edit the two shots so that the movement of the woman tilting her head down from the screen to the keyboard and back up again starts in cut 3 and ends in cut 4. Here's how that would be done in this example.

The establishing shot of the woman sitting at the computer (cut 3) is dragged from the Project window into video track B in the Construction window and placed right next to the salesperson intro cut. The audio portion of the clip automatically goes into audio track B.

 Note   **Editors often refer to a particular cut as a "shot." Therefore, the words** *cut* **and** *shot* **are used interchangeably in this section.**

Next, the over-the-shoulder shot (cut 4) is dragged into the Construction window and placed next to the establishing shot:

	Cut3....	Cut4.avi [1]		B
				A
				B

What we want to do now is set the Out point of cut 3 and the In point of cut 4 so that part of the movement of the woman's head appears in cut 3 and the rest of the motion appears in cut 4. To find the correct Out point for cut 3, we open it in the Clip window. We won't worry about the In point right now; we'll set it later when we add the narration. Playing the cut, we stop at the point where the woman tilts her head down. The Out point is set at the frame where her head has stopped moving downward:

The Clip window is kept open.

We then open cut 4 in the Clip window and scroll through the cut until we see the woman tilt her head down. The In point for this clip is set where her head stops moving downward:

By referring back to cut 3 in the Clip window, we can confirm that the woman's head is in about the same position in both cuts.

Because we've changed the length of both cuts, we go back to the Construction window and drag cut 4 to the left so that it sits against cut 3. When the cuts are previewed, the woman's head should start down in cut 3; then in cut 4 it should pause briefly and then move back up to the screen.

One reason for editing these two cuts together this way, besides making the edit smoother, is that the motion of the woman's head from the keys to the screen in cut 4 leads the viewer to the screen, which is shown in the next shot, shot 5.

If, in your situation, the motion seems too abrupt or jerky, either set the Out point of the first cut later or the In point of the second cut earlier. If there seems to be too much of a pause, then either set the Out point of the first cut earlier or the In point of the second cut later.

Now that we've got the visual edit the way we want it, we add the narration.

Matching the Video Edit to the Words

Cuts 3 and 4 should last the same amount of time as the voice-over cut, which lasts about seven seconds. At this point, the video cuts are much too long and probably not in the correct position. The question is, Where should the change of shot (the edit) occur in relation to the voice-over?

A general rule is to change shots during a pause in the audio. In this case, there is a pause between the words "solutions" and "to" in the sentence, "Now you can create integrated solutions to your most difficult data management problems."

 We could have chosen the pause between "integrated" and "solutions" or between "data" and "management." The reason we're using the pause between "solutions" and "to" is because it is in the middle of the voice-over chunk, and we want to cover the narration with two shots of about equal length. If you were going to use three shots to cover this chunk of narration, you would need to find two pauses (for two video edits); in that case, the two other pauses just mentioned would work fine.

We need to change the length of cut 3 so that the video edit occurs between the words "solutions" and "to." The first audio cut is opened in the clip window. We set the In and Out points. There should be about a five-frame pad at the beginning and end of the cut. The cut is then played at normal speed to find the pause between the words "solutions" and "to." A place marker is set at this point:

Dragging the clip into the Construction window, we place it in audio track A underneath video cuts 3 and 4 and align the place marker with the edit between the video cuts:

The part of the narration before the place marker doesn't last long enough to cover all of video cut 3. We don't want to leave such a large gap in the audio track, so we shorten video cut 3 with the stretch pointer so that it begins at the same time as the audio cut:

Then we slide video cuts 3 and 4 and the audio cut to the left to remove the gap in the video track:

You can use a special tool called the multi-track selector to move several tracks to the left or the right. It is designated by the double-arrow icon in the bottom-left corner of the Construction window. Click on the tool to select it and then click on the first clip in video track A you want to move. Drag the cuts to the left or right and then release. When you're done, remember to click back on the pointer icon to return to normal editing mode.

Cut 4 is then shortened by using the stretch pointer on the end of the cut and dragging it to the left. The end of cut 4 should line up with the end of the voice-over cut.

By previewing the cuts, we see the establishing shot while we hear the first part of the voice-over; then after the word "solutions" the shot changes to the over-the-shoulder shot and we hear the rest of the voice-over.

In this case, the background sound (*ambience*) for cuts 3 and 4 is so loud that we can't hear the voice-over clearly. This problem is fixed by reducing the volume of the background sound with the audio fade control located at the bottom of the audio cuts:

This might seem like a lot of work for two shots, but adding subtle touches such as editing on movement makes the final piece much smoother and easier to follow.

Matching Actions to Words   Whenever possible, you should try to match an action in a shot with a particular word in the audio track. In this case, the first screen shot shows a pull-down menu appearing, and someone choosing the Add Movie item from the menu:

Options Window	Options Window	Options Window	Options Window
Add Field	**Add Field**	Add Field	Add Field
Delete Field	Delete Field	Delete Field	Delete Field
Add Image	Add Image	**Add Image**	Add Image
Delete Image	Delete Image	Delete Image	Delete Image
Add Movie	Add Movie	Add Movie	**Add Movie**
Delete Movie	Delete Movie	Delete Movie	Delete Movie

To match this action with the word "commands" in the phrase "with easy-to-use commands you can quickly add," we take the following steps:

Voice-over cut 2 (chunk 2) is dragged into the Construction window and placed in audio track A. We position voice-over cut 2 about a second to the right of the current end of the movie (to give us a little room to work):

We open it in the Clip window and set its In and Out points with five frames of pad at the beginning and end. Then by listening to the cut we find the point where the word "commands" starts. A place marker is set at this point.

Now we go back to the Construction window and drag the menu-selection clip (cut 5) into video track B and position it just after cut 4. The cut is then opened in the Clip window and we can find the frame where the "Add Movie" option is first highlighted. We set a marker at this frame.

Going back to the Construction window, we position the cursor directly over the marker in cut 5, click on the mouse, and drag the cut to the right until the video marker is aligned with the marker in the audio clip:

Cut 5 extends before the beginning of the audio cut, so we use the stretch pointer to align the beginning of cut 5 with the beginning of audio cut 2. We then slide both cuts to the right to eliminate any gaps:

The item should just be highlighted as the word "commands" is heard.

Covering the Rest of the Voice-Over Cut   Now let's say we want to add a new shot to cover the part of the voice-over from the word "digital video" to the end of the sentence. We again match an action in the video with a particular word in the audio track. In this case, the action is a digital video clip appearing and the word we'll match to is "movies."

First we shorten cut 5 so that it ends after the word "add." We open voice-over cut 2 in the Clip window and place a marker (2) at the pause between the words "add" and "digital."

Going back to the Construction window, we use the stretch pointer to adjust the end of cut 5 until it lines up with marker 2:

The next cut, cut 6, shows a digital video clip appearing in a database record. We want to match this action with the word "movies." We open cut 6 in the Clip window, find the frame where the video clip first appears, and place a marker (3) at that point. We open voice-over cut 2 in the Clip window and find the point where the word "movies" begins and set a marker (3) there.

Cut 6 is dragged into the Construction window and placed in video track B. We set a later In point for Cut 6 so that we have room to align the markers. Then we align the marker in cut 6 with marker 3 in the voice-over cut 2:

We then use the stretch pointer to eliminate any gap between Cut 6 and Cut 6 and to match the end of cut 6 with the end of voice-over cut 2:

For this example, these cuts would look as follows in the final movie:

- We see the menu bar appear as we hear the phrase "with easy-to-use."

- As we hear the word "commands," we see the Add Movies item highlighted.

- As the item is clicked, we hear the phrase "you can add."

- After the word "add," the shot changes and we see a database format and hear the word "digital."

- As we hear the word "movies," we see the video clip appear and then hear the rest of the voice-over, "to individual records in your database."

Although all this seems a bit complicated (on the written page), once you try it a few times yourself, you should be able to get the hang of it.

We follow the same steps for adding video cuts 7–10 and voice-over cuts 3–6 to the movie. The basic steps are:

1. Drag the voice-over cut into the Construction window.

2. Set the In and Out points in the Clip window, remembering to add five frames of pad to the beginning and end (you might want to have a 15-frame pad for short voice-overs, such as numbers 4, 5, and 6).

3. Pick a word to match the action in the video cut and set a marker at that point.

4. Drag the video cut for that voice-over into the Construction window and place it next to the last video cut in the movie.

5. Open the video cut in the Clip window, find the action we want to match to the audio, and set a market at that point.

6. Align the markers in the video and audio cuts. You may have to set a later In point on the video cuts to give yourself room.

7. Use the stretch pointer to remove any gap between the video cuts.

8. Use the stretch pointer to match the end of the video cut with the end of the voice-over cut.

9. Reduce the background sound of the video cut so that we can hear the voice-over clearly.

 Remember to save your project every now and then so you don't lose all your work if the computer goes down.

Adding the Customer Testimonials

Adding the customer testimonials is easy compared to what we've just been through. Essentially, all we have to do is set the In and Out points and add them to the end of the movie. The only wrinkle is that we're going to add a little flash by using a wipe transition for the transitions into and between the customer testimonials.

The first testimonial (cut 11) is dragged into the Construction window and placed in video track A (so we can overlap it with cut 10, which is in track B). We open the cut in the Clip window and set the In and Out points so that there are 30 frames (one second) of pad at the beginning and end of the cut. We need these large pads because we want the transitions to occur before and after the cut, not during the cut itself.

Going back to the Construction window, we increase the resolution of the time ruler so we can line up the cuts more precisely.

We position cut 11 so that it begins at the end of cut 10:

8:00	0:00:42:00	0:00:46:00	
		Cut11.avi [1]	A
V I D E O			T
9.avi...	Cut10....		B

Using the stretch pointer, we extend the end of cut 10 so that it overlaps cut 11 by 30 frames:

We then open the Transitions window and locate the Push transition. Its icon is dragged into the Construction window and placed in the T track between the overlap of cuts 10 and 11. Then, the length of the effect is adjusted to match the length of the overlap:

The reason we used 30 frames of overlap for this transition it that the Push transition moves too quickly if the overlap is shorter.

Okay, that's it for the first testimonial. Now we add the second one using the same steps, but we place the second testimonial in track B:

This time, we need to make several adjustments to the Push transition. We click on the right edge selector so that cut 12 pushes in, moving from right to left:

We also set the track selector so that the transition is from track A to track B. Previewing the last few cuts, we see the first testimonial push in from the left; when it ends, the second testimonial pushes in from the right.

Adding the Salesperson Outro

Now we use another transition for the transition from the second testimonial into the salesperson outro. The salesperson outro (cut 13) is dragged into the Construction window and placed in video track A after the end of cut 12. We open it in the Clip window and set the In point with 20 frames of pad and the Out point with 15 frames of pad. Now we go back to the Construction window and position cut 13 so that it overlaps cut 12 by 20 frames:

We drag the Cross Dissolve transition from the Transitions window and place it in the overlap between cuts 12 and 13. The Track Selector arrow is adjusted so that it points upward. We then adjust the length of the effect to match the overlap.

Adding the Close

The close is the same as the open so all we have to do is copy each cut from the beginning of the movie (with the Copy command in the Edit menu), move to the end of the movie, and then paste the cut in the same order as in the open. The only difference is that we have to dissolve into the blue matte from cut 13 and then end on the blue matte. The Construction window should look like this:

Previewing the last few cuts, we see the first testimonial push in from the left, then the second testimonial push in from the right. This shot then dissolves into the salesperson outro, which then dissolves into the closing animation.

All the cuts are assembled in their correct places in the Construction window, so we can make a movie of the project using the Make Movie command in the Project menu.

 You might want to adjust the Output Options (in the Project menu) to reduce the quality—and therefore the size—of the movie, so it doesn't take up too much space on your hard drive. You then increase the quality setting when you make the final movie.

Editing the Final Cut

Going back to our fictitious example . . . you've shown the rough cut to your boss and he loves it. There are only a few minor changes he wants you to make:

- He'd like you to switch the order of the shots at the end of the voice-over, so the real estate example is last.

- He wants you to add music to the beginning of the piece and have it last until the customer testimonials, then begin again under the salesperson's outro and continue to the end of the piece.

Based on all the work you put into this project, these are fairly minor changes. Maybe showing him the shooting script worked after all. Let's step through each change in order.

Switching the Order of the Shots

This change involves six cuts: cuts 8, 9, and 10 and their associated voice-over cuts. We aren't changing the length of any of the shots, so all we have to do is switch the order of the cuts—they should fit back into the same space in video track B and audio track B. Here's how it's done:

1. We adjust the time ruler so that we can see all three cuts.

2. Cut 8 (the real estate example) is selected and dragged into the Super track; its audio track moves to audio track C:

3. We drag cut 9 to the left until it rests against cut 7.

4. We drag cut 10 to the left until it rests against cut 9 and reset its Out point to remove the 20 frames of pad we added to create the transition to cut 11:

5. Cut 8 is dragged from the Super track A and placed next to the end of cut 10.

6. We extend cut 8 so that it overlaps cut 11 by 20 frames:

7. We switch the order of the voice-over cuts (using audio track C) so that they match the video cuts.

In this example, the cuts appear as shown in Figure 8-5. You should note that the Cross Dissolve transition (formerly between cuts 10 and 11) is now between cuts 8 and 11. You don't have to reset the transition.

Figure 8-5.   Switching the order of cuts–Step 3. Cut 8 is dragged from video track A and placed to the right of track 10. The audio cut for cut 8 is moved from audio track C and placed under cut 8. Now the order of cuts is cut 9, cut 10, and then cut 8.

Adding Music

You were going to add music anyway, but you wanted to give your boss the satisfaction of making changes, so you didn't bring that up. You have a friend who's a musician, and he's given you some samples of his work that you can use.

 If you want to use copyrighted music in your piece, you must get permission first. How do you know if it's copyrighted? If you can buy it in a store, it's probably copyrighted. Look on the label. Using copyrighted material without permission is against the law, and you could wind up getting sued. If you are really dying to use a particular piece of music that's copyrighted, contact the owner of the copyright and ask for permission to use it (this process is called *getting the rights*). The fees can range from a few bucks to a few thousand dollars. An attractive alternative is to look for collections of *clip music.* You can usually purchase the rights to use this kind of material for a hundred dollars or so—and you'll never have to worry about getting tangled up in legal battles.

We are using music in two different sections of the video piece, so we need to pick two separate pieces of music. For the beginning of the video, we want a section of music that begins cleanly. For the end of the piece, we want something that either has a definite end or something we can fade out nicely, such as a rhythmic pattern.

 In case you were thinking that you could simply match the music at the end of the piece with the beginning so that it could loop when the piece starts again, be forewarned that this is difficult to do because our ears are good at picking out edits in music. It's much easier to simply fade up at the beginning and fade out at the end. Silence is easy to match.

Once we select the sections of music we want to use, we digitize them, making sure we have a few extra seconds at the beginning and end of each clip to give us some flexibility in editing. The clips are imported into Premiere. Music cut 1 is dragged into audio track C and placed at the beginning of the movie.

The music is faded in under the opening animation by using the audio fade control located at the bottom of the music cut. By clicking the pointer on the middle line of the audio fade control, we create a *handle* at about the one-second point on the timeline:

This handle sets the end of the audio fade-in; that is, the music is at the normal level within one second of the beginning. We then click on the handle located the beginning of the cut and drag this handle down to the bottom of the box:

We also want to reduce the volume of the music while people are talking; so we need to create a handle at the beginning of cut 2:

Then we create another handle about one second later and drag this handle down about halfway between the middle line and the bottom:

We could also have the music fade in only to the background level used during clip 2—as opposed to fading in to normal level and then back out.

Now we want to make the music last until the beginning of the customer testimonials. To see the whole piece, we reset the time ruler to 10 seconds. Then we extend the music cut with the stretch pointer so that it reaches the end of cut 8. To set the music at the same level throughout the salesperson and voice-over sections, we find the end of the music cut. We then create a handle in the music cut about 20 frames before the end of cut 8 and drag this handle down to about the same point as the previous handle:

This point is also where we want to fade the music out so that we don't hear it over the customer testimonials. To do this, we click on the handle at the end of the music cut and drag it to the bottom of the audio fade control box:

These two handles set a 20-frame audio fade-out. If we want a longer fade-out, we should set a new handle farther back (to the left) and drag the middle handle down to make a smooth fade from the new handle to the end of the cut.

Adding the second section of music is done the same way, with two exceptions:

- We should fade the music in to a low level because the music comes in under the salesperson's outro.

- We should fade in to full volume at the beginning of the product logo.

Replacing the Scratch Narration

We're almost there. All we have to do is record the narrator and replace the scratch narration. To make sure you don't have to re-edit a piece because the real narration is longer or shorter than the scratch narration, you should go through the movie (either in the Construction window or in the movie itself) and write down how long each chunk of narration lasts (next to its position in the script). Then record the narrator, using a stopwatch to time each chunk, and have the narrator redo each chunk until it matches the time on the script. This way, you know each chunk fits.

Back to our example. The new chunks of narration—the final narration—are imported into Premiere. Then each piece of scratch narration is replaced with the final narration as follows:

1. A new chunk of narration is opened in the Clip window. The In and Out points are set with five frames of pad.

2. The corresponding chunk of scratch narration is selected and then deleted by pressing the $\boxed{\text{D}}$ key.

3. The new chunk of narration is dragged into the Construction window and placed where the scratch narration was.

4. The stretch pointer is used to eliminate any gaps.

We work our way through the movie, replacing each piece of narration as we go. When we're done, we preview the entire movie to make sure there aren't any mistakes.

Then the Output Options settings are reset to the highest-quality settings, and the final movie is created using the Make Movie command.

Wrap-Up

If you work on a project like this, it will probably look a lot different because it will contain different elements than the example used in this chapter. But the basic techniques used in pre-production, production, and post-production are similar for most video projects. As a quick review, the basics steps are listed below:

Pre-Production

- Writing the treatment
- Writing the shooting script

Production

- Shooting the necessary footage, making sure to get enough extra shots and cutaways

Post-Production

- Logging the footage
- Writing the script (in this example, the script didn't change)
- Preparing for the edit, transferring the footage and audio clips
- Editing the rough cut
- Editing the final cut

This example concludes the discussion of continuity editing. We're now going to move on to a freer form of editing—montage cutting. But as you'll find out, freer doesn't necessarily mean easier.

CHAPTER 9

Montages and Mixed Formats

he previous three chapters discussed continuity editing. This chapter examines the more impressionistic and subjective world of montage and mixed-format editing.

Comparison of Editing Styles

Visual storytelling through the use of continuity editing is an extremely powerful way to deliver a message. By creating or fabricating a reality, you provide the viewer with a detailed context for the message. You can convey specific information, facts, opinions, etc., using dialog or narration to support the visual story.

In addition, it's a comfortable style to watch because it's a facsimile of reality. The pacing is often leisurely, so the viewer can absorb the information and follow the story. This is why continuity editing is used for a wide range of video formats, from news reports and documentaries to sitcoms and full-length movies.

In contrast, the objective of montage and mixed-format editing is to convey an impression or a feeling.

A *montage* consists of a series of short, disconnected shots and conveys its message primarily through imagery and often music. Examples of montage include certain types of commercials, impressionistic MTV segments (where the singers aren't shown singing the song), and video art pieces. If used in documentaries or movies, montages are usually short segments that amplify the central theme of the piece, condense a passage of time, or enhance the emotional message of a particular segment.

A *mixed-format* piece is similar to a montage in that it is a series of short, disconnected images, but it differs from a montage in that it can include shots with dialog. It often delivers specific information in narration. Examples include most commercials (either for products or politicians), sales promotions, and movie previews.

The advantage of these editing styles is that they can deliver their messages quickly. This makes them an attractive method for editing commercials and other types of short video segments. The disadvantage is that video segments edited in these styles are not rooted in a story or along a narrative line, so it's hard for viewers to stay connected for long periods of time. Eventually, most viewers want some kind of structure.

If you've read the previous chapters, then you already have most of the physical editing skills to cut pieces in any of the formats. The mechanics of putting the shots together and timing them to music is fairly straightforward. The more difficult part is making sense of what you're doing, which is the subject of this chapter.

Montage Basics

In a montage, the individual shots don't matter as much as the overall effect. You are trying to convey a feeling, an impression, which is created by the combination of images more than by the images themselves. For example, consider the visual elements described in Figure 9-1. The shots, which show various aspects of San Francisco, don't tell a story. There aren't any characters and there isn't a plot. But if you saw this series of shots on television, you'd probably come away with a general impression of San Francisco as an interesting, fun, and beautiful city.

The shots used in a montage differ from those of a narrative segment in several ways. Generally speaking, they rarely last longer than a few seconds. This keeps the montage moving along, preventing the viewer from dwelling on any particular shot (which might detract from the overall effect). Another difference is that shots in a montage usually do not show someone talking on camera. If there is narration, it is not

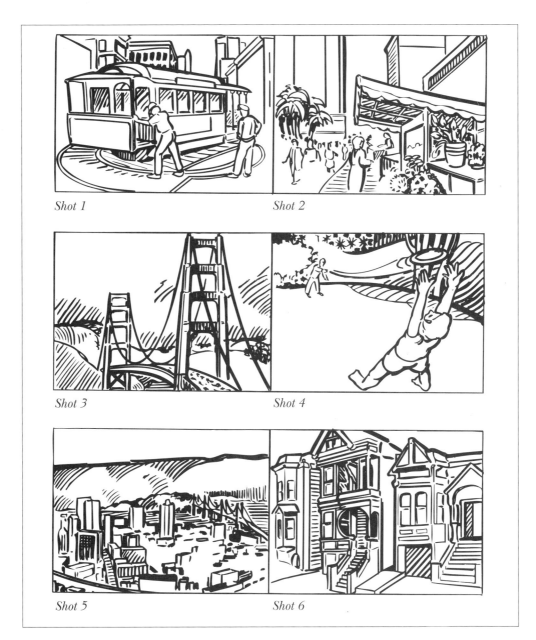

Figure 9-1.   San Francisco montage. Shot 1: full shot of cable car turning around. Shot 2: long shot of shoppers wandering along an outdoor market. Shot 3: extreme long shot of Golden Gate Bridge. Shot 4: long shot of people playing frisbee. Shot 5: extreme long shot of San Francisco skyline. Shot 6: long shot of "Painted Ladies" houses in the Haight district.

tied to any one shot because the shots don't appear on the screen long enough for the viewer to make a specific connection.

You may notice that there are few hard-and-fast rules with montage editing; i.e., "the shots are usually this or that" and "generally speaking, the shots do this or that." This isn't ambivalence on the part of the authors, it's an indication that montage editing is very subjective. What works for you might not work for someone else. The general rules are just that— general rules—and should be deviated from as often as warranted.

The visual and audio clips used in a montage are rarely linked or in synch. The video clips don't necessarily have an audio component, and the audio components generally don't include their own video component. The video and audio tracks are linked through editing, and through the pacing and timing of the video and audio edits.

This unlinking of the video and audio tracks can be a bit disconcerting at first because of all the options it allows. But the flip side of this unlinking is a tremendous creative freedom. As you edit more and more montages, you will develop your own personal style. But in the beginning, it's a good idea to start off with some basic concepts and then deviate from them as you develop more confidence.

Types of Montages

There are two loose categories of montages: those in which the various images support and supplement each other, and those that use contrasting imagery to produce conflict and, through that conflict, convey a message not inherent in the images themselves.

Montages with Supporting Imagery

This type of montage conveys its message or impression through the compilation of similar shots; that is, shot 1 plus shot 2 plus shot 3 plus shot 4 convey the idea. Each shot adds a little bit to the overall impression. The montage of San Francisco images discussed previously is one example of this type of montage.

There are many different ways of using a set of supporting images to convey a larger concept or impression. A few common methods are discussed in the next sections.

Progression in Space or Time

A common motivation for using similar shots in a montage, which has fallen into disfavor of late, is to convey a sense of movement in space or time. For example, Figure 9-2 describes several shots that show different points in a person's travel from Chicago to New Orleans. In a way, these shots tell a story, so they don't fit the strict definition of a montage. But because they don't include dialog and are not linked by strict spatial continuity, the sequence is considered a montage.

There isn't one correct set of shots for this montage. Anything that conveys the sense of movement or progression works. If, however, you are trying to convey two movements—the physical travel and an emotional transition corresponding to the trip—then the shots must satisfy both progressions.

For example, if you want to convey the sense that the person is dreading his or her arrival in New Orleans, then the early shots would show the person looking normal or rested, and the later shots would show him in an agitated state (tapping his fingers, looking pensively out the window, etc.).

Notice that this example also contains a second type of progression—passage through time—that can be used by itself. For example, the shots shown in Figure 9-3 convey the often frantic and hectic life of a TV director. The early shots show the director in command, upright in his chair, his actions crisp. Over the course of the montage, he looks increasingly tired until finally he slumps in his chair and closes his eyes.

Again, this montage is telling a story, so it doesn't fit the strict definition of a montage. But here the basic rules of continuity are broken on almost every edit—the director jumps from one position to another (a dissolve is used to soften the edits). This is not a reality that can exist. It is an impression, an artistic compression of that person's experience.

The freedom from having to maintain continuity is one of the strongest reasons for using a montage. You can condense time to a greater extent in a montage than in a segment edited for continuity. In addition, you can change camera angles at will to impart a surrealistic quality to the montage.

Shot 1   *Shot 2*

Shot 3   *Shot 4*

Shot 5   *Shot 6*

Figure 9-2. Trip montage. Shot 1: overhead wide shot showing station name (Chicago), main character, and train. This shot lays a base for the montage. Shot 2: medium shot of man on train indicates that the main character is going somewhere. Shot 3: long shot of railroad car with conductor indicates the start of the journey. Shot 4: close-up of watch hints at the passage of time. Shot 5: medium shot of conductor announcing the arrival at another station indicates a passage of time and progression. Shot 6: medium shot of main character shows that he is taking a long journey.

Shot 7

Shot 8

Shot 9

Shot 10

Figure 9-2 (continued). Shot 7: medium shot of main character sleeping implies that this is a long, long journey. Shot 8: medium shot of man acting restless shows that he is getting impatient. Shot 9: long shot of train arriving in New Orleans sets up the conclusion of the montage. Shot 10: overhead shot of main character leaving the train matches the first shot of the montage and provides closure.

Preponderance of the Evidence

Did you ever have a friend who argued by spouting one fact after another until he or she won the argument with the sheer weight of his or her knowledge? You can do the same with a montage.

Let's say you want to discuss (in a video piece) recent positive reviews of your product. You could interview an industry pundit who praises your product, or you could take shots of the headlines from the articles

Figure 9-3.   Progression—day in the life of a TV director. Shot 1: wide shot of control
room shows the characters and the location. Shot 2: over-the-shoulder
shot of director focuses attention on him. Shot 3: medium shot of director
in profile narrows the focus. Shot 4: dissolve to medium shot of director at
a later time. This shot is from a different angle to contrast it with the
previous shot. Shot 5: dissolve to a medium shot of director at a still later
time (from a different angle). Director is looking more and more tired. Shot
6: dissolve to another medium shot of director from another angle. The
camera is moving around the director to create a sense of progression.
Shot 7: dissolve to another medium shot of director, opposite profile. The
camera angle has moved 180° around the director, which provides a sense
of closure to the montage. This sets up the end of the montage. Shot 8: full
shot of director shows him asleep at the control panel.

about your product and edit them into a montage (Figure 9-4). By doing the latter, you deliver an even more powerful message—in just 10 seconds, you've shown the viewer that many critics like your product.

This is a particularly powerful technique when you want to show a sensitive or controversial topic. A montage of shots of different homeless children living on the street can often convey a more powerful message than a shot of just one child. In contrast to the previous type of montage (sense of progression), this type of montage works because the shots are so similar. They make their argument by showing how widespread something is.

But there is a flip side to this type of montage: Viewers are smart, and if they think they are being manipulated, they quickly turn on you and become skeptical of the images. You must, therefore, walk a fine line between a potent delivery and overkill.

Different Facets of the Same Idea

Another common use of montages is to show different facets or parts of a place, person, or idea. The montage of San Francisco described earlier in this chapter is an example of this type of montage.

Another montage of this type is shown in Figure 9-5. In this case, the shots depict different parts, or facets, of a manufacturing plant. Because each shot contains some kind of action, the overall impression is one of bustling activity. You could build a sequence that has continuity between the various pieces of equipment, but your goal here is not to describe the actual manufacturing process but to convey the more general sense of bustle and motion.

You could use this type of montage to give credit to all the people who worked on a particular product. For example, if you use a two-second shot of each person, you'd give recognition to everyone on a small team in 20 or 30 seconds. Put a piece of triumphant music underneath the montage, and you'd give the team a nice plug.

As mentioned in Chapter 6, it often helps to analyze television and movies to see how the experts do it. For montages, two of the best places to look are MTV and sports programs. Both of these formats use montages extensively. You don't have to copy their styles, but analyzing them might give you ideas about your own montages.

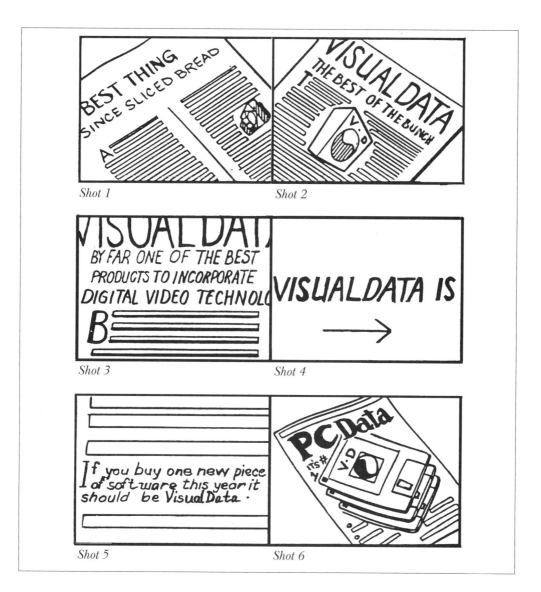

Figure 9-4. Product review montage. Shot 1: close-up of product review. Angle shot to convey energy and action. Shot 2: close-up of product review. Opposite angle adds action to the montage. Shot 3: extreme close-up of product review delivers specific information about a critic's review. Shot 4: quick pan of headline that includes the word "VisualData" adds motion to the montage. Shot 5: extreme close-up of product review delivers more specific information about the review. Shot 6: medium shot of magazine showing the product on the cover pulls viewers back out of specific text and prepares them for the end of montage.

Shot 1   Shot 2

Shot 3   Shot 4

Shot 5   Shot 6

Figure 9-5. Factory montage. Shot 1: medium shot of circuit board spinning in front of camera. Shot 2: medium shot of robot arm moving down changes the direction of motion. Shot 3: full shot of factory floor shows a variety of movements. Shot 4: medium shot of circuit boards moving toward the camera on a conveyor belt. This shot again changes the direction of movement and places the viewer in the middle of the action. Shot 5: robot arm swings across the scene. This shot keeps the viewer close to the action. Shot 6: extreme close-up of circuit board. The last shot of the montage should match the beginning of the next scene. In this case, a person is going to talk about a new kind of microprocessor that is selling very well; hence this shot.

Montages with Conflicting Imagery

In most of the preceding examples, a rough idea of the overall concept of the montage could be guessed from any one of the individual shots—not so in the case of a montage built from conflicting images. In this type of montage, the overall impression is created by the collision of several images. The juxtaposition produces tension that is relieved to some extent by the synthesis of a new concept—the main point of the montage.

Generally speaking, these montages work when the conflict is fairly obvious, as in the montage comparing winners and losers in a sports contest depicted in Figure 9-6 (pp. 212–213). This doesn't mean you shouldn't try to make comparisons on a subtle or subliminal level, but you might not reach as many people with that type of approach.

Because the message of this type of montage lies in the collisions between dissimilar imagery, one group of shots can be used in two different montages to different effect. For example, consider the images of wealth and poverty in Figure 9-7 (pp. 214–215). The overall effect of this montage is to contrast haves with have-nots. This montage can make the viewers feel guilty or angry, or can be used to prod the viewers into helping the poor.

But if the same shots of the homeless man are interwoven with shots of a hard-working auto mechanic (Figure 9-8, pp. 216–217), the overall message changes. In this case, you might summon up feelings of resentment toward the homeless.

A real-life example of this duality involves the footage of the 1992 Los Angeles riot. This footage has been used by liberal reformers to call for more financial assistance for inner city neighborhoods. The same footage has been used by conservatives to call for more law and order.

As mentioned before, bold, powerful montages can backfire if the viewers feel manipulated. The longer a montage lasts, the greater the chance the audience will tire of the message and become distant or, worse, skeptical.

Tapping the Power of Images

Montages work when people can extract meaning from the images themselves. The images do not need interpretation. In fact, sometimes the image taps into the context of the viewers' lives and produces an impression deeper and richer than the information carried by the image itself. For example, consider each of the following separate images:

- A man searching through the wreckage of a burned-down house
- A mother cuddling her newborn baby
- Neil Armstrong stepping off the lunar module
- President Nixon getting into a helicopter, waving good-bye
- Looters running through the streets of Los Angeles
- Dan Quayle smiling

All these images trigger a chain of ideas. Just what kind of ideas are triggered depends on the type of image. Some images are universal; that is, they evoke similar thoughts and impressions in all people. In other cases, the connection is limited to a particular part of society, a particular time, or a specific place.

Universal Images

Everyone can understand universal images because they deal with common human experiences, such as life, death, health, sickness, hunger, and poverty. Although montages consisting of just these types of images might seem a little empty or lightweight because they're not presenting anything new, these types of montages, used within the context of a narrative video segment, can establish a mood or add emphasis. Usually, the emphasis only applies to a concept or a message already established within the narrative section of the video segment.

Context-Dependent Images

Some images produce an impression only within a certain group of society—people of a certain age, background, or vocation. But what these images lack in reach, they make up in power. Images that depict specific actions, places, or people can evoke more powerful associations.

For example, let's say you are marketing a new personal computer, and the audience for the video you are making is already familiar with personal computers. The images of the IBM and Apple logos are all that's needed to depict the competition. If you are building a new word process-

Figure 9-6.   Contrasting images—winners and losers. Shot 1: medium shot of player
spiking ball in the end zone signals a touchdown. Shot 2: medium shot of
a fallen opponent sets up the contrast between winners and losers. Shot 3:
full shot of players from the winning team hoisting the player in panel 1 on
their shoulders shows that the game is over. Shot 4: medium shot of
players on the losing team looking sad provides contrast.

ing program, the image of Bill Gates produces the same effect. You don't
need to explain what these companies are or who Gates is—your audience knows. And by using just these images, you give the viewers plenty of
room to add their own interpretations and associations to the images.

 In a way, this is similar to the conceptual compression used in building
visual stories with continuity editing, but in this case, you are using specific images to represent larger ideas as opposed to compressing time.

Shot 5

Shot 6

Shot 7

Shot 8

Figure 9-6 (continued). Shot 5: full shot of fans cheering reinforces the euphoria of the winning side. Shot 6: extreme close-up of losing player crying heightens the emotional drama. Shot 7: overhead shot of losing coach with no one else around stresses the difference between solitary sadness and group celebration. This shot follows another shot of the losing team so that the montage ends on the winning team. Shot 8: full shot of winning team and coach celebrating wraps up the montage. If you were rooting for the losing side, then you could switch the order of shots 7 and 8 to end on "your" team.

You can also get the advantage of letting the viewer "in on the joke." Images that tap into concepts close to the viewer's concerns help the viewer identify with the video piece. But an inside joke is only good for insiders. That's the disadvantage of specific images—they must be geared for particular audiences.

Shot 1   *Shot 2*

Shot 3   *Shot 4*

Figure 9-7.   Contrasting images—wealth vs. poverty. Shot 1: full shot of large, expensive car cruising up to the entrance of a fancy restaurant. Shot 2: zoom in as chauffeur opens the rear door to focus on wealthy couple. Shot 3: medium shot of homeless man on street. Shot 4: close shot of homeless man as he clutches one of his few possessions in the world.

Here's another example: An image of Bobby Kennedy giving a speech, or of an antiwar protester sticking a flower in the muzzle of a soldier's gun means different things to people born in the 1950s and those born in the 1970s. In one case, the audience lived through turmoil of the 1960s; in the other case, they might have only read about it.

A picture of Dan Quayle means different things to people of varying political persuasions. To liberals, a picture of the former vice-president might call up memories of his various gaffes and blun-

Shot 5

Shot 6

Shot 7

Shot 8

Figure 9-7 (continued).   Shot 5: wealthy couple drinking champagne inside fancy restaurant. Shot 6: homeless man getting his dinner at a soup kitchen. Shot 7: wealthy couple preparing for bed in their spacious bedroom. Shot 8: homeless man preparing to go to sleep under a bush.

ders. To conservatives, they see a put-upon, nice guy who championed their causes. His image is also time dependent. Fifteen years from now, people might not remember who he was or what he did. (Quick, who was Gerald Ford's vice-president?)

So if you're going to use specific, context-dependent imagery, make sure the central message of the montage is clear. This can be done in a narrative section preceding the montage, in narration or lyrics during the montage, and/or in universal images interspersed within the montage.

Figure 9-8. Contrasting images—homeless vs. working man. Shot 1: long shot of the exterior of an auto mechanic's shop. Shot 2: medium shot of auto mechanic working underneath a car. Shot 3: medium shot of homeless man on street. Shot 4: close shot of homeless man as he clutches one of his few possessions in the world.

As in continuity editing, the ultimate goal is delivering a message to the viewer, in this case, an idea or impression. With specific images, you need to take extra care to tailor the piece to the audience.

The Importance of Music and Pacing in Montages

A montage without a sound track can seem empty. In contrast, adding a piece of music, particularly one with lyrics, can transform the images

Figure 9-8 (continued).   Shot 5: working man eating dinner with his family. Shot 6: homeless man getting his dinner at a soup kitchen. Shot 7: working man playing with his family in the bedroom. Shot 8: homeless man preparing to go to sleep under a bush.

into an interesting, sometimes powerful piece of video. For example, consider the following short montage:

- Shot of a young girl just learning to walk

- Shot of the young girl (age 5) with her family at a carnival

- Shot of the girl (age 8) throwing a ball to her dad

- Shot of the girl (age 12) with several friends

- Shot of the girl (age 17) getting her high school diploma

Now, try to remember the music and words to the songs "Born in the U.S.A." or "My Home Town" by Bruce Springsteen. Once you've got the words in your head, read through the list of shots again. The lyrics help tie the shots together.

Let's combine the same shots with a different piece of music—the current theme music for the United Airlines commercials ("Rhapsody in Blue" by George Gershwin). In this case, if you hear that music and see those pictures, you probably expect to see a shot of an airplane next and then a sales pitch.

Again, same shots, another piece of music—the title soundtrack from the movie *Jaws*. A bizarre selection, I'll admit, but it does add a strange wrinkle to the montage. Now, you might wonder what catastrophe is about to occur.

 Music, like specific images, often works only for particular audiences. If you didn't watch much TV or listen to the radio, then you wouldn't be familiar with the United Airlines TV ads and their use of Gershwin's music.

The whole point of the previous exercise is to point out that music can influence a montage in powerful ways. It can support the message of the video (Springsteen), de-emphasize the video by drawing attention to the music (United Airlines), or put the video in a different context (*Jaws*).

You can also set up a contrast between the music and the montage. For example, using "America the Beautiful" with pictures of poverty and crime creates a strong sense of irony and cynicism.

These are extreme examples primarily because the music clips are well known. But even generic music adds a distinct flavor and tone to a video segment. Because music can have such an impact, you should match the music to the style and the message of the montage.

Matching Music to the Montage Style

If you are working with similar images that support each other, you generally want to use rhythmic music that has a melody. This type of music helps tie the images together and does not call attention to itself. If the music has lyrics, then the words of the song should work in concert with the images. This doesn't mean they have to describe the people and places shown in the video. In fact, it's better not to make such literal connections, but there should be something in common between the words and pictures.

For example, the shots listed earlier about family life would be enhanced by a rock-and-roll ballad but probably not by a piece of avant-garde jazz.

If your montage consists of conflicting images, then a piece of music with a strong beat can help call attention to the conflicts. For example, a piece of rap music could turn a montage showing the rioting in Los Angeles into a powerful call for reform.

 Next time you watch a movie, try to pick out each piece of music. Editors of feature films use music extensively to set the mood of scenes, and you'll probably be surprised at how often music has been added. If edited well, the music sits in the background, subtly setting the mood. You should also note how different styles of music are used (active vs. slow, simple vs. complex, major chords vs. minor chords) to match the visual and emotional content of the montage.

Setting the Pace with Music

If you are using music, then the pacing of the montage is often determined by the tempo of the music. In fact, you generally add the music to the audio track first and then edit the shots to match the music.

A piece of music with a quick beat, such as a rock-and-roll song, calls for short shots with lots of action. A graceful section of new age music calls for longer shots. This means you need to think about the mood and the tempo of the music when you are picking a song for your montage.

 You might have to try many different pieces of music before you find one that works with the images you want to use. One way to shorten your search time is to assemble the shots for the montage into a rough cut and then test the music against the rough cut. Then, once you find a piece of music that works, go back and edit the montage again, this time matching the shots to the beat of the music.

Matching Special Effects to Music and Visuals

Few montages are edited together with simple cuts; often, some kind of special effect is used to smooth out the transition (dissolve, wipe, etc.). Because different special effects affect a montage in different ways, you should use effects that match both the mood of the music and the style of the montage.

Flowing Music

When you use classical or new age music (soft, flowing pieces), you might want to use dissolves between shots. These types of music usually don't have a strong beat, so the gradual transition produced by a dissolve matches the flow of the music.

For example, let's say your montage consists of the nature shots shown in Figure 9-9. A piece of flowing classical music would add a sense of serenity to the montage, which is accentuated by the dissolves.

Here's another example: Let's say you want to create a montage that portrays a factory in an ominous way. The shots for the montage are shown in Figure 9-10. You choose a dark piece of music—one with a slow tempo, lots of low notes, and in a minor key. If you simply edit the shots together with cuts, the abrupt shot changes work against the flow of the music. Dissolves de-emphasize the transitions between the shots and match the music better.

Active Music

When you use a piece of music with a strong beat, you generally want to use more active special effects, such as *pushes* (where one image pushes the other image off the screen) or wipes.

 In some situations, a simple cut works fine. Try the edit as a cut first, then experiment with special effects.

For example, let's say you are creating a montage of shots from a baseball game. You decide to use a fast-paced, rock-and-roll song (such as "Centerfield" by John Mellencamp). You could use dissolves between each shot, but you'd fit the action of the shots and music better if you used simple cuts and active special effects (such as pushes and wipes) for the transitions.

 When editing montages with active effects, you should try to match the motion of the effects to the action in a shot. For example, if you're adding an effect between a shot of a catcher throwing a ball to second base, and a shot of a base runner running from right to left toward second base, you'd want to use a push left to match the runner's motion. Matching the actions of special effects is covered in more detail in the next chapter.

Shot 1   Shot 2

Shot 3   Shot 4

Shot 5   Shot 6

Figure 9-9. Matching music and effects—nature scene. Shot 1: extreme long shot of a forest and stream establishes the scene. Shot 2: dissolve to long shot of forest and stream from slightly different angle. Shot 3: dissolve to medium shot of stream showing dead log. This shot emphasizes the death of a tree in the forest. Shot 4: close shot of leaf floating downstream represents the flow of nutrients from the dead log. Shot 5: close shot of stream bank showing leaf represents the movement of nutrients from the dead log to other plants. Shot 6: close shot of sprout. Life reborn.

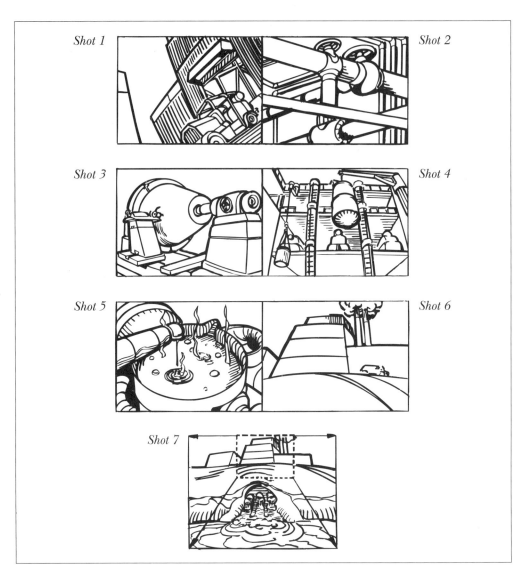

Shot 1 Shot 2 Shot 3 Shot 4 Shot 5 Shot 6 Shot 7

Figure 9-10. Matching music and effects—ominous factory. Shot 1: angled long shot of truck and factory. The angle of the shot adds tension to the scene. Shot 2: medium shot of pipes criss-crossing the screen. Shot 3: full shot of a large piece of equipment. The shots aren't describing how the pipes and equipment are connected, which provides a sense of mystery. Shot 4: long shot looking up at factory. The camera angle emphasizes the size and complexity of the factory and makes it appear imposing. Shot 5: medium shot of boiling vat adds to the mystery. Shot 6: long shot of factory exterior. Shot 7: zoom out to reveal sewer pipes releasing chemicals into stream.

Extremely Active Music

If the music you're using has a driving beat, such as a rap song, you might not need to use a special effect at all—a simple cut might suffice. But you need to time the shot changes (the edits) so that they occur on the beats of the music. That way, the music and pictures work together.

Unusual Situations in Matching Music to Images

The previous paragraphs described some general rules for matching special effects and music. But whenever possible, you should try to match an effect to whatever is going on in the music at a particular time. For example, going back to the baseball example, let's say you time an edit to occur just as a cymbal crash takes place. You could use a wipe, but how about a fast zoom open instead? The motion of this effect would heighten the impact provided by the cymbal. Keep your eyes open for these opportunities. These subtle touches add zing to your montages.

Learn the Rules, Then Break Them

As mentioned at the beginning of this chapter, there are few hard-and-fast rules for editing montages. What matters is the final piece and whether it reaches your audience. So after you get the hang of the more conventional ways of editing described here, experiment. Here are some styles you might want to try:

- **Dissolve through a color**: Place a solid-color matte between each pair of shots, and dissolve between the shots and the mattes.

- **Intersperse black-and-white shots with color**: Use a filter to turn some of the shots into black-and-white images, and intercut them with color shots.

- **Gradually decrease the length of the shots**: This works best when the music builds to a climax.

- **Intersperse still images (freeze frames) with moving video**: You might also want to try freezing a shot at the end, fading to black, then fading up the next shot that then freezes at the end, and so on.

- **Deliberately mix soft music with hard cuts**: This creates a tension between the pictures and the sounds.

- **Use *swish pans* at transitions**: A swish pan is a pan that moves so quickly that the image seems smeared. When inserted into a montage and dissolved in and out of, it adds a sense of motion to the segment.

Mixed-Format Basics

Mixed formats sit in the middle between the structured approach of continuity editing and free-flowing montage cutting. Here, you can focus on individual shots to add impact or specific information to a segment. For example, you might insert short sections of talking heads in the middle of several impressionistic shots, or you might use graphics containing text to deliver specific information.

But unlike a narrative segment, the shots in a mixed-format piece do not necessarily relate to each other in terms of a location or by continuity. There's no attempt to fabricate a reality.

So in a sense, the mixed format borrows some of the best features from the other two styles (continuity and montage). It can deliver specific information, but the piece isn't tied to telling a visual story. However, a disadvantage of this style is that without some kind of structure—a rough storyline or visual style—a mixed-format piece can end up as visual fast food: It looks good as you're watching it, but a minute later, you're left with no impression.

Turning a Montage into a Mixed-Format Piece

In many cases, you can transform a montage into a mixed-format piece by simply adding a talking head. For example, let's go back and review the nature montage discussed earlier (Figure 9-9). By adding some shots of a naturalist talking on camera about the cycle of life, death, and rebirth in a forest, we add specific information to the montage (Figure 9-11, pp. 242–243).

You don't have to show the person every time he or she talks. Once you've shown the person once or twice, you can then use his or her audio as a voice-over and cover the person's image with some of the nature shots. Using voice-overs is discussed in more detail in Chapter 11.

Going back to the product review montage from before, you could put short quotes from industry pundits in between the shots of the headlines (Figure 9-12, p. 244). This way, you could combine the power of on-camera testimonials with the weight provided by a collection of print reviews.

Using Text in Place of Narration

An increasingly common type of mixed-format piece uses graphic elements with text, in place of narration. For example, let's say we are re-editing the software demonstration piece described in Chapter 8. Instead of using a salesperson, we take his or her words and place them in a graphic. These words can appear by themselves, or we can superimpose them over a shot of the computer screen.

The advantage of this style is its novelty. People aren't yet accustomed to seeing text interspersed with video. Sooner or later, though, the novelty will wear off, and you'll need to come up with a new trick or style to capture the audience's attention.

Experiment, Experiment, Experiment

The mixed-format style gives you a tremendous amount of freedom, so use it. Combine techniques from montage cutting with continuity editing. Intercut long shots with short shots. Place text in different parts of the screen. Have text carry over from a graphic shot into a piece of video.

The best place to get new ideas about mixed-format editing is television. Movies aren't generally edited in mixed-format style because they are trying to tell a story. MTV, commercials, and art videos are a better source.

 When you're scanning the airwaves for new ideas, put a tape in the VCR, and record what you're watching. That way, you're able to go back and step through the material shot by shot.

Figure 9-11.   Mixed-format—nature segment. Shot 1: extreme long shot of a forest and
stream establishes the scene. Shot 2: dissolve to long shot of forest and
stream from slightly different angle. Shot 3: dissolve to naturalist
describing the cycle of death and rebirth in a forest. Shot 4: dissolve to
medium shot of stream showing dead log. This shot emphasizes the death
of a tree in the forest.

Getting Advice

With continuity editing, there's a good chance that if you follow the
basic grammar of visual storytelling, the audience will understand the
scene and get your message. However, with montages and mixed-format
pieces, you're working on a more impressionistic level and taking
greater risks; so, you might be the only person who understands your

Figure 9-11 (continued). Shot 5: close shot of leaf floating downstream represents the flow of nutrients from the dead log. Shot 6: dissolve to naturalist describing how nature is constantly in flux, with nutrients and energy constantly flowing from the dead to the newly born. Shot 7: close shot of stream bank showing leaf represents the movement of nutrients from the dead log to other plants. Shot 8: close shot of sprout. Life reborn.

brilliant idea or concept. Therefore, it's important to show your work to friends, colleagues, or people similar to the intended audience.

When you show your piece to these people, try not to argue or defend your work, just listen. You don't have to take their advice, but their opinions are important, especially if you don't like what they're saying. It's better to get negative feedback early, before you spend a lot of time on the piece.

Figure 9-12.   Mixed-format—product demonstration. Shot 1: industry pundit talking about the VisualData product. Shot 2: special effect (push left) to newspaper article. Shot 3: close shot of newspaper article about the product. Shot 4: special effect (push left) to another industry analyst. Shot 5: medium shot of industry analyst talking about the product. Shot 6: close shot of magazine cover showing product.

Wrap-Up

Montage and mixed-format editing are powerful methods for creating impressionistic messages. Each style offers the editor a tremendous amount of freedom in the choice of images and pacing. But these types of segments only work for short periods of time; viewers can get overwhelmed or bored if the piece lasts too long. Used in small doses, they can embellish a narrative piece with powerful impressions and feelings.

CHAPTER 10

Special Effects Wizardry

W orking with video on your PC can be a bit of a pain. It takes up lots of memory, it often doesn't run as fast as you would like, and the window isn't big enough (yet). But having video on your computer in digital form opens up a world of possibilities. Because it's digital information, you can change the image just as you would any other image on your PC. You can bend it, stretch it, change the colors, move the image around the screen, almost anything you can think up.

This isn't the first time people have been able to play with digital video. High-end video post-production houses have offered digital video technology, such as the Harry and Paintbox systems from Quantel, for a number of years. But these devices by themselves rent for $200 or more an hour. And you have to rent the online editing system as well (another $250/hr). So spending just one day fooling around with these systems can cost you upward of $4,000.

With Video for Windows or QuickTime for Windows and a video-editing program, such as Premiere, however, you have the capability of performing many of the same special effects of the more expensive professional systems. In addition, programs such as Digital Morph let you produce bizarre and intriguing effects that aren't even possible in many high-end suites.

In this chapter, we review a number of different tricks and techniques you can use to create dazzling and mind-bending effects. This area of digital video is changing very rapidly with new special effects programs appearing nearly ever other month. In this chapter we'll focus on the effects you can perform with Premiere and the morphing capabilities of programs like Digital Morph.

Creating Special Effects with Premiere

There are two basic kinds of special effects: those that work with two clips (transitions and superimposing) and those that affect only a single clip, such as filters.

Making New Tricks with Transitions

In earlier chapters, we examined how a transition can create a smooth and interesting flow from one video clip to another. Here, we're going to look at some other ways that transitions can be used.

Using Several Transitions in a Row

Sometimes you have a set of video clips that you'd like to join together. You could use the same transition between each pair of clips, but a more interesting method would be to use a group of transitions that complement each other.

For example, let's say you are producing a CD-ROM that contains a huge number of different video clips. You want to create a short introductory segment that displays portions of several clips to give the user an idea of what's on the rest of the disk.

Here's how you could use different variations of the Push transition (in Premiere) to combine the clips into a dynamic segment:

1. Import the clips you want to use and move them into the Construction window. We're using only four clips in this example, but you can use as many as you like. Here, the clips are each about three seconds long, and the overlap between each pair of clips is one second:

2. Add a Push transition between clips 1 and 2. By default, it pushes from left to right.

3. Add another Push transition between clips 2 and 3. Double-click on the effect to set the track selector and the edge direction as shown here:

   This makes the clip in track A push up from the bottom.

4. Add a third Push transition between clips 3 and 4. Set the track selector and edge direction so that the transition is from track A to track B, and the push happens from right to left:

5. Preview the work area. The new clips should come in from different sides (left, bottom, and then right).

There are a number of other combinations of effects that work well together:

- A succession of revealing effects such as Barn Door, Iris, and Split (the combination draws the viewer's eye farther into the segment)

- A succession of Radial Wipes, with each one starting at a different corner in a rotating pattern

- A succession of Clock Wipes

- Matching Spin Away effects

Making Incomplete Transitions

So far, we've been performing complete transitions; that is, the transition starts with the video in one track and ends with the video in the other track. But by changing the parameters, you can perform incomplete transitions (i.e., start with the clip in track A, and end with a combination of the clips in tracks A and B.) For example, you can set up a half dissolve to blend two images together, say, a clip of a windsurfer and a clip of a cloud:

1. Import both clips and position them in the Construction window, then place a Cross Dissolve effect between the clips as shown here:

2. Double-click on the effect to call up the Effects dialog box. Move the slider bar under the End box until it reaches the 66% point. This means that when the effect ends, the screen is made up of 66 percent of clip B and 34 percent of clip A (Figure 10-1).

3. Go back to the Construction window and put another Cross Dissolve effect immediately after the existing one. Set the effect's duration so that it ends with the clips.

4. Double-click on the second effect and set both the start and end sliders to 66%. This freezes the effect in that position (Figure 10-2).

5. Preview the work area.

The preview starts with the image of the windsurfer, then the image of the cloud fades in until both images can be seen, then the combined image of both clips continues to the end.

Figure 10-1.

By setting the end position of a transition to a partial value (in this case 66%), you create an incomplete transition. In this example, the effect is a cross dissolve, so the incomplete transition gradually superimposes one video cut on top of another.

Figure 10-2.

Setting the start and end positions of a transition to the same partial value (66%) freezes the effect. In this example, the incomplete transition superimposes one video cut on top of another.

This is similar to superimposing one clip on top of another, which is described in "Superimposing Images" later in this chapter.

You can also use an incomplete Wipe transition to combine two clips side by side. By stopping the wipe before it's finished, you break the screen into two parts, one part for each clip. The trick is to figure out what you want the combined image, the *split screen*, to look like and then work backward:

1. Import two clips into the Construction window and position them with an overlap, as shown:

2. Open clip 1 and find the position you want to end on for the split screen. The main subject of the clip should be on the left half of the screen. Set this as your Out point.

3. Do the same for the other clip, with the exception that the main subject should be on the right half of the screen.

4. Make a freeze frame of the last frame of clip 1 using the Export Frame as BitMap command. Import the freeze frame and place it next to clip 1 in track A. Extend the freeze frame to match the end of clip 2:

5. Place a Wipe transition in the overlap between clip 1 and clip 2. Extend the Wipe so that it covers most but not all of the overlap, as the next picture shows:

6. Double-click on the effect and set the end position to 50% and the Wipe direction so that the Wipe moves right to left:

7. Place a second Wipe effect in the remaining overlap and set its start and end positions to 50%.

8. Preview the work area.

The preview starts off with just clip 1, then clip 2 should start to wipe in from the right side. As clip 2 continues to move in toward the center, clip 1 freezes. Then the wipe finishes (stops moving) and clip 2 plays to its end (Figure 10-3).

Note Although this movie contains several events—an incomplete Wipe, a freeze frame, and a frozen Wipe—none of them starts at the same time. The Wipe starts before clip 1 freezes, then the Wipe freezes, then clip 2 ends. By making these events happen at different times, we smooth out the effects. Keep your eyes open for ways to use this technique in other situations where you are combining several effects and edits.

Figure 10-3.

A split-screen is created by performing an incomplete Wipe. The second video clip comes in from the right. The Wipe then freezes when it reaches the middle point.

Working with Filters

Filters perform a transformation on some or all of the pixels in the image. Applying filters to a video clip is tricky, however, because the image changes over time and the effect of the filter can change as well.

In Premiere, you apply a filter to a clip by selecting the clip in the Construction window and then choosing the Filters option from the Project menu. Click on the name of the filter you want to apply from the Available list on the left side of the dialog box and then click on the Add button to place the filter in the Current list on the right side:

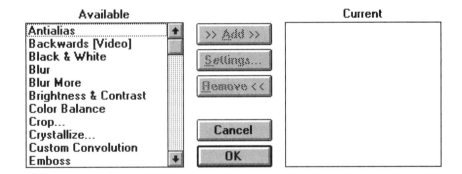

To remove a filter, select the filter you want to remove from the Current list and click on the Remove button. You can add more than one filter to a clip. For example, you can add several Blur filters to make the clip extra blurry, or you could combine a Sharpen filter with a Color Pass filter.

Premiere offers a bewildering array of filters, too many to go into detail on each one of them here. The best advice is try them all yourself so that you have an idea of what they do (or you can refer to the Premiere manual). Test them on a title, grid, or color bars so that you can clearly see their effects.

There are two basic types of filters: *static filters*, whose effects remain constant through the course of the entire clip, and *dynamic filters*, whose effects change over time.

Static Filters

There are three static filters you might use fairly regularly to correct for differences in lighting and camera quality:

- **Color Balance:** This filter reduces the intensity of one or more of the three colors that make up the video image. If the image has a greenish cast, you can reduce the tint by moving the green slider to the left. However, this reduces the overall brightness of the image, so you may have to offset the reduction with the Brightness & Contrast filter.

- **Brightness & Contrast:** This is really two filters (brightness and contrast) that work the same way as the brightness/contrast adjustments on your television. These filters are good for increasing the overall intensity of the image.

- **Gamma Correction:** The gamma correction can enhance a picture by changing the brightness levels of the *midtones* (pixels with a medium level of intensity).

Dynamic Filters

With dynamic filters, the image changes over time. There are two ways to achieve this effect. *Constant-effect filters* change the image over time, though the level, or amount, of the effect remains constant. *Progressive-effect filtering* increases or decreases the level of the effect over the course of the clip.

Constant-Effect Filters These filters distort the image based on a transformation that varies over time. The transformation is usually based on a mathematical formula, such as a sine wave. Examples include Wave and Ripple.

Progressive-Effect Filtering With this technique, you vary the level of the effect over the course of the clip. This allows you, for instance, to apply a filter at the beginning of the clip and gradually reduce its level, so that by the end of the clip, the filter effect is gone. There are two ways to accomplish progressive-effect filtering: *simple dissolve* and *incremental progression*.

Simple Dissolve   Let's say you want to apply the Blur More filter to the beginning of a video clip of a windsurfer and then gradually fade the effect out so that at the end, the clip is seen clearly. Here's how you do it:

1. Place the video clip of the windsurfer in video track A.

2. Make a copy of the clip, put the copy in video track B, and align it with the original clip in track A:

3. Apply three Blur More filters to the clip in track A.

4. Place a Cross Dissolve transition between the clips in tracks A and B:

5. Set the work area to include both clips and preview the work area.

At the beginning, the clip appears blurry and then becomes gradually clearer over the course of the clip:

This technique works for some of the less complex filters (such as Blur, Color Balance, and Black & White). For more complex filters (such as Crystallize or Pointilize), it is sometimes better to change the effect of the filter over a freeze frame of the first or last frame of the video clip. That way, the image isn't moving while the filter effect is changing.

For example, you could make a freeze frame of the first frame of a video clip of a windsurfer (using the Export Frame as BitMap command). Import the freeze frame back into Premiere. Place it in video track A, and make an aligned copy in track B. Repeat the steps described earlier for the Blur More dissolve effect, using the one Crystallize filter instead. Then put the video clip of the windsurfer after the freeze frame in track A. The end result: the crystallizing effect fades away, revealing the still image of the windsurfer, which then moves.

Incremental Progression   If you want to change the effect of a complex filter while the video clip is playing, then you need to change the effect of the filter in small, incremental steps. This is similar to the way animators represent motion by breaking up a movement into separate steps. In this case, you are adding or taking away a filter in small steps.

Let's say you want to apply the Spherize filter to a video clip of a person's face, then gradually fade the effect out:

1. Import the video clip and place it at the beginning of track A.

2. Put an aligned copy of the freeze frame in track B.

3. Set the time ruler to one second.

4. Use the razor blade icon to split the clip in track A. In this example, we split it at the one-second point on the timeline.

This creates two new clips, one that lasts for one second, another that is three seconds long:

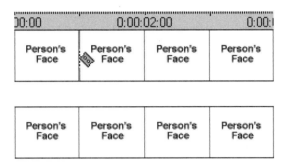

5. Apply the Spherize filter to the first clip in track A. Set the Spherize amount to 100 in the dialog box shown next:

6. Use the razor blade icon to split the clip in track B at the two-second point on the timeline.

7. Apply the Spherize filter to the first clip in track B. Use a setting of 75 for this clip.

8. Add a Cross Dissolve transition between the first clips in tracks A and B:

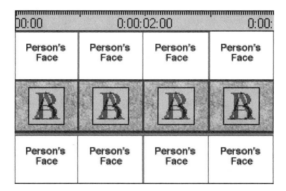

9. Repeat these steps for the second clips in tracks A and B, reducing the amount of the filter by 25 each time and inserting a Cross Dissolve effect between the clips. The track selectors for the effects should be set so that the tracks alternate: track A, track B, track A, etc.

The movie starts with a rather strange face, then gradually transforms into a normal-looking face (Figure 10-4). You can make the change more gradual by increasing the number of steps. Here we used four one-second steps, but we could have used eight steps, each 15 frames long. Of course, this means twice as much work.

Figure 10-4.

Progressive filtering with the Spherize filter. The cut starts out with the image of the face looking like it is stretched over a ball. The filter is then gradually removed until the image is unfiltered (looks normal) at the end of the cut.

 If you try this technique on your own material, you might notice that the rate of filter fading is a bit uneven. You can smooth out the fading by clipping four frames or so before and after the points o the original edits, in this case: 1:00, 2:00, and 3:00.

Slide the remaining clips back together. The fade should be much smoother.

Superimposing Images

In superimposing, you're basically combining one image with another. The superimposed image could be a title and the other a video clip, or it could be two different video clips.

The key step is determining which parts of the superimposed image to use. You do this by making transparent the parts you don't want . It's like making a stencil. You're cutting out the parts of the superimposed image in which you want the main video (in track A and/or B) to show through.

Setting the Transparency

There are a number of different ways to set the transparency. You can specify a particular part of the superimposed image or a particular range of colors. Each editing program has its own methods for setting the transparency.

The most extensive set of transparency options can be found in Premiere, so we'll go into those options in detail. There are seven different options for superimposing an image: a None option that lets you specify a particular area of the image as transparent and six options called *keys* in which you specify the transparency based on a range of colors or intensities or on a particular matte.

We use a video clip of a windsurfer as the main video and a title consisting of the word *Windsurfing* as the superimposed image. The images are imported into the program and placed in the Construction window, as shown in Figure 10-5.

None Option   The simplest way to superimpose an image is to use a garbage matte, which sets a particular region in the superimposed clip as transparent. Click once on the image in the superimpose track and then choose the Transparency option from the Clip menu.

In the middle of the dialog box that appears is the Key Type drop-down list box (Figure 10-6). We'll get to other options in a minute. For now, let's just work with the None option.

There are four small squares in the Sample box (upper-right corner). These squares define which parts of the images are transparent. Click the square in the top-left corner of the Sample box and drag it down until it is just above the word *Windsurfing*. Click and drag the square in the top right until it is level with the square on the left side.

Figure 10-5.

Superimposing a title over a video cut. The title cut is placed in the Super track and lined up with the video cut.

Figure 10-6. Key choices in Adobe Premiere for Windows. Each option lets you set a different portion of a clip as transparent.

Then click anywhere in the Sample box to make the transparent parts of the image appear black:

This sets the garbage matte that specifies the parts of the image that will be transparent. In this case, only the long, flat rectangle containing the title will be superimposed. The remaining black area will be transparent and will show the clip of the actual windsurfer.

Click the OK button, then set the work area to include just the two clips and preview the work area. The word *Windsurfing* appears against a white background:

Notice that at the bottom of the superimposed clip in the Construction window is a thin horizontal line. This is the fade control for the superimposed image. If you move the pointer onto the line, it turns into a finger. Click the finger on the line to create a handle, then drag the handle down to fade the image out and up to fade the image in:

 This is similar to the way you fade audio in and out.

Preview the work area again. This time the superimposed image fades in, and then after a couple of seconds it fades out (Figure 10-7). This technique of fading in and out a superimposed image, or *super*, can be used with any of the transparency options.

Chroma Key   The Chroma option sets a color or a range of colors in the superimposed image to be transparent. Using the Key Type list box in the Transparency dialog box, select the Chroma option. Move the cursor into the Color box. As the next illustration shows, the pointer turns into an eye dropper that you use to pick the color you want to be transparent:

Figure 10-7.

Fading a superimposed title in and out.

Because we want to use white as the transparent color, click anywhere in the white areas of the image in the Color box (white is the default color, so you don't actually have to use the eye dropper in this case). Then click anywhere in the Sample box to see the regions of transparency:

 Make sure the squares for the garbage matte are in their initial positions (one at each corner).

Click OK and preview the work area. This time, only the letters of the word *Windsurfing* are superimposed, along with some spaces around the letters:

It would be nice just to have the letters superimposed and not the spaces between them. Open the Transparency dialog box. Under the Key Type list box, there is the Similarity slider bar. This sets how broad a range of colors you want to be transparent. A None, or zero, similarity means that only the color selected with the eye dropper is transparent. A medium similarity means that colors similar to the selected color are transparent. Move the Similarity slider to the right and notice what happens in the Sample box (make sure the transparent areas appear black). As you move the slider farther to the right, less and less of the space between the letters is visible, which means they will be transparent in the assembled movie (Figure 10-8).

Figure 10-8.   Setting the similarity for a Chroma key. Increasing the similarity expands the range of colors in the superimposed image (in this case the title) that is set as transparent.

Click OK and preview the work area. Now only the letters appear:

Let's look at another example that demonstrates the features of the Chroma key. Instead of a title on a white background, we'll use a video clip of a person standing against a blue background.

Open the Transparency dialog box and use the eye dropper to select the blue background as the transparency color (the key). Adjust the similarity setting until just the person appears in the Sample window. You might also want to adjust the position of the Blend slider to smooth any rough edges (Figure 10-9).

Preview the work area. You should see the image of the person appearing in front of the windsurfer (Figure 10-10).

This technique, called *blue screening*, is used extensively in television—for example, to project an image of a weather map behind a weather forecaster. The person is actually standing in front of, and pointing at, a blank, blue screen. The weather maps are then added to the image electronically. A particular color, *chroma blue*, is used for the screen because human skin does not contain that shade of blue. The person, however, should not wear a blue shirt; otherwise, the weather map (or whatever the video clip is) will appear through his or her shirt.

RGB Key   This key sets a range of colors and intensities (brightnesses) to be transparent. It is a bit more specific than the Chroma key, which does not take into account how bright a color is, only its hue.

Luminance Key   The Luminance key sets a range of intensities (brightnesses) to be transparent. You can use this key to add texture to the main video clip.

Figure 10-9.   The Blend slider smoothes out abrupt changes in color. Increasing the blend amount helps remove rough edges around superimposed objects.

Figure 10-10.

Person superimposed over a video clip using a Chroma key. The person was shot against a blue screen, which was then made transparent using a Chroma key. The timing of the superimposed image was set so that the person appears to turn his head to follow the windsurfer.

Alpha Channel   This is useful when working with graphics produced from a graphics program that creates an *Alpha channel* for the graphic (such as Adobe Photoshop). An Alpha channel is a custom mask that matches the contours of the graphic.

Let's use another title on a white background to demonstrate this key. With the Alpha Channel key, the sliders for Similarity and Blend are disabled. That's because the Alpha channel matches the borders of the title, so no adjustment is needed. This produces the cleanest borders for a title:

The Alpha Channel key also lets you reverse the transparency, making the title itself transparent:

Now the main video, the windsurfer, shows through the letters of the title:

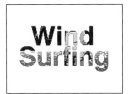

Blue Matte   The Blue Matte is used when you've created a graphic against a blue background and don't have an Alpha channel to work with, or when you've shot someone against a solid blue background.

Green Matte   This key is similar to the Blue Matte except that it is used for graphics set against a green background.

The Superimpose Controls

You can modify the superimposed transparency in a number of ways. The Similarity and Blend controls have already been discussed. You can use the Threshold and Cutoff sliders to increase or decrease the presence of shadows in the superimposed image (available only on the Luminance and Chroma keys).

The Reverse Key check box allows you to make the transparent portions of the superimposed image nontransparent, and vice-versa. This option is available only for the None, Alpha Channel, Image Matte, and Difference Matte key options.

The Drop Shadow check box allows you to add a drop shadow to the superimposed image. This is available only for the RGB and Difference key options.

The Smoothing list box lets you reduce rough edges in the transparent areas by averaging the pixels along the edges. This is useful when attempting to blue screen a person into a background.

Slowing Down (or Speeding Up) a Clip

Sometimes you need a clip to be just a little bit longer to match a piece of music or a particular transition. With the Speed option in the Clip menu, you can slow the rate at which the clip plays so that it lasts longer. For example, if you set the speed of a two-second clip to 50%, the modified clip lasts four seconds. You can also speed up a clip by setting a speed value greater than 100. A value of 200% makes the clip play twice as fast.

The frame rate isn't really changed when you change the speed. The program creates a virtual clip based on the new speed value, then selects the appropriate frame from the original clip for each frame of the speed-adjusted clip. This can produce uneven motion if you slow down or speed up the clip using irregular values (i.e., 27% or 160%). Regular values form common fractions or integers, so 25% (or 1/4) slows the clip down by using each original frame four times. At 300%, every third frame is used.

Compositing

One of the great advantages of digital editing over traditional analog video editing is that you can re-record a video clip as many times as you want without degrading the quality of the image. This means that you can add, or *layer*, one clip (or title) after another to the same shot. Each time you add a new element, you composite it by making a new movie. The final movie is the end result of several intermediate movies, or *passes*. Because each pass can involve any one of the techniques discussed in this chapter, the possibilities are limitless. The following is a fairly standard example, but it's only meant as a guide to what is possible. You should experiment with your own ideas.

Overlapping Multiple Titles

Let's say we want to add several titles to a clip and have them overlap at various points in time. We'll use the windsurfing clip and three titles: *Wind*, *Surfing*, and *Windsurfing*. The tricky part is that we want the titles to appear as if they were sitting on top of each other.

When compositing, you need to build from the back towards the front—in other words, build the background first, add the next farthest away layer, and so on until you get to the foreground. Figure 10-11 shows the relationship of the clip and titles for this example.

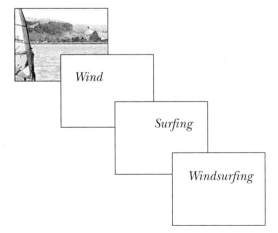

Figure 10-11.   Building a composite requires starting with the background image, then adding layers to it until you end up with the foreground layer.

To build the first layer we superimpose the Wind title on the wind-surfing clip with the following steps:

1. Place the windsurfing clip in video track A and place it at the beginning of the movie.

2. Place the Wind title in the superimpose track and position it to start at the 1:00 point on the timeline:

3. Use the stretch pointer to extend the duration of the title to three seconds.

4. Set the transparency of the title clip using the most appropriate key (in this case, the Chroma key)

5. Use the fade controls in the superimpose track to create a one-second fade-up and one-second fade-out of the Wind title:

6. Make a movie, giving it the name Pass1 (if possible, don't use any compression):

7. Import the Pass1 clip into Premiere.

8. Delete the clips in the Construction window.

9. Place the Pass1 clip in video track A and position it at the beginning of the movie.

10. Place the second title, Surfing, in video track B and position it so that it starts at the 2:00 position on the timeline:

11. Use the stretch pointer to extend the duration of the Surfing title to three seconds.

12. Set the transparency of the title using the most appropriate key.

13. Use the fade control in the superimpose track to create a one-second fade-up and one-second fade-out of the Surfing title.

14. Make a movie (with the name Pass2) with the same settings as before. The second movie, or second pass, shows the second title fading in before the first title has faded out (Figure 10-12). Because the second title was added after the first title, it appears in front of the Wind title.

Figure 10-12.

In this movie, the second title, *Surfing*, fades in before the first title, *Wind*, fades out completely.

15. Repeat steps 7 through 14, using the third title and Pass2 clips in the Construction window, and positioning the third title to start at the 3:00 point on the timeline.

The final movie shows one title fading in on top of the existing titles, which are gradually fading out (Figure 10-13).

You can also use the technique of compositing to build very complex transitions involving three or more clips. In the first pass, you would create a transition between clips 1 and 2. Make a movie of this transition. You would then bring in that movie and make a transition between the movie and the third clip. Make another movie of the second transition. You then bring in the second movie and make a transition between it and a third clip, and so on.

Compositing is time-consuming and it can use up a lot of space on your hard drive. But making the effort can dramatically improve the look of your pieces, elevating them from simple digital clips to professional-quality movies.

Figure 10-13.

In this movie, the third title, *Windsurfing*, fades in before the first two titles, *Wind* and *Surfing*, fade out completely.

Morphing

Morphing is one of the most bizarre effects you can produce on your computer. A *morph* is a short video clip in which a person's face or other object transforms into another object. Michael Jackson's music video, "Black and White," used this effect to switch from one person to another. A Chrysler commercial used this technique to transform an old model of a car into a new version. Those effects were created on high-end computers and cost tens of thousands of dollars to produce. But you can create similar effects with new morphing programs on your PC.

There are a number of morphing programs. The following section examines one of them, Digital Morph (from HSC Software), which should give you a good background in the basic technique of morphing.

Working with Digital Morph

Digital Morph allows you to import two still images and then produce a gradual morphing transition between them. The beginning image is called the *source image*. The image you're morphing to is called the *destination image*. In this example, we use a shot of a young boy for the source image and a shot of a young girl for the destination image (Figure 10-14).

Figure 10-14.   Digital Morph allows you to morph from one still image to another. Here we are morphing a boy into a girl. The large window shows an intermediate image in the morphing transition.

We're covering only the basic techniques of morphing in this section. Please review your Digital Morph manual for specific instructions (i.e., how to start a new morph, import images, etc.).

To create a smooth morph, you need to tell the program how to change the source image into the destination image. In Digital Morph, this is done with *field lines*. You place field lines around recognizable features in the image. In this example, we're morphing between two faces, so the first step is to put field lines around the boy's eyes:

We then move the boy's field lines to the girl's image:

and shape them around the girl's eyes:

 Moving the field lines tells the program to move the pixels inside and nearby the lines (the boy's eyes) to a new position (the girl's eyes). When the final morph is created, the program will not only move the pixels, but will also create a dissolve between the source pixels and the destination pixels. This combination of moving and dissolving between pixels is the whole secret behind morphing.

Finally, we place field lines around other features of the boy's face and then move these field lines to match the respective features on the girl's face (Figure 10-15).

Figure 10-15.   Field lines drawn around features of the boy's face are moved to the girl's image and formed around features of the girl's face.

    It is important to add field lines to any identifiable features, particularly those that form lines or edges in your image. These can be smile lines, eyebrows, ears—whatever creates a change in brightness or hue.

Reviewing Your Progress   You can preview the morph transition at any point by using the Do Morph command (in the Morph menu). You select the part of the transition to preview using the slider bar and then click the OK button to create the preview:

If parts of the morph preview image are blurry it means that you haven't added enough field lines to that area. Add more lines to the source image and move them to the correct place in the destination image. Then preview the morph again. Once you're satisfied with the morph image at one point in the transition, move the transition slider in the preview dialog box to another point in the transition and preview the morph again. Spot-checking the morph transition like this ensures that the final morph transition, which consists of 20 or more frames, will look right.

After you've spot-checked the morph, you can create the actual morph transition (called the *animation* in Digital Morph). Choose the Animate option in the File menu, type in the length of the transition (in frames):

Click on OK to make the morph. If you set the field lines correctly, your morph should look great (Figure 10-16).

Advanced Morphing Techniques

Morphing is a powerful technique for creating intriguing transitions. But it is as much an art as a science. The following is a collection of tips and tricks I've accumulated through my professional work—but it is far from complete. Each morph is a new challenge and a new opportunity to develop another technique.

Figure 10-16.   A complete morph from a boy to a girl

Tips for Morphing Faces

- For starters, use a program like Adobe Photoshop to align the source and destination images so that the two heads appear in about the same place in the image. This reduces the amount of motion in the morph transition, which leads to a smoother morph.

- Use four to six field lines for each eye. If it is a close-up, use four field lines for each eye's pupil.

- Use three lines for each eyebrow (if they are visible).

- Use at least six lines for the mouth. If the mouth is open, use another three lines for the teeth. If the shot is a close-up, use two sets of lines for the top part of the lip and another two sets of lines for the bottom lip.

- Don't forget the ears; use four to six lines for each ear.

- If one of the people is smiling, use three field lines to mark each smile line, then position these field lines in about the same relative position in the destination image.

- Trace the edge of the hair line but don't try to match every lock of hair.

- Morphing between a person with glasses and a person without glasses is tricky. Outline the glasses in the source image and then position these field lines in about the same relative position in the destination image. You may have to remove lines outlining the eyebrows.

- Put a number of field lines in the background and don't move them in the destination image. These lines, called *anchor lines*, help smooth the edges of the faces during the transition.

Morphing between Two Objects

- As with faces, it's important that the two objects appear in the about the same position in the image. Use Photoshop to align the objects.

- Use a similar or identical background. If the background is changing, the viewer may be distracted from the main event, the foreground.

- Outline all areas of high contrast and color change. The human eye is very good at seeing edges (in either brightness or color). Focus on these areas first, then add points to other features.

- Start with a few lines, preview the morph, and then add lines where the image seems smeared. Adding unnecessary lines at the beginning not only takes a lot of time, but also increases the time to create the animation.

A Handbag of Tricks

Whew! Lots of stuff to play with. Well, if you've gotten this far into the chapter, you're probably hungry for more. Here are brief descriptions of some other tricks you can try. If you're not sure how to make a certain trick happen, try to break it into its parts: What is the transition? What are the filters? Is there a superimposed image? Then review the sections earlier in the chapter that deal with the techniques used.

The Heartbeat of (Anything)

Using the progressive filtering technique with the Spherize filter, you can make any object have a visible heartbeat. Apply the filter and produce a clip that gradually fades it out (in incremental steps). Then take a piece of that clip, copy it, and reverse it (using the Backward filter). Pump in, pump out. Play with the timing of the clips until you get a realistic heartbeat. Add the sound of a heartbeat in the sound track, and you've got a seriously weird piece of video.

Layering Transparent Clips

With the current small video window, this technique works best with titles, but as the window gets larger, you can try video clips as well. The end effect is that of several elements appearing on the screen at seemingly different distances from the viewer; for example, large titles going in front of titles in the back. An artistic touch is to make the titles transparent so that you can see the other titles underneath. Then layer them, starting with the farthest clip.

Wrap-Up

The techniques described in this chapter have barely scratched the surface of what is possible. We didn't even discuss how you can use separate effects from different programs (such as Premiere and Digital Morph) on the same piece of video. It's all too easy, however, to get seduced by all the digital gadgetry and effects and lose sight of the main goal—delivering a message. The effects you use should work with, not against, the message of your piece. Don't just throw in one effect after another. Have a reason. Your piece will not only look better, but it may also affect your viewers more deeply and memorably.

PART III

BECOMING A PROFESSIONAL

You now have all the tools to create clear and informative digital movies. But this is just the beginning. Through the use of various techniques covered in Part III of this book, you can improve your digital videos and incorporate them in other formats, such as videotapes and interactive multimedia programs. Chapter 11 covers advanced audio-editing techniques. Chapter 12 is a comprehensive primer on video production. Chapter 13 covers the details of digital video and compression. Chapter 14 discusses the use of digital video in interactive applications.

Advanced Audio-Editing Techniques

S ound is one of the great unsung aspects of video, primarily because most people think of video as solely a visual medium. True, the pictures attract people's attention. But the right soundtrack embellishes the visuals with presence and a mood. It can mean the difference between a merely average piece and a truly spectacular one.

Elements of Audio

The audio you hear in a digital video clip, or on a videotape for that matter, is not just one piece of sound. The audio track usually consists of a combination of many different sound elements. The most common elements are narration or dialog, background sounds, music, and audio special effects (Figure 11-1). These different elements are mixed to produce the final audio track—the sound you hear in the finished piece. Sometimes as many as four or five elements are mixed for a single shot. The soundtrack for a feature film, for example, can consist of as many as 20 different sounds—all occurring at the same time. Each type of sound element poses unique challenges for the editor, so we discuss each one in turn.

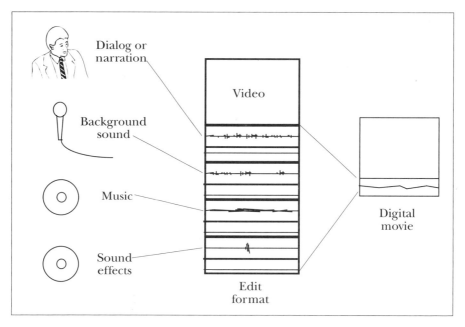

Figure 11-1.   There are four major types of sound elements that can be used in a digital video movie: speech (either dialog or narration), background sound, music, and audio special effects.

Dialog and Narration

Dialog and narration are the most important sound elements in any segment in which they are heard. That's the point, isn't it? You are putting them in so that the viewer can hear what the actor or narrator is saying. The volume of these elements is set high enough so that they are always the loudest, most easily heard elements.

Although both of these elements involve someone talking, there are significant differences between them. One obvious difference is that you don't see the narrator. His or her words are laid under the video (if you are using a person as both an on-camera host and a narrator, then the previous comment applies only to the narrated portions).

Another difference between narration and dialog is that a recording of dialog always includes some of the background sound of the recording location. This can be the hum of an air conditioner in an interior location or the buzz of traffic in an outdoor location. This extra sound is always there, although it can be minimized by the placement of the microphone and the choice of a quiet location. By contrast, narration is usually recorded in an extremely quiet place. In professional productions, the narrator sits inside a sound-proof booth to make sure there is no extraneous noise.

If you are not going to be recording narration in a sound booth but still want to have clean narration—that is, without any extraneous sounds— you might not want to record directly into your PC. It's better to record the narration on a standard cassette recorder in a quiet room and then transfer the narration from the cassette tape to your PC using a sound digitizing board.

Because narration does not usually include any ambience or background sound, video clips that are used with narration should have their own background sounds. This is why you should record audio when you are shooting a scene.

Here's a quick exercise that points out the difference between narration and a piece of dialog. Record some narration in a quiet room. Digitize it and then import it into a video-editing program. Then import a clip of dialog and place it after the narration in the editing program. Remove the video portion of the dialog clip. Then listen to both clips. The difference you hear in the dialog clip is the background sound.

Using Dialog as a Voice-Over

You don't necessarily have to use a shot of dialog as a combined video/audio clip. A common technique is to use the audio portion of one part of a dialog shot as a voice-over. For example, let's say you shot a scene of two people talking at a restaurant. As the following illustration shows, the most straightforward way of editing this scene is to have each shot last as long as the dialog for that shot:

Video	Medium shot of man talking	Medium shot of woman talking
Audio		

Another way to edit this scene to make it more interesting is to cut to the shot of the woman before the man stops talking:

This way we can see her reaction before she starts to speak. In the television industry this is known as an *L cut* and it is used extensively to create smoother scenes.

Background Sound

As mentioned before, microphones pick up not only the primary source of sound such as a person talking but also the ambience that is present in almost all locations. We don't usually notice this sound, but it's there and the microphone always picks it up.

The amount of sound that passes by us unnoticed is amazing. Our brains filter it out so that we can concentrate on what someone is saying. But because the microphone picks up all the sounds of a location, you need to become adept at recognizing background sounds. Here's a quick exercise that can help you to listen better:

1. Close your eyes and try to pick out as many different sounds as you can in a room. Listen for at least 30 seconds to give your brain a chance to switch to a different mode of listening.

2. Turn your head and determine if the sounds change in intensity.

3. Try to locate the source of the sounds without opening your eyes.

4. Go to another location and repeat these steps.

5. If you haven't gone outside yet, step into an outdoor location and try to pick out the background sounds.

After a while, you should be able to pick up background sounds without closing your eyes. It's important to be able to hear the ambience of a location because it can add unwanted sounds to the interview or dialog and, ultimately, to the video piece. For example, let's say you were interviewing your grandmother about her experiences during the Depression. She tells you a wonderful story about the first time she drove a car. You dig through the family album and find an old black-and-white picture of that event. You decide to combine the audio portion of her interview (as a voice-over) with the old photos. You carefully edit her words and the pictures together, only to find that the refrigerator hum (picked up during the interview) seems extremely out of place while you look at the shots of her behind the wheel.

 You don't have to worry about background sound if the dialog is always going to be used as a combined video/audio clip. For some reason, our brains don't seem to mind hearing background sound when we see the person talking on the screen. But because you don't always know beforehand when you might want to use dialog as a voice-over, it's a good idea to conduct interviews in quiet locations.

Although every location has its own blend of background sounds, there are some standard problems that pop up regularly in various locations. Here are a few examples:

Office: Air conditioning, computers, people talking nearby, telephones

Shopping mall: Air conditioning (everywhere), escalators, fountains

Hospital: Intercom, air conditioning, refrigerators and other machinery, people talking

City street: Traffic (particularly motorcycles), fire engines, airplanes, subway rumble, people talking, construction

Suburban street: Traffic, children playing, lawn mowers

You won't able to eliminate background sound in every circumstance, but you should try to minimize it as best you can. You'll save yourself a few gray hairs when you get into the editing phase.

Using Background Sounds for Best Effect

Although background sound is a nuisance when recording interviews and dialog, it is an essential part of video clips that don't include someone talking. Imagine a shot of a mountain stream without the gurgling sound of the water. Imagine a basketball game without the roar of the crowd, the squeak of the sneakers on the wood floor. Imagine the space shuttle lifting off without the thunder of its engines.

These types of background sounds, often called *nat sounds* (for "natural sound"), add texture and fullness to a video clip. For this reason, it's not uncommon to use a shot with rich nat sound to introduce a new scene. For example, you might use the sound of a stream (under a long shot of a mountain meadow) to introduce a scene of two people talking in a meadow:

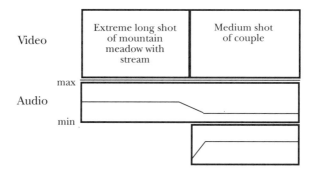

The sound of a stream works in concert with the establishing shot to set the scene. It is an audio cue that helps orient the viewer. Just

before the woman starts talking the volume, or level, of the stream sound is dropped down so it does not interfere with the woman's dialogue.

A nat sound that is used to start a scene can also be interwoven with the dialog for dramatic effect. Let's say you are editing a scene of a father and son starting a tense conversation in a kitchen. The scene begins with the father cleaning some tools in the sink (Figure 11-2). Let's step through each shot to explain how the nat sound of the water in the sink is integrated into the scene:

Shot 1: Father is at the sink. The sound of the water in the sink is used near full, or normal, to help set the scene (Figure 11-3 describes the conventions used for audio levels).

Shot 2: Son walks in. The sound of the water is continued through this shot. The sound of the son's footsteps is kept low so that the viewer can hear it. The implication is that the father hasn't.

Shot 3: Son sits down. The water sound continues; the sound of the son sitting down is set louder in this shot to set up the father's reaction.

Shot 4: Father turns and talks. The sound of the water in the sink continues under the father's dialog, which is used full.

Shot 5: Son doesn't respond. The sound of the water continues at the same level because it is the only sound in the scene.

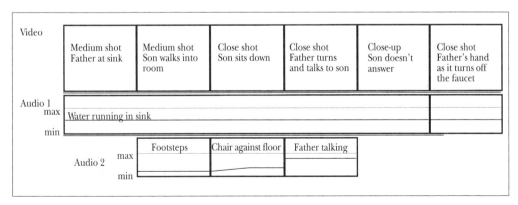

Figure 11-2.   The background audio should continue through a scene to tie it together. Here the background sound of water running in a sink is continued under the shots of the son.

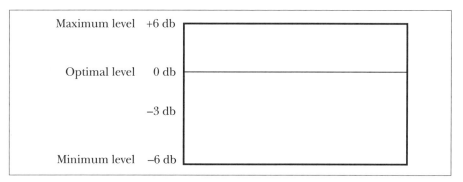

Figure 11-3. The optimal level for a final audio track is 0 db distortion. Audio peaks between 0 db and 9 db can be tolerated, but peaks at 9 db cause a type of distortion called *clipping*. Audio levels below 0 db sound quieter.

Shot 6: Father turns off faucet. Here's the payoff. The sound of the water is increased because the faucet is seen in a close-up. This then emphasizes the silence that occurs when the water is shut off. The obvious implication is that the father is upset.

The viewer is so used to hearing the water throughout the first five shots of the scene, that in shot 6 an element of tension is added when that sound is removed.

A background sound, such as the faucet in this example, is usually kept at about the same level, unless (as in shot 6) the source of the sound is seen in a close-up. If we were to back away from the scene—for example, with a shot taken from outside looking in through a window at the father and son—then the sound of the water would be decreased.

As you edit, keep an ear out for natural sounds that can be used to introduce a scene or to accentuate the storyline. Think of it as another dimension in which to work. Your viewers might not notice why a scene that integrates nat sounds works so well, but you will.

Maintaining a Smooth Background

In the previous example, we carried the sound of the water through the first five shots to maintain a smooth audio track that ties all the shots to that location (the kitchen). In reality, the shot of the son walking through the door (shot 2) might have been taken in another place, at another time, so it would not have any of the sound of water in the sink.

Imagine what would happen if we didn't carry the water sound through shots 2 and 3, if we just used the background sound that came with each shot when it was taken (Figure 11-4). At the end of shot 1, the water sound would stop suddenly. We would hear the footsteps, then the son sitting down. At shot 4, the sound of the water would suddenly be present again (underneath the father's voice). Editing the scene this way prevents the shots from seeming like they were all of the same place. In addition, the sudden change in the audio (the water sound dropping out then back in) distracts the viewer. Differing levels of background sound also distract the viewer.

Difficulties in maintaining a smooth audio background can occur in many different situations. The following is a selection of common problem situations and ways to get around them.

Figure 11-4. If a continuous background sound is not laid under an entire scene, then the audio changes with each shot. This emphasizes the edits and makes the scene seem choppy.

Removing Unwanted Sounds

Let's say you are editing a scene of two people putting together a piece of machinery. The order of the shots is defined by continuity; i.e., the machinery is assembled in order:

Shot 1	Shot 2	Shot 3	Shot 4
Audio 1	Audio 2	Audio 3	Audio 4

Unfortunately, the background sound for shot 2 includes the sound of the lunch whistle blowing. The easiest way to fix this is to get rid of the sound for shot 2 and replace it. You can use extra sound from shot 1:

Shot 1	Shot 2	Shot 3	Shot 4
Audio 1		Audio 3	Audio 4

You can also use extra sound from shot 3:

Shot 1	Shot 2	Shot 3	Shot 4
Audio 1	Audio 3		Audio 4

Either option involves a few steps, so let's go through how you do the first option in an editing program, such as Adobe Premiere for Windows. We start with the four shots lined up in order in the Construction window (Figure 11-5):

1. Move shot 1 down so that the video portion sits in video track B and the audio portion in audio track B:

2. Using the stretch pointer, extend shot 1 until it reaches the beginning of shot 3:

3. Delete the audio portion of shot 2 by clicking on it and pressing the (Delete) key:

Now the audio for shot 1 extends through shot 2. The video edit hasn't changed because video track A has priority over video track B. So the video of shot 2 starts at the same point in the final piece.

Handling Changes in Background Sound

Most of the time the background sounds for two shots are different— even if they were taken in the same place. Although these changes aren't usually apparent, there are some situations where a noticeable change occurs.

For example, let's say that in the previous example the audio for shot 2 doesn't include the lunch whistle, but includes the hum of a different piece of machinery instead. If you simply cut from shot 1 to shot 2, the audio changes abruptly because of the new sound.

In this case, you don't need to get rid of the sound for shot 2; you need to smooth out the transition between the two audio portions. The easiest way to do this is to *cross-fade* the audio of shots 1 and 2. Figure 11-6 shows a completed cross-fade in Premiere. The audio of shot 1 is faded out as the audio of shot 2 is faded in.

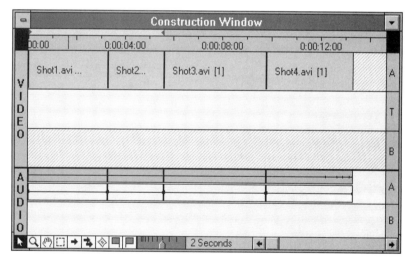

Figure 11-5.   At times you will need to remove a section of background audio because it contains a sound that distracts the viewer. In this case, shot 2 contains the sound of a lunchtime whistle, which doesn't appear in shots 1 or 3. The solution is to remove the background audio for shot 2 and replace it with audio from shot 1 or 3.

Figure 11-6.   Cross-fading the audio between two cuts helps even out any differences in background audio between them. In Premiere, you create a cross-fade by extending the audio for each cut so that they overlap, and then fade down the audio of the first clip while fading up the audio of the second clip.

Here's how you perform a cross-fade:

1. Move shot 2 down so that the video portion is in video track B and the audio portion in audio track B:

2. Open the Transitions window (in the Window menu), choose the Direct transition, and place it above the video portion of shot 2. Align the edges of the Direct transition to match the edges of shot 2:

3. Using the stretch pointer, extend the left edge of shot 2 to the left by about 15 frames. Then use the stretch pointer to extend the right edge of shot 1 to the right by 15 frames. This creates a 30-frame audio overlap::

4. Create a handle in the audio portion of shot 1 at the point where the extended shot 2 begins. Drag the handle at the right edge of shot 1 down to the bottom of the level control box. Modify the audio portion of shot 2 in a similar way so that the two audio portions look like this:

Now the audio of shot 1 starts to fade out as the audio of shot 2 fades in. The cross-fade starts before the video edit occurs to smooth out the transition. The Direct transition is used to maintain the timing of the original video edit.

Filling in Missing Background Sounds

If you're working with someone else's video clips or with material from a clip media disk, you might find that some of the clips don't have any background sound. As mentioned earlier, if one shot in a scene has background sound, then the rest of the shots in the scene should as well.

Let's say you edited the scene depicted in Figure 11-7. Shots 2, 3, 4, and 5 are without background sound. Your first option is to try to extend the audio from a previous shot (as done in the section on removing unwanted sounds). This option works in a large number of cases but not this one. The audio for shot 1, the forest, won't fit any of the other shots because it doesn't include the specific sounds needed for each shot (truck, door closing, footsteps, and power saw).

Your second option is to avoid using background sounds entirely and use a piece of music throughout the whole scene. To do this, you need to choose a piece of music that suits the message or story you are trying to convey. If you are making a piece about the need for lumber, then you could use music that had a strong, upbeat mood to convey industriousness. But if you are making a video that is protesting against logging, then you might use music of a more ominous nature.

Figure 11-7.   If one shot in a scene has background audio, in this case shot 1, then you need to create background sound for the rest of the scene.

The use of music without background sound gives the scene a sur-realistic quality. If that's what you're looking for, then using a single piece of music throughout the scene is an acceptable solution. But if that's not your goal, then you have to try to find a way to put in the appropriate sounds.

The third option is to find replacement audio for each shot that is missing it. Let's say you found another tape that has shots of a different kind of truck in another forest. It also has a shot of a different person using a power saw. You could borrow the audio from the alternate truck shot and put it under shot 2 (Figure 11-8). It doesn't have to be a perfect match, just close. Test it out and you'll know if it works.

You could also borrow the sound of the alternate power saw shot and put it under shot 5 (Figure 11-9). In this case you need to synch the sound of the audio to match the movement of the saw (the sound of a power saw changes when it cuts into wood).

That leaves shots 3 and 4. These are a bit more difficult because they include actions that call for specific sounds: the closing of the truck door and the sound of the man's footsteps. Because you don't have alternate shots for these shots, you need to create the back-ground sound for these shots from scratch with sound effects, which is the subject of the next section.

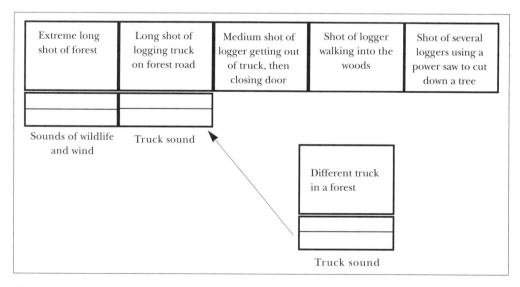

Figure 11-8.   You can copy the sound of a truck from another shot and place it under the shot of the truck in this scene to create a segment of background audio.

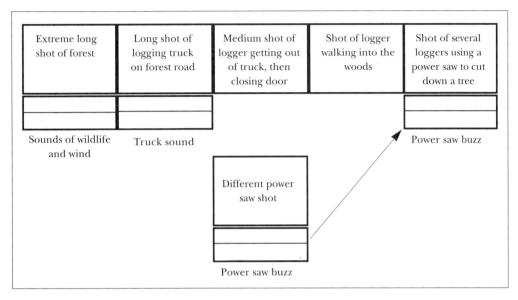

Figure 11-9.   By using the sound of a power saw from another shot, you can create a background sound for the saw in this scene.

Adding Sound Effects

Creating sound effects is one of the most tedious, yet most magical parts of editing audio. The right sound effect can save a shot from the trash bin or add sparkle to an otherwise average shot.

In the previous example, we faced the problem of creating background sounds for two shots that didn't have any audio: a man getting out of a truck and closing the door and a man walking in a forest. We look at each one in turn.

Adding the Sound of a Truck Door

The sound of a car door closing is fairly similar to the sound of a truck door closing; so all you need to do is find a quiet spot where there isn't a lot of background sound and close a car door several times (while you record). Try to close the door harder on each try to give yourself some options. Digitize those sounds and import them into your editing program.

You now need to synch the sound of the door closing to the action in shot 3. Here's how you do it in Premiere:

1. Open the sound effect in the Clip window.

2. Set the In and Out points so that there is only about 10 frames of pad before and after the door slam.

3. Add a marker at the exact point where the sound of the door slam occurs. Open shot 3 in the Clip window and add a marker at the exact point where the door closes. Move the sound effect into audio track A slide it under shot 3 until the markers for the sound effect and shot 3 are aligned:

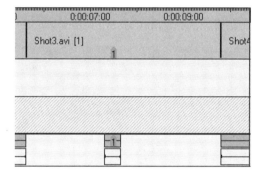

4. Set the work area to include just shot 3 and preview the work area.

5. Adjust the position of the sound effect (right or left) until the door slam sound is in synch with the video.

Now that you've matched the specific action of the door closing, you can fill in the rest of the audio with a more general type of audio. Because the truck is in the woods, the basic background sound would be similar to the audio you used in shot 1. Make a copy of the audio portion of shot 1 and place the copy in audio track B under shot 3:

Preview the work area. Adjust the volume, or level, of the door slam audio so that you can hear it clearly and it fits the video. That is, if the truck is a long way from the viewer (i.e., the camera), the sound should not be very loud. If the truck is close to the viewer, the sound should be louder.

Adding Footsteps

Creating a sound effect to match a person's footsteps can be fairly tricky. The difficult part is matching the pace of the steps. You could record the sound of one step and use that one sound for each step in the shot, but it would be better and would require less editing time to match the whole walk. That means that you have to *foley*, or imitate the person's walking speed, when you record the effect.

The easiest way to do that is to figure out how many steps the man takes over the course of the shot. Let's say, in this case, the man takes six steps in five seconds. Then when you are recording the effect, have your assistant (or whoever is the surrogate walker) walk at a pace so that he or she takes the same number of steps in the same amount of time (six steps in five seconds). Record several versions to give yourself some options later on.

 A more involved method would be to play the tape of the man walking in the woods as your assistant is walking. Then by listening to your assistant's footsteps as you're watching the tape, you could tell if the walks are similar.

Matching the pace is only one part of the solution—not all foot-steps sound the same. The sound of high heels on a wood floor is dramatically different from work boots in a forest; so you have to try to match the situation when you record the sound effect. In this case, an obvious option is to find a patch of dry leaves. But let's say it's summer, and there isn't a dry leaf to be found. Now you have to get creative. Every sound editor has his or her own war stories of improvised sound effects. In this case, having someone walking on a piece of carpet covered with potato chips would create a fairly close substitute for a person walking on dry leaves.

Once you're satisfied that you matched the pace and the tonal quality of the footsteps, you record the effect, digitize it, and import it into your editing program. Place the sound effect in an audio track under the shot in question and adjust its position, right or left, until the effect is in synch with the video.

 You can use the arrow keys to move a clip one frame at a time. The left arrow moves the clip one frame earlier in the Construction window. The right arrow, one frame later.

If you haven't matched the pace of the walk exactly, try splitting the sound effect into two parts and adjusting each part. The holes in the sound are filled by the background sound of the woods.

Each tricky situation calls for a unique solution. But over time you'll collect your own bag of sound effects tricks, and matching sounds will become easier.

Using Prepackaged Sound Effects

If you're going to be working with a lot of sound effects, you might want to look into acquiring a set of prepackaged sound effects. These are collections of typical sounds, such as closing doors, speeding cars, and fire engines. The British Broadcasting Corporation has produced probably the most extensive collection, which offers everything from the buzz of a World War I biplane to the sound of someone scraping toast.

Audio Sweetening

Sound effects aren't just for fixing problems. You can also use them to add sparkle and texture to particular shots or whole scenes. For example, if you edited a scene of two people talking at an outdoor café, you could introduce an artificial background sound of city traffic to make it seem as if they were in the middle of a city. This bed of sound would be played at low volume, so it would not conflict with the dialog.

 You might wonder why you should go to all the trouble to eliminate background sound in dialog shots if you're going to put background sound back in. The reason is that you might want to use a different background sound in the final piece. By making sure the dialog is clean, you give yourself more options in the editing room.

You can also use sound effects to boost the sound for particular parts of a shot. For example, let's say you took a long shot of someone knocking on the front door of a house. Because it's a long shot, the audio for the shot probably won't pick up the sound of the door well (to do that, the microphone would have to be near the door, and it might be visible in the shot). You can fix this by replacing that part of the audio with a sound effect of a door knock.

How much sweetening you should do depends on where your piece will be shown, how much time you have, and how much money you have. Audio sweetening plays a big role in feature films, but the subtleties added by sweetening are lost if your piece is going to be played at a noisy trade show.

Adding Music

Of all the techniques in the sound editor's tool kit, music is the most powerful and manipulative. The right piece of music can turn an average scene into an emotional tour de force. In contrast, the wrong piece of music can deflate a powerful scene into a mishmash of conflicting signals.

Music works in mysterious ways. It somehow taps into a different part of our brain and creates associations that often work on a subconscious or subliminal level. Try to remember a scene from one of your favorite movies. It's likely that music played a major role in making that scene memorable.

Imagine *Star Wars* without John Williams' soundtrack (if you saw the movie, you can probably still remember the theme music). The haunting, threatening music of *Jaws* is burned in the minds of millions of Americans. "Lara's Theme" from *Dr. Zhivago*, the soundtracks for *Rocky*, *Chariots of Fire*, *The Sting*, the list goes on and on. And from the world of television, it's scary how many of us can recall songs for old television shows. Anyone remember the theme songs to "The Jetsons," "Green Acres," the original "Star Trek," and "M*A*S*H"?

Film and video professionals have known for a long time that music can create a new experience for the viewer—one that is richer, deeper, and more memorable. Now it's your turn.

Setting the Right Mood

Every type of music produces a different mood. A classical piece can "color" a scene differently than hard-edged rock-and-roll; so you need to choose your music carefully.

Most of us are already familiar with how music can affect a scene. A tune in a minor key lends a somber or sad edge to the visuals. Soft, flowing music—maybe just a classical guitar or a flute—adds a peaceful sense to a scene. A loud and boisterous saxophone injects energy. A full orchestra, with its emphasis on stringed instruments, creates a sweeping sensation. A heavily synthesized piece, with lots of electronic sounds, imbues the scene with futuristic tones.

Because music can have such an impact, you need to match the mood of the music with the mood of the scene. You also need to consider the style of editing you are using. Music with a strong beat and fast tempo suggests a series of quick shots. A piece of music with longer notes and a diminished beat calls for lengthier shots.

You should start thinking about what kind of music you'll use at the beginning of a project. Too many people leave it to the end when there isn't enough time.

Using Music as an Active Element

If a scene doesn't include narration or dialog, you have a lot of freedom in your choice of music. It can be majestic and sweeping, it can include lyrics, and it can have a strong beat. If the ambience of a shot is important—say, the sound of a mountain stream—then the music should not be so loud and active that it clashes with the background sound. How loud is too loud? That depends on the situation. If you're editing a car chase scene, the music can be very loud because the background sound will be as well.

As was described in Chapter 9, in these types of sections the video and music are edited at the same time. You first lay down the music, then you edit the pictures (as opposed to laying the music in after the pictures are edited). The music's beat and tempo suggest ways to edit the video. This can complicate things if your video edit points are determined by continuity. In most cases, the visual continuity is more important.

 In feature films, music is often added after the film is edited. The composer scores the music so that it fits the edited film. You might not have the budget to commission music specifically for your piece, so you should edit the music and visuals at the same time.

Give yourself a lot of time when editing scenes that use music as an active element. You might re-edit the same section several times before you are satisfied. Many times you may find out that that perfect piece of music wasn't so perfect after all, and you need to find another piece that fits the images better.

Using Background Music

In scenes with dialog, the music takes a back seat to the words. Therefore, you should use music that doesn't compete with the dialog but supports it. Generally speaking, background music is fairly simple; it does not contain a large number of instruments. The type of melody used varies from editor to editor and scene to scene. But the important point to remember is that the music is there to embellish, not to call attention to itself.

Although it does not play an active role in a scene, background music still can add a great deal to the mood. It can add an emotional element not present in the dialog (or in the acting). It can also serve to make a transition from one mood to another. For example, the scene of the two people sitting by a mountain stream discussed earlier could start with calm, soft music. As the scene progresses and the people start to argue, the music could switch to a minor key to introduce a sense of tension and conflict.

 As with editing, one of the best ways to learn how to use background music is to hear how it's used on television and in movies. Train yourself to listen for the music and hear how it sets the tone of a scene.

Incorporating Music into Your Movies

Unlike background sound, which is tied to a particular shot or scene, music can be introduced and removed at any point in time. You can use a piece of music to introduce a scene by starting the music just before the scene begins. You can also add a piece of music in the middle of a shot. For example, in the logging scene described earlier, you can fade up a piece of music halfway into the long shot of the forest.

Most of the time, you fade up a piece of music at the start and fade it down at the end. The length of a music fade can vary, but on average it lasts for at least several seconds and usually more.

If the music is an active element, it should be played full—that is, at the 0 db level. Above that level, you start to get distortion. Background music should be set low enough so that it doesn't overwhelm the dialog, but loud enough so that it can be heard. Often a single piece of music is used as an active element in one part of a scene and then as a background element in sections with dialog. In these situations, you should start to fade the music down gradually so that it is at the proper level when the dialog begins.

Sources of Music

If you plan to use a piece of music from a record or CD you bought in a store, then it is probably copyrighted and you must get permission from the copyright holder to use that music. Most of the time, the music publisher holds the copyright, so you have to negotiate with the company over how much to pay for the permission.

An attractive option is to use *clip music*, also known as *needle drops*. This is generic music that was produced solely for the purpose of being licensed. A large number of these CDs have already been produced; you purchase the rights to use the material when you purchase the disc. Given the wide range of music styles available on clip discs, you should probably not consider using well-known songs unless you have a large budget for music.

Yet another option is to compose the music yourself. There are a number of new music-composing programs that let you create generic music of your own. These programs contain algorithms for different styles of music (samba, ragtime, big band, etc.). You can have the programs create compositions at random or by following the key, melody, or tempo you determine. The programs then create the music and store it as a digital file. Your compositions won't sound as professional as store-bought music or even as good as clip music, but they probably sound a lot better than what you could bang out on a piano (unless, of course, you're a musician).

Mixing Several Audio Tracks

Combining several sound elements into a final, single audio track is as much an art as it is a science. In the film and television industry, this process is known as a *mix down*, and there are professionals who specialize in this process alone. Entire books have been written about the art of sound mixing. Here we just examine the technical aspects of working with several tracks of audio.

On the face of it, sound mixing involves setting the level of each sound element so that it can be heard clearly among the others. The tricky part is making sure the various sounds don't clash or overwhelm one another. If you're working with only three elements, that should be a manageable task.

Your main concern, not surprisingly, is with the primary audio. If someone is talking, you need to hear him or her clearly, so the level of dialog and narration should be set at 0 db (Figure 11-10).

Next you should set the level of any sound effect that needs to be heard clearly (i.e., that is not used as background sound). For example, if a door closing appears prominently in a shot, then you want to hear that sound. Most of the time, these types of sound effects occur between sections of dialog, so they won't interfere.

Third, adjust the level of the background sound so that it is present but low enough so that it doesn't conflict with the dialog and primary sound effects. If you are working with a music track as well, drop the background sound level down a bit lower than you would otherwise (to make room for the music).

Last, adjust the music level. You might want to change the beginning and ending points of the audio fades at this point to accommodate the other audio tracks.

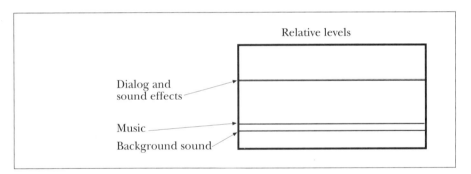

Figure 11-10. Dialog and narration are set near the 0 db level because you want to hear them clearly. Audio special effects that are tied to an action in the video are set fairly high as well. Background sound and music are set lower so they don't conflict with dialog or narration. However, if there isn't any dialog, music or background sound can be set at 0 db.

If you want to use four audio tracks in Premiere, you need to do the mix down in two stages. Set the levels of the dialog and primary sound effects first. Set the work area to include only the section where you want to use four audio tracks, and make a movie of this section. Import this movie back into your project and save the project under a new name. Then replace the track of dialog with the composite track you just made and delete the track of primary sound effects (since it's included in the composite track). This gives you the extra audio track you need.

If you are going to be working with more than three audio tracks, you might want to consider exporting the various sound elements to a sound-editing program. In addition to giving you more control over several audio tracks, these programs let you apply a wide range of special effects, such as filters, reverb, pitch shift, and tempo change. Once you mix down in the sound-editing program, import the mixed-down track into the video-editing program and place it under the appropriate shots.

As with sound mixing, a detailed discussion of how to use sound effects is beyond the scope of this book. If you are interested in getting involved in this area of production, you should buy a book devoted to this issue (please refer to Appendix A for a list of books on video and audio production).

Wrap-Up

In this chapter we focused on how to make the audio portion of a digital movie as compelling as the video part. Too often an afterthought, audio editing is an essential part of professional productions for producing the proper balance of dialog, background ambience, sound effects, and music. If you take the time to make the audio track support and enhance the video, your movies will stand out from the crowd.

CHAPTER 12

Getting Good Stuff to Work With

N o amount of editing can ever completely correct for poor camerawork, bad lighting, and shoddy sound recording. Starting with good material makes the job of editing much easier because you can spend more time fine-tuning your video segments and less time cutting around problems. In this chapter, we review some of the basics of proper camera, lighting, and sound-recording techniques.

Before the Shooting Starts

Production tends to be expensive. Unless you're acting as a one-person production team, you'll probably be working with two or three other people. And these people will probably want to be paid (you can only beg favors from friends for so long).

Even if you're not spending a lot of money, production is still time-consuming. A general rule in documentary production is that each day of shooting produces three minutes of edited video, that is, footage that ends up in the final piece. For scripted productions, such as a training video, you can get as much as five or six minutes of edited video per day; so, a 12-minute piece requires at least two days of shooting. And that's just an average for an experienced production team. You might need to spend more time in the field than that.

So it's a good idea to think about what you're going to shoot before you pack up the camera and start shooting.

Have a Plan

Earlier chapters discussed the importance of developing a shooting script for your production. This document is a kind of blueprint for the final piece. If you don't write a shooting script, at least write down a list of shots you think you'll need.

Such a list is invaluable if you have to shift your plans in the middle of a shoot day. You will be able to modify your plans more easily and more efficiently if you've got a good sense of what you absolutely have to shoot.

 A shoot day is like those supermarket sweepstakes where you're allowed to grab as much as you can within a certain period of time. You want to get the best items, so you check out the store beforehand to make sure you know where your favorite items are. That kind of planning works for video production as well.

Scout the Location

If you have the time, you should try to scout all locations (places you're going to shoot) several days before the actual shoot day. This gives you time to identify and resolve any unexpected problems. There is a basic set of items to check for indoor and outdoor locations.

Indoor Locations

- The number of windows (this affects your lighting plan)
- The number of electrical outlets (which affects the number of extension cords you need to bring)
- Whether the outlets are on separate circuits (this is especially important if you're going to be using many lights, because you shouldn't put more than three lights on one circuit)

- Background sounds (Can annoying appliances be turned off? Do special arrangements need to be made? Do you need to bring sound blankets to muffle the sound?)
- Parking (What is the best place to off-load your equipment so that you're close to an entrance?)

Outdoor Locations

- Position of the sun (with regard to your likely camera position and the time of day you'll be shooting)
- Background sounds (construction and traffic noise, again with regard to the time of day)

Some of these items might seem pretty trivial, but working out potential problems beforehand will make your shoot day go smoother, and that will lead to better material.

Check Your Equipment

You are totally dependent on your equipment. If it doesn't work, you might as well pack up and go home. Therefore, a cardinal rule is to make sure the equipment is working before you go out on location. That means putting in a battery, turning on the camera, recording some footage and audio, and playing it back to verify the quality. Don't assume a cable works; make sure.

Video production equipment falls into two main categories: studio production and field (or remote) production. Most of the time you won't be working in a studio, so we'll focus on remote production equipment. Appendix A contains a list of books on video production, some of which focus on studio production.

The basic parts of a remote production system are discussed in detail in the following sections.

The Camera Package (Camera, Recorder, Tripod, Extras)

There are a wide variety of cameras and lenses that can be used for video work. You should make sure the camera you choose has at least an 8:1 zoom ratio (for more flexibility in framing a shot), a lens iris that you can set automatically or manually, and a white-balance button. Most of the top-end cameras have these features.

In addition to the camera, you want to have the following items to round out the camera package:

- Recorder (if it is not attached)
- Batteries (enough for all exterior shooting, plus two extras)
- AC adapter/battery charger
- Camera case
- Tripod
- Camera-tripod plate (This connects the camera to the tripod. Some tripods don't use plates, but if yours does, make sure you have it, or you won't be able to use the tripod.)
- Monitor
- Power cable for monitor
- Video cable to connect monitor to the recorder or the camera

The Lighting Kit (Lights, Light Stands, Power Cords)

The kind and number of lights you need depends on where and what you're shooting. A basic lighting kit, which meets the needs of most indoor and outdoor shooting, includes the following items:

- Four lights (two lights of 650 Watts, two lights of 1,000 Watts)
- Four light stands
- Two umbrella reflectors
- Extra bulbs
- A power cord for each light
- Extension cords
- Power strip (multiple outlets on a single extension cord)
- Gaffer's tape (2-inch wide gray tape, which is stronger than duct tape)
- White card reflector (large piece of white poster board)
- Flexfill (a flexible circle of aluminized plastic, which is used in outdoor situations)

The Sound-Recording Package (Microphones)

Although most camcorders come with a microphone attached, you should also bring along at least one other microphone. The on-board mike won't be close enough to the action to give you crisp, clear audio.

As with the lighting package, your particular needs for sound-recording equipment vary according to your production. The following package covers most situations:

- Two Tram or Lavalier microphones (small microphones that can be clipped onto a person's shirt for an interview)

- Microphone batteries (the size depends on the mike; make sure you have at least two extras)

- Additional microphone (see optional-elements list that follows)

- Microphone cable and spare

- Headphones

That's the basic package, but if you want the audio in your piece to grab people's attention, then you should consider using one or both of the following mikes:

- Hypercardioid microphone, such as a Schoepps or a Sennheiser 416 (These microphones are designed to pick up sound from only a small region in the front of the mike. These are the standard mikes for getting natural sound. They are also a popular choice for recording interviews or scripted dialogs on a set. In these situations, the mike is hung from a boom.)

- Shotgun mike (This microphone is designed to pick out sounds that are far away. In general, it should not be used indoors because it often picks up unwanted echoes.)

Extras (Videotape, Phone List, Appearance Releases)

You should always bring more videotapes than you need. They don't weigh much, and you'd hate to run out. You should also bring a list of phone numbers of people to contact in case you have trouble with the equipment.

If you are going to be shooting footage of people, you should bring along *appearance releases*. These are legal documents giving you permission to use a person's face or voice in your final piece.

Familiarity Breeds Contempt

After you've been shooting for a while, you might start to slack off on your equipment check-out procedure—not a good idea. Take a tip from professional camera operators. They check out their equipment every day, even if they shot with it the day before. Pieces of equipment malfunction, parts break, cables wear out, and people borrow pieces of equipment and don't return them.

Plan to spend 15 minutes checking out the equipment. That's a short period of time compared to the hours that can be lost when a key piece of equipment breaks or is forgotten.

Camera Basics

The basic goal of production is to get the material you need to convey your story or message. Beyond that, you should try to get the best material you can. It's not enough simply to mechanically tick off the shots on your shot list. You need to compose your shots so that they emphasize the right elements. You might want to perform camera moves and zooms to add movement to the shots. You need to take into account the vagaries of lighting (particularly in outdoor locations).

Many books have been written about the craft of videography. A partial list can be found in Appendix A. This section only covers some of the more basic rules of shooting. Then, we examine some common situations you're likely to face.

 The word "scene" is used here in the standard sense of a place or a location. The "frame" is the image in the camera's viewfinder at any point in time.

Choosing a Composition

The standard composition for a shot follows the *rule of thirds*, which is shown in Figure 12-1. Key elements in a shot, such as people, are placed

Figure 12-1.

Whenever possible, the major element in a shot should be positioned off-center along imaginary lines that divide the screen into thirds.

along lines that divide the screen into three equal parts or at their intersections.

You can experiment with other compositional schemes, such as dividing the screen into fifths and placing key elements along the two-fifths and three-fifths lines. But you should avoid placing people directly in the center of the screen because that creates a boring image (with the exception of someone talking to camera; see section entitled "Shooting Someone Talking to Camera").

With video, what you see is *not* what you get. The image in the camera's viewfinder includes more than what is seen on a normal television. This is because most televisions enlarge the picture slightly to make sure that the picture fills the screen; so you should maintain a 10 to 15 percent safety border for all shots (Figure 12-2).

Some of the newer camcorders indicate the safe action area in the viewfinder. If not, you have to remember to avoid placing important elements at the edge of the screen.

Note   **Some video capture boards use the entire frame, not just what's within the safe action area.**

Figure 12-2.

The safe action area is the portion of the screen that appears on a standard television set.

◄——*Safe action area*——►

◄———*Viewfinder frame*———►

You should avoid flat compositions. These usually occur when all of the key elements are the same distance from the camera. Either move the camera or move one of the elements to add depth to the scene. Another way to add depth is to include an interesting background or a piece of the foreground in the shot. But the foreground or background should not interfere or conflict with the key elements. For example, you should make sure that the background doesn't contain any bright sources of light that might attract the viewer's eye.

Taking Level and Steady Shots

Whenever possible, use a tripod. Your shots will be much steadier, and you will be able to plan your compositions more carefully.

If your tripod comes with a level gauge, make sure the tripod is level first, then place the camera on the tripod. If you are working with a tripod that doesn't have such a gauge, find a true horizontal line in the scene and align the camera frame with that line.

If you are going to be shooting without a tripod—that is, *hand held*—try to steady yourself on a solid object (desk, chair, etc.) whenever possible. This is especially important if you are zooming into something because any movement on your part is exaggerated.

If you are going to be walking a lot while shooting, you might want to rent a Steadicam Jr. (from Cinema Products). This is a special mount for lightweight camcorders that uses a counterbalancing system to keep the camera steady. Practice with it a bit before you start shooting to get the hang of it.

Lens Aperture and Exposure

The lens in a video camera is similar to one in a still camera. You control how much light comes in by adjusting the aperture. Almost all video cameras have an *auto-iris* feature that automatically adjusts the lens aperture to optimize the exposure. This works fine as long as you're shooting a fairly static scene. But if the lighting changes for some reason (the sun goes behind a cloud, a bright object moves into the frame), the auto-iris might react too slowly or in an undesirable way. You should be alert to these situations and control the aperture manually.

Although a video camera seems to take realistic pictures, it is no match for the human eye or even a film camera. The main difference is its limited ability to record information from bright and dark areas simultaneously (areas of high and low tonal value). The human eye can discern tones over a range of 100 to 1; that is, the brightest element is 100 times brighter than the darkest one. By contrast, most video cameras have a tonal latitude of only 20 to 1 (Figure 12-3).

 One way to get a sense of what the camera is seeing is to squint your eyes. This approximates the tonal range of the camera.

When faced with a scene that has high tonal contrast, you must choose which part of the tonal spectrum you will focus on. You can *stop down* by decreasing the aperture, which will provide more detail of bright objects, but the dark areas will blend together (the top image in Figure 12-3). This is equivalent to underexposing in a film camera.

You can *open up* by increasing the aperture, which gives you more detail of the dark elements (the bottom image in Figure 12-3). This is generally not a good idea because the bright areas will be overexposed and will bleed into other parts of the picture.

The best solution is to position the camera or use lights to narrow the tonal range of the scene. Avoid bright objects in the background. Use reflectors or lights to lighten up overly dark areas. Other techniques for getting the best picture out of a video camera are discussed in "Lighting Basics" later in this chapter.

Focusing

Most camcorders come with an automatic focus feature. This helps reduce the amount of work you have to do in shooting footage, but you should wean yourself off this feature as soon as possible. The device that controls the automatic focus doesn't know what is the most important element in a shot and, therefore, what should be in focus.

This can be a problem when there are a number of elements at different distances from the camera, i.e., a scene with depth. The automatic focus often emphasizes the largest or brightest element in the frame.

It might take you a while to get familiar with *manual focusing*—which way to turn the focus ring to bring things into focus. But by focusing the camera yourself, you'll know that the key elements are in focus.

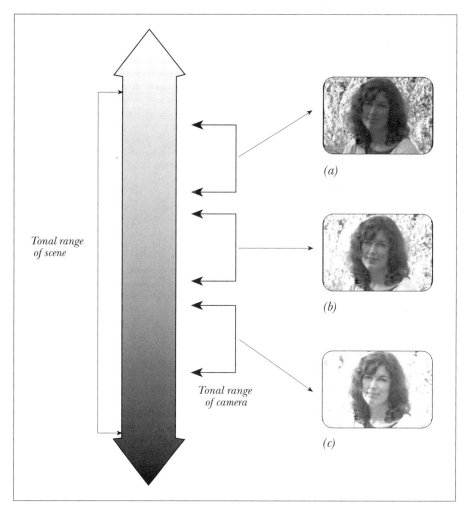

Figure 12-3. A video camera has a limited tonal range; it cannot accurately depict both the extremely bright and dark areas of a scene. In a scene with a bright background and dark foreground, the position of the iris determines which part of the scene will be properly exposed.

(a) Stopping down the iris provides a good exposure for the bright areas, but you lose detail in the dark regions of the shot.

(b) Setting the iris in a middle range provides a fair amount of detail for both bright and dark regions of the shot.

(c) Opening up the iris provides good detail of the dark areas of a shot, but the bright areas become too bright. This is generally not a good idea because overly bright areas bleed into other parts of the shot.

Depth of Field

Another thing you need to consider when shooting a scene that has depth is that most of the time some of the elements are out of focus. Each configuration of *lens angle* (the position of the zoom lens) and aperture produces a different *depth of field*—a certain range of distances in which objects are in focus.

 If you are an experienced still photographer, you can skip the next two sections. The relationship between depth of field, lens angle (focal length), and aperture is the same for still and video cameras.

Aperture and Depth of Field

Basically, a large aperture creates a short depth of field and vice versa (Figure 12-4). This means that with a large aperture (low *f*-stop), the

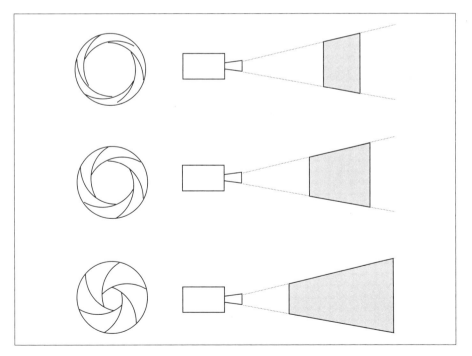

Figure 12-4.   Effect of aperture on depth of field. A wider aperture produces a shorter depth of field.

key element is in focus, but the background is not. With a small aperture, both the key element and the background are in focus.

 The practical result of this is that you probably want to shoot with a fairly low aperture ($f5$ to $f8$) to keep the background in focus. Unfortunately, this means that you need to have a lot of light to get a correct exposure, which can be difficult in indoor locations (that's why television lights are so bright).

Lens Angle and Depth of Field

The basic rule is the wider the lens angle, the greater the depth of field (Figure 12-5). This means it is easier to keep the key element in focus if you are shooting with a wide angle, particularly if the key element is moving in the shot.

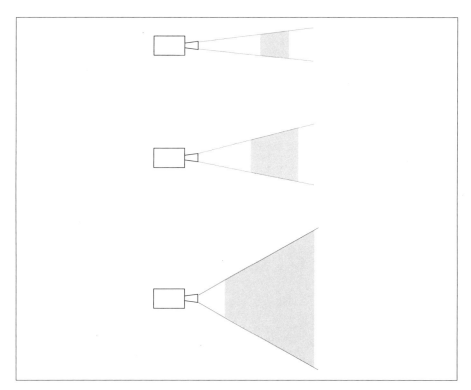

Figure 12-5. Effect of lens angle on depth of field. A wider camera lens (zoomed out) produces a larger depth of field.

On a camera with a zoom lens, the wide-angle setting is the one that shows the largest area; so, you "zoom in" from a wide angle to a tight angle.

The depth of field changes as you zoom in or out on a shot. As you zoom in, the depth of field decreases; as you zoom out, the depth of field increases. As a practical matter, this means that before you start recording, you should always zoom in to the key element in a scene, focus, and then zoom back out. That way, you will be able to zoom in and know that the focus is correct.

Changing Focus

The viewer's attention is drawn to whatever is in focus in a shot. You can shift the viewer's attention to other elements in a shot by changing which elements are in focus.

For example, let's say you have a shot that involves two people: One in the foreground, the other in the background (Figure 12-6). Because of the distance between them, you can't have both people in focus at the same time. Instead, you can start the shot with the foreground person in focus and then change the focus, or *rack focus*, to bring the background person into focus (Figure 12-6). The person in the foreground then goes out of focus.

 This shot does not work if you are shooting with a small aperture; i.e., shooting with a lot of light. You need to have a short depth of field, which requires a large aperture.

 Some of the more recent camcorders come with a "shutter feature." This allows you to decrease the amount of light entering the camera, independent of the aperture. By setting a high shutter speed, you are able to use a larger aperture than normal (lower *f*-stop), which helps when trying to create a short depth of field.

In a static shot, like the one of the two people discussed earlier, you decide where you want to move the focused plane. But if you are shooting a person who is walking toward the camera, then the focused plane is defined by the distance between your subject and the camera. You need to gradually adjust the focus to keep the person in sharp detail (Figure 12-7).

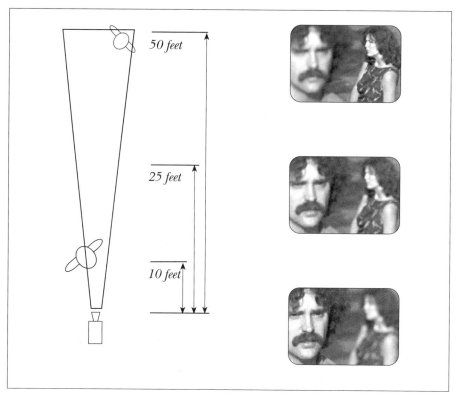

Figure 12-6.   Rack-focusing between two people. The shot starts with the
foreground person in focus. The lens focus is then changed so
that the person in the background comes into focus and the
foreground person becomes blurry.

One of the most difficult camera shots to perform is of a person walking toward the camera as you zoom out to keep the person's size approximately the same within the frame, and you move the camera to keep the person in the center of the frame. For example, let's say you are shooting a man as he walks down a hallway (toward camera) and then turns right down a connecting hallway. This shot involves a zoom out, a rack focus, and a pan (as the man turns).

This type of shot is accomplished by having an assistant change the focus as you control the zoom and the camera movement. The assistant marks the beginning and ending focus points (on the focus ring) and then gradually adjusts the focus as the subject comes forward. Although this seems complicated, it is often more practical than the

Focus plane 20 feet

Focus plane 15 feet

Focus plane 10 feet

LEGEND:

Depth of field (decreases as subject approaches camera)

Figure 12-7.   When someone is walking toward the camera, you need to readjust the focus to match the person's position. Shooting with a wide lens angle gives you a larger depth of field and requires less focus readjustment

alternative of using a dolly and tracking in front of the person as he or she walks down the hallway.

You can deliberately throw a shot out of focus to produce an interesting special effect. Record 5 to 20 seconds of the subject, then quickly rotate the focus ring until the image of the subject goes completely out of focus. When coupled with a dissolve in editing, this shot can produce an interesting transition.

Camera Height and Angle

Most of the time, you position the camera at the same level as your subject (Figure 12-8). This is the most natural viewpoint for the camera (and ultimately the viewer). Shooting down on a subject can minimize its importance or, in the case of a person, indicate a lack of authority. A low angle makes the subject seem more powerful and imposing. However, you should not use this camera angle when shooting a close shot of a person's face because it exaggerates the person's neck and emphasizes unwanted elements, such as nostrils.

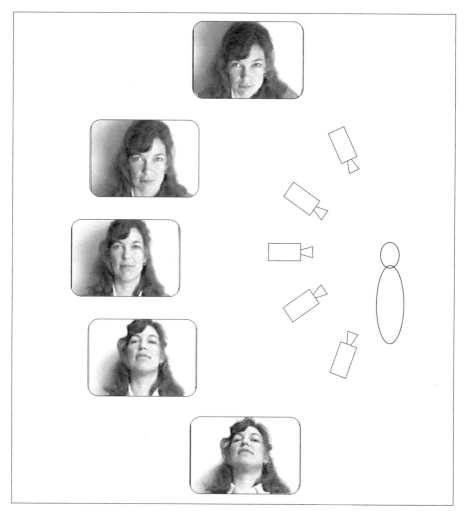

Figure 12-8.   Most of the time you want to have the camera at the same height as the subject. This produces the most natural-looking image. Camera angles from above tend to make a person look small and insignificant. Low camera angles make a person seem more imposing.

Camera Moves (Tilts, Pans, and Zooms)

When you move the camera during a shot, do it slowly, more slowly than you think is necessary. After you review your footage in the editing room a few times, you'll get a better idea of the proper speed.

You should practice a camera move once or twice before you start recording. This saves you from having to sift through a bunch of worthless takes in the editing room.

When *tilting* or *panning* (going up/down or pivoting side to side), you should frame the beginning and end of the camera move ahead of time. Don't just start moving and decide where to end on-the-fly. You should also make sure that the middle of the shot is interesting. If there is a lot of dead space in the middle, change the position of the camera so that dead space is minimized (Figure 12-9). Another way to correct for dead space in the middle of a pan is to follow an object (such as a car or a person) during the pan. This distracts the viewer from the dead space in the middle of the pan.

Using a Monitor

It's often a good idea to bring a color monitor along. You will get a better idea of the colors in a scene. The monitor will also reveal when key elements are in danger of being lost outside the safe action area.

Shooting Tips for Common Situations

Every situation has its own challenges, some more difficult than others. The following sections describe how to shoot some of the more typical shots. You should deviate from the suggestions given for any particular example as your needs warrant.

Shooting Someone Talking to Camera

Most of the time, people do not talk directly into the camera and, thus, directly to the viewer. They are usually looking at someone else. The exceptions are as follows:

- A host of a program

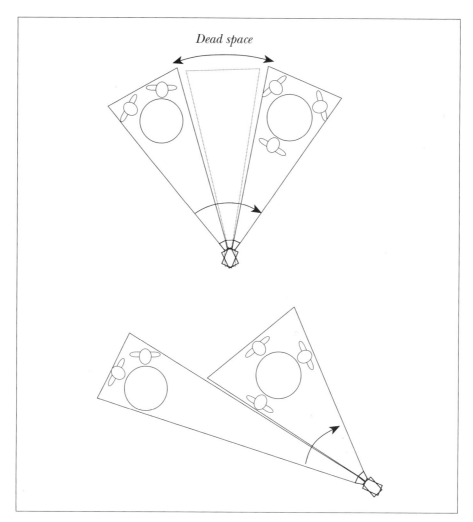

Figure 12-9. When panning between two different elements—in this case, two groups of people sitting at tables—position the camera so that there isn't too much dead space between the two elements.

- A television news reporter or anchor
- Someone making a televised address, such as a politician
- A salesperson in a commercial

Because of the special nature of these situations, a person talking to camera is usually placed in the middle of the frame (Figure 12-10).

Figure 12-10.   When a person is speaking directly at the camera lens (talking to camera), he or she should be positioned in the center of the frame.

The only time the subject moves off center is when graphic elements are used, as in the case of a graphic appearing over the shoulder of a television news anchor (Figure 12-11).

Shooting Interviews

The typical camera setup for an interview is shown in Figure 12-12. The person being interviewed, the interviewee, is placed to one side of the frame and looks across the center line. The camera should be at the same level as the interviewee's eyes. The interviewer should sit as close to the camera as possible so that the interviewee is looking toward the camera (but not directly into it). There are four standard framings for

Figure 12-11.   When incorporating a graphic with a person talking to camera, position the person to one side of the frame.

an interview: a full or wide shot, a medium shot, a close shot, and a close-up. These framings are shown in Figure 12-12.

The *wide shot* is generally used to establish the scene. Because it lacks the intimacy of the closer shots, you should not use this shot when the interviewee is saying something important. This shot often includes a portion of the interviewer.

The *medium shot* is used when a person talks with his or her hands or moves about in the chair. These movements would extend beyond the frame in closer shots. Because of the small size of current QuickTime movies, you should use this shot sparingly.

The *close shot* provides an intimacy with the interviewee but is not so close that the viewer feels uncomfortable.

A *close-up* adds a sense of drama and tension. If the person is not saying something all that important, stick with a close shot.

Another shot that is often taken in interview situations is the *reverse shot*, which shows the interviewer (Figure 12-13). If you want the final piece to look like a conversation between the interviewee and the interviewer (as opposed to just a set of answers), then you should shoot the interviewer's questions again on the reverse shot.

 Remember to stay on the same side of the line of interest when shooting the reverse shot.

Now for a brief digression on interviewing techniques: Here are a few tips that can help you get good "sound bites" from interviews:

- Make sure the interviewee looks at you. Wandering eyes can make the person look devious.

- Ask the person to incorporate your question in his or her answer. For example, if the question is, "How long have you been working on product XYZ?" the person's answer should be something like, "We've been working on product XYZ for more than three years," not "more than three years." This allows you to omit your questions from the edited video if desired.

Wide shot   Medium shot   Close shot   Close-up

Figure 12-12. Typical camera setup for interview. The interviewer sits close to the camera. The interviewee looks at the interviewer, not at the camera.

Figure 12-13.   A reverse shot shows the interviewer looking towards the interviewee. The camera position must be on the same side of the line of interest.

- If the person gives an incredibly long answer, ask the question again. You'll be surprised at how much people can improve their answers on retakes.

- Try to develop a conversational style in asking your questions. Don't be afraid to digress into other areas if it helps make the interviewee feel relaxed and speak naturally.

- It's not particularly comfortable sitting in front of all those lights with a camera pointed at your head. Try to make the interviewee feel as relaxed and at ease as possible.

Shooting Groups of People

You have two main concerns when shooting a group of people: keeping up with the flow of the conversation and getting enough cutaways. The first concern deals with making sure the camera catches people talking (as opposed to just after they finish talking). The easiest way to do this is with multiple cameras. But because you might not have that kind of a budget, the following discussion assumes you are shooting with only one camera.

Primary Placement of the Camera

The best way to cover the action is to place the camera in front of the group of people and near the center. For example, let's say there are three people talking at a table. The primary camera placement, shown in Figure 12-14, allows you to get six different kinds of shots: a three-shot, two different two-shots, and three close-ups.

You would gradually switch between these shots as the conversation moves from person to person. Let's say you are shooting the person on the right (person 2) in a close-up (shot 4). That person stops talking,

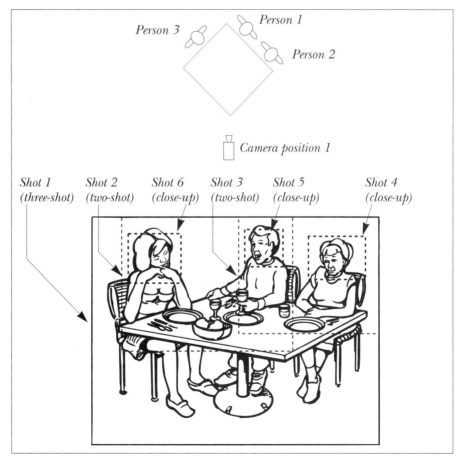

Figure 12-14.   Primary camera placement for shooting a group of people. A direct shot provides a good overview of the scene. You can also get cutaways of individual people from this angle.

and the person in the middle starts to talk. You would zoom out while you pan left until you are framed for a two-shot that includes the middle person (shot 3). Then you could stay on the two-shot, or if the middle person talked for a while, you could zoom in to a close-up of him (shot 5).

You would continue in this fashion, zooming in and out while panning, to cover the people talking. This is better than moving the camera quickly from one person to another. This technique also allows the editor to use the camera moves instead of always having to switch to a new shot when someone starts talking.

This technique is used for unscripted conversations. If you laid out exactly who is going to talk when, then you would use the same camera position, but you would reframe the camera before each new piece of dialog. You would shoot all the shots from this camera position, before moving to the other camera positions.

Getting Cutaways

This type of scene needs lots of cutaways. Even with smooth camera moves between the speakers, you still won't catch all the action. Unless you're working with professional actors, it is hard for speakers to repeat their words; so it's best just to have the speakers talk naturally while you shoot reaction and listening shots for cutaways.

You can get listening shots from all three close-ups (shots 4, 5, and 6 in Figure 12-14). Make sure you get several shots of people turning their heads from one person to another (i.e., following the conversation).

In addition, you should shoot cutaways from two other camera positions (Figure 12-15). From the framings shown in the figure, you get the following shots:

- **Cutaway 1, shot 1:** Person 1 listening to person 3
- **Cutaway 2, shot 1:** Person 1 listening to person 3 (closer shot)
- **Cutaway 2, shot 2:** Person 1 turning head toward person 2
- **Cutaway 3, shot 1:** Person 2 listening to person 1
- **Cutaway 3, shot 2:** Person 2 listening to person 3

You get a similar set of cutaways from camera position 3.

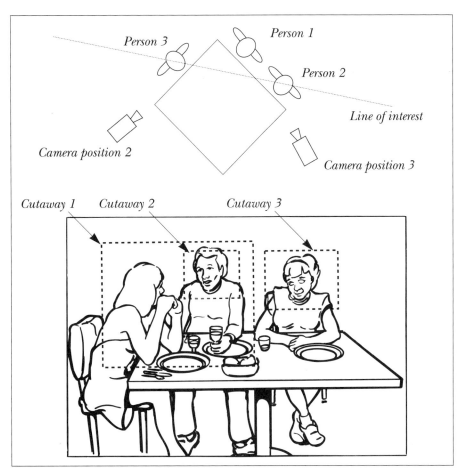

Figure 12-15.   The best cutaways are shot from a different position than the primary camera position. In this case, the camera is moved to the left to get various cutaways of the group. Moving the camera to the right, camera position 3, would produce a similar set of cutaways.

 You must stay on the same side of the line of interest when shooting cutaways.

These cutaways not only give you plenty of options when you get into the editing room, but they also help you get out of binds when the camera missed something important.

Shooting a Person Handling a Prop

The main trick to shooting this type of scene is getting shots that allow the editor to focus on the action quickly. You also need to provide shots that allow the editor to condense time in case the action takes a long time.

Let's assume we're shooting a man playing a piece of music on a piano (Figure 12-16). From camera position 1 you shoot the entire performance from beginning to end. This is called a *master shot* because it is a verbatim recording of the entire action. The master shot should start with the person walking into the frame and sitting down and end with the person walking out of the frame. As long as the entire action (the performance in this case) doesn't last too long, it's a good idea to get a master shot because it gives you more options in editing. After the master shot is complete, you can then get cutaways from this camera position using shots 3 and 4 (Figure 12-17).

Note   Some film purists suggest that you can *edit* your piece in the camera, that is, shoot exactly the shots you'll need and no more. This is efficient in terms of the amount of videotape you shoot but a poor use of resources and your time. Videotape is cheap; production is expensive. It is much wiser to cover yourself by shooting extra material and then picking the best shots when you are editing the piece together.

Next, you move to camera position 2 and have the man repeat the performance, this time getting shots 5, 6, and 7 (Figure 12-18).

Last, you move to camera position 3 and get close shots and close-ups (shots 8, 9, and 10) of the man's hands as he plays (Figure 12-19). When you take close-ups of particular actions (finger playing a single key, etc.), make sure the shot starts with the man's hand out of frame. This gives you a lot more leeway in terms of matching continuity later on.

A typical sequence that could be edited from these shots is shown in Figure 12-20.

The basic technique of shooting a master shot, a reverse shot, and then close-ups works for a wide variety of situations, such as a person at a computer, a person using a shovel—basically any scene where a person is interacting with a prop.

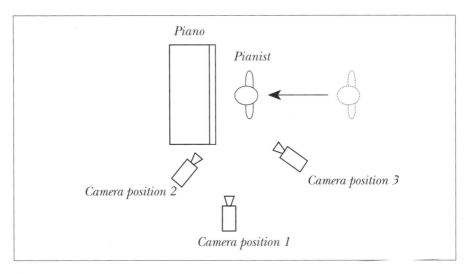

Figure 12-16.   Camera positions for shooting a pianist at a piano. Camera position 1 provides the master shot for the scene. Camera positions 2 and 3 are used to shoot cutaways.

Figure 12-17.   Various shots from camera position 1. This is the most natural view of the scene (as if you were in the audience). You should shoot a master shot of the entire performance from this camera position.

Figure 12-18. Various shots from camera position 2. This camera angle allows you to focus on the pianist.

Figure 12-19. Various shots from camera position 3. This camera angle allows you to focus on the piano and the pianist's hands.

Figure 12-20.   By shooting the performance from several camera angles, you can create an edited segment that has a lot of visual variety.

 Tip   **You might get bored with this standard technique after a while, so experiment with different camera angles (high or low). Try shooting a person's reflection in a computer screen or on the varnish of a piano, use tilts and pans—anything to inject something new into the sequence.**

Movement into and out of the Frame

When you are shooting a walking shot in which a person is shown walking into or out of somewhere (a room, a house, a car, etc.), there are several things to keep in mind.

Entering and Leaving the Frame

You should always make sure that the person is not in the frame either at the beginning or end of the shot. This makes it easier to edit the shot into a sequence of other shots. If possible, the shot should include the person entering and leaving the frame (Figures 12-21 and 12-22). Later you can always use just the part of the shot with the person already in the frame if you want.

Figure 12-21.

When an element in a scene is moving, in this case a person, you should try to have the shot begin with the moving element out of the frame. The moving element then moves into the frame and exits the frame before the shot ends. Shooting the shot this way gives you more options during editing.

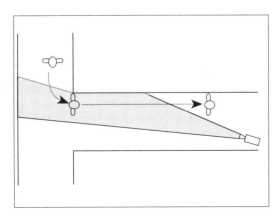

Figure 12-22.

Even if you are certain that you want a shot to start with a person in the frame, in this case a person walking down a hallway, try to start the shot without the person in the frame. It takes a little more time to shoot a shot this way, but it will give you more flexibility later on in editing.

Providing Internal Edits

It helps to give the editor a way to shorten the shot. Let's say you're shooting a woman leaving an apartment and walking to her car (Figure 12-23). That shot would last about 20 seconds, but the editor might decide to spend only 10 seconds getting the woman from the door to the car. By shooting a close-up of the woman's face from the front (Figure 12-24), you give the editor the option of condensing the action, as shown on the next page.

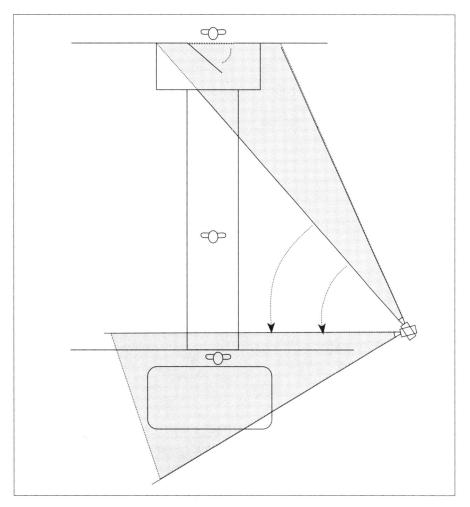

Figure 12-23.   Shooting a woman walking to a car in one continuous shot. There is no easy way to shorten the duration of this shot.

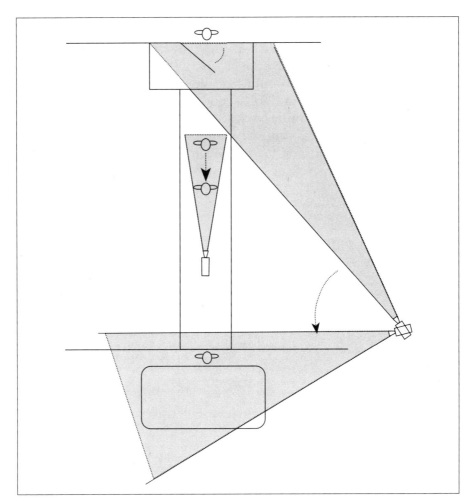

Figure 12-24. Shooting an internal cutaway. Shooting a close-up of the person's face gives a cutaway that you can use to shorten the panning shot in Figure 12-23.

- **Shot 1:** Woman leaving apartment (3 seconds)
- **Shot 2:** Close-up of woman's face (3 seconds)
- **Shot 1:** Woman getting into car (4 seconds)

Any close-up of the person (feet, hands, etc.) will give the editor this option.

Another way to shoot this action is to break it into two shots. In shot 1, the woman leaves the apartment and exits the frame (Figure 12-25). In shot 2, she is already in the frame as she walks toward the camera (and the car). Now, because the shots are from different angles and because the woman leaves the frame in shot 1, the editor can start shot 2 at any point without worrying about a break in continuity (although it helps to match her stride).

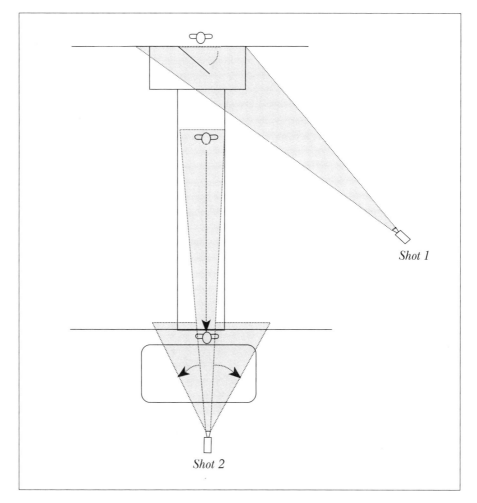

Shot 1

Shot 2

Figure 12-25. Shooting a woman walking to a car in two shots. After you have established the woman in shot 1, you can cut to any point in shot 2 to finish the scene.

Remembering the Line of Interest

When a person leaves the frame in one shot and re-enters the frame in a following shot, he or she should re-enter on the opposite side of the frame from which he or she left. This way, the person keeps moving in the same direction. This is a variation on the line-of-interest rule for shooting cutaways. Let's say you're shooting a person walking across the screen. You break the walk into three shots (Figure 12-26). The line of interest is the line of the person's walk, so all the camera positions are on the same side.

It gets a bit more confusing when the person walks toward and past the camera as he or she goes out of the frame (Figure 12-27). The person should still enter the frame on the opposite side in the next shot.

 If there is an intermediate shot between two walking shots, such as a close-up of the person's face or something not connected with the person at all, then you can cross the line of interest without confusing the viewer.

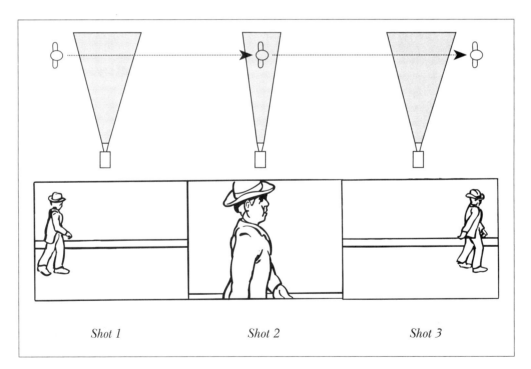

Shot 1   *Shot 2*   *Shot 3*

Figure 12-26. Line-of-interest example 1. The camera remains on the same side of the person for all three shots.

Shot 1   Shot 2

Figure 12-27. Line-of-interest example 2. If a person leaves the frame in one shot, he or she should enter on the opposite side of the frame in the next shot. This way the person will continue to move in the same direction, in this case from left to right.

Unusual Situations and Techniques

Here's a collection of short tips for particular situations. Use whatever fits your needs.

Shooting Computer Screens

If you are shooting a computer and want the viewer to be able to read what's on the screen, try to make the room as dark as possible to eliminate reflections in the screen. If there is still too much reflection of the room, move the camera as close as possible to the screen and hold a large dark cloth behind the camera.

Most computer screens roll or flicker when shot with a video camera. This has to do with the difference between refresh rate of the monitor and the frame rate of the tape deck, which is 29.97 frames per second.

Vérité

Some situations don't occur in a controlled way. These include protest marches, sporting events, and community meetings. You probably won't be able to get someone to repeat what he or she did or said in case you missed it the first time, so you have to get what you can at the moment, constantly keeping an eye out for cutaways that will help you edit the scene together.

For a cutaway to work, it shouldn't be tied directly to the action or event because it will be hard to match continuity. Shots of onlookers work well, as do signs.

This type of shooting is called *vérité*, and it is demanding, both on the camera operator and the director. And if you're acting as both, you need to take your eye out from behind the viewfinder from time to time to see what is going on outside the camera's viewfinder.

Another thing to keep in mind is that the line-of-interest rule still holds. The protest marchers can't suddenly march in the other direction! The easiest way to cover yourself is to take neutral shots (in front of or behind the march) that will allow you to cross the line during editing.

The Poor Man's Tracking Shots

You should be alert for any type of people mover that can act as a dolly. These include wheelchairs, carts, escalators, and moving sidewalks. Put yourself on the people mover and let it move you through a location. You can also have a person walk alongside. The advantage of this shot is that it conveys a sense of motion while maintaining close connection with the subject.

Special Effects in the Camera

By exaggerating a camera move (a tilt, pan, or zoom), you can create a kind of special effect that adds a sense of visual excitement to a sequence of shots:

Swish Pan: This is a pan that moves so fast that the image is blurry. By intercutting a swish pan between two static shots, you can give the impression of simultaneity, as if you had just whisked the camera from one place to the other.

Snap Zoom: This is a zoom that moves so quickly from a wide-angle shot to a close-up (or vice versa) that the middle of the shot is smeared; only the beginning and the end of the shot can be seen clearly. With a sound effect added, this shot can bring a strong punch or climax to a scene. You must turn the zoom lens manually to perform a snap zoom. The motorized zoom doesn't move fast enough.

Vertigo Shot: This bizarre shot is a combination of a zoom with a contrary dolly forward or backward. When executed correctly, the main subject remains the same size (as if nothing is changing), while the background expands or contracts unnaturally (Figure 12-28). Alfred Hitchcock's *Vertigo* popularized this effect as a means of conveying a subject's confusion.

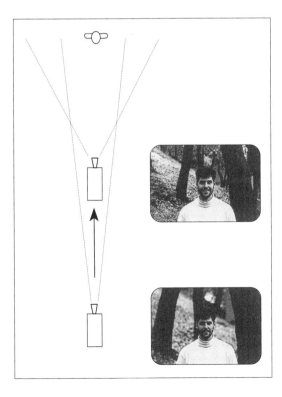

Figure 12-28.

In a vertigo shot, the camera is dollied back while the lens is zoomed in (or vice versa). The main subject in the scene stays the same size in the frame, but the perception of depth in the background changes significantly.

Wiggle Cam

This style of shooting, made popular by AT&T commercials several years ago, involves a constantly moving camera. The camera weaves and bobs throughout the shot, never settling on a particular framing. The theory behind this style is that a constantly changing image is more likely to hold the viewer's attention. If you're facing a situation where getting and holding the viewer's attention is likely to be a problem, then you might consider using this technique. A disadvantage of this type of shooting is that it can't be easily edited together with footage shot in more traditional ways.

Common Directing and Shooting Mistakes

If you follow the advice mentioned in the previous sections, you'll probably stay clear of most of the obvious mistakes. But some mistakes occur so often, even to professionals, that we mention them again here.

Not Enough Cutaways

When it comes time to edit your material, it seems as if you never have enough cutaways. Of course, figuring out what will be a useful cutaway is difficult in the field. That's why you should plan the shoot carefully.

Shots That Don't Last Long Enough

You can edit a shot to make it shorter, but you can't make it longer (at least not easily). Make sure your shots last for at least 5 seconds (10 seconds is better).

Starting Too Soon

Once you turn on the camcorder, it takes five seconds before the deck comes to speed and you can record usable video. This doesn't apply if you put the camera in pause mode (but that chews up batteries). Get in the habit of counting down from five to one after turning on the camera before you ask someone a question or cue someone to move. If you're directing a camera operator the dialog goes like this:

Director: "Roll tape!"

Operator: (after five seconds) "Speed!"

Director: "Action!"

Lighting Basics

There is an infinite number of ways to light any particular scene. We cover the most standard ways here, but once you get the hang of these techniques, feel free to experiment.

The primary goal of lighting is to make sure there is enough light on your subject that it can be seen clearly on the videotape. Sometimes this can be accomplished with *available lighting*, that is, the light naturally occurring at a location. Outdoor scenes shot in the early morning and late afternoon don't usually need additional lighting; the available lighting is sufficient.

 Sufficient lighting doesn't mean that your camera tells you it's bright enough to shoot. It means that your subject (a person or an object) is bright enough that it can be seen clearly and with detail. Most camera light meters evaluate the entire frame, not individual items within it. You could place your subject against a bright wall, and the camera would say there's enough light, even though your subject would be almost black.

The other functions of lighting are to emphasize or conceal particular elements in a shot, to add a sense of depth to a shot, and to even out the range of bright and dark objects in the shot to compensate for the limitations of video cameras.

A basic fact of video production is that the camera is no match for the human eye in terms of picking out detail in bright and dark objects. Professional cameras get close, but they cost $30,000. Consumer camcorders, particularly Hi-8 models, are getting better. As mentioned earlier, the main problem is that video cameras have a narrow tonal range, that is, the ratio between the brightest and the darkest object in which detail can be seen (Figure 12-3). The human eye has a tonal range of about 100 to 1; a video camera can manage only about 20 to 1. The solution is to reduce the tonal range of the shot by avoiding bright objects and backgrounds and by using lights to brighten dark areas.

Terminology

Lights come in a dizzying array of sizes and types. In addition, there are a number of ways a light can be used in a particular scene (and well-defined terms for each type of use). Here's a quick rundown on some basic lighting terms.

Available Light

This is the light occurring naturally at a location. It can be sunlight; a fluorescent, incandescent, or halogen lamp; fire or a candle; or a mixture of any of these types.

Hard Light vs. Soft Light

Hard light is direct light that throws strong, distinct shadows. Hard light is used to define surfaces and features and increase the overall illumination of an object. Direct sunlight is an example of hard light.

The opposite of hard light is diffuse, or soft, light, which casts soft shadows. *Soft light* is used to diminish the strong shadows produced by hard light. It can also even out the lighting in a scene. Sunlight on an overcast day is an example of soft light. Figure 12-29 illustrates the difference between hard and soft light.

With professional lighting equipment, any light that projects directly onto the subject will cast hard light. By putting a piece of acetate (known as a *diffuser*) between the light and the subject, you turn the hard light into soft light. Another technique for creating soft light is to bounce a light off a reflector, such as a lighting umbrella or a large piece of white poster board.

(a) Hard light   *(b) Soft light*

Figure 12-29.

(a) Hard light emphasizes edges and produces dark shadows. (b) Soft, diffuse light produces even lighting. People generally look better under soft light.

Light Placement

The placement of a light in relation to the subject dramatically affects the subject's appearance. Figure 12-30 shows the effect of different lateral placements of a light, and Figure 12-31 shows the effect of different vertical placements. Lighting that is overhead and in front of the subject tends to be the most natural. Low lights tend to make a person seem dark and sinister.

Most professional lighting setups use several lights in different positions to create a mix of hard and soft light that adds texture to a scene.

The Key Light

This is the primary light for illuminating the subject. It is often referred to as just "the key," as in, "We'll use sunlight as the key." Typically, the key light is the strongest light: It is placed to one side of the camera, set fairly high, and is often used as a direct source of light (light 1 in Figure 12-32).

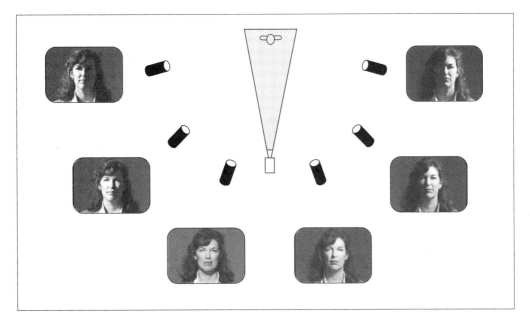

Figure 12-30.   The position of the key light dramatically alters the look of a shot. A key light to the far right or left produces a dramatic, moody shot. The most common position is just off center to the right or left.

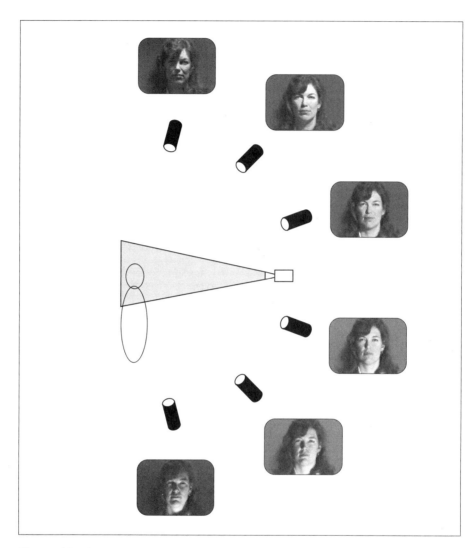

Figure 12-31.   The vertical position of a light changes the mood of a shot. A light directly over a person is generally not used because it casts shadows over the eyes. A low light position tends to make the person seem dark and sinister.

The Fill Light

This light evens out the light on the subject by casting a soft light that softens the hard shadows created by the key light (light 2 in Figure 12-

32). The fill is usually placed on the opposite side of the camera from the key light and usually has a lower wattage than the key.

The Back Light

This light is used to cast light on the back edge of the subject. It is also known as a *rim light* because it provides a rim of light around the edge of the subject (light 3 in Figure 12-32). A back light helps separate the subject from the background. It is usually placed on the opposite side of the camera from the key light.

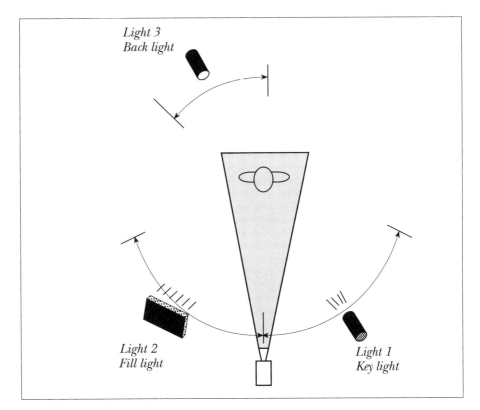

Figure 12-32.   The key light is usually placed to one side of the camera and the fill light is placed on the opposite side. This allows the fill light to fill in the shadows created by the key light. The back light is usually placed on the same side as the fill light but behind the subject. If the subject is not looking directly into the camera, then the key light should be placed so that the person is looking toward the key light.

Diffusers, Scrims, and Gels

There are a number of attachments that can be applied to lights to alter their lighting characteristics. As mentioned earlier, a diffuser is a translucent piece of material that converts direct light into diffuse light (hard to soft). A *scrim* is a piece of wire mesh that decreases the overall intensity of a light without diffusing it. A *gel* is a colored filter that adds color to a light. A translucent gel can also act as a diffuser.

Color Temperature

Lights differ in the color of the light they produce. Our eyes and brains filter out these differences, but the camera doesn't. That's why normal light bulbs look orange when compared to sunlight in a video image.

A light is defined by its *color temperature*, which is related to the actual temperature of the light-emitting element (Table 12-1). When seen in the same video frame, lights with higher color temperatures will appear to have a bluish cast, while lights with a lower color temperature will appear orange or yellow.

 Most lights used in video production use tungsten elements.

Table 12-1.   **Light Sources and Their Color Temperatures**

Source	Temperature (in K)*
Candle	1,930
Tungsten lights	3,000
Halogen lights	3,200–3,400
Fluorescent	3,200–5,000
HMI arcs	5,600–6,000
Sunrise, sunset	2,000–3,000
Midday sun	5,000–5,400
Overcast sky	6,800–7,500

*K = Kelvin; 273K = 0°C

White Balance

Although the camera picks up all the shades of color in various types of light, you can get around this problem by tuning the camera to one particular type of light. This is done with the white-balance adjustment on the camera. By pointing the camera at a white piece of paper and then pressing the white-balance button, you are telling the camera "this is white." Thus, if you are shooting outside, the camera is then tuned for the bluish cast of sunlight. If you move indoors, you must white balance again, so the camera is tuned to the lower-temperature "white" produced by the tungsten elements (otherwise, your video will have a strong orange cast and almost no blue).

Camera Filters

Unfortunately, the white-balance adjustment won't correct for the entire range of color temperatures between sunlight and indoor lights. Some consumer camcorders and all professional video cameras come with a set of filters for different lighting situations. By using the correct filter and setting the white balance, you can accommodate almost any type of lighting situation.

Tips for Outdoor Lighting

The main advantage to outdoor shooting is that it doesn't take long to set the lights. In most cases, you just pick a camera position and start rolling. The disadvantage is that your production is subject to the vagaries of weather.

The primary thing to keep in mind when shooting outside is to shoot with the sun behind you, preferably over one shoulder, not directly behind. Having the sun off-axis a bit creates a more interesting picture by creating shadows on the subject.

You should also position your subject so that he or she is not in front of a bright background. The viewer's eyes are drawn to the brightest object on the screen, and that should be your subject, not the background.

The exception to this is a *silhouette* shot where you are trying to focus on the contrast between the dark subject and a bright background.

The color and quality of sunlight changes over the course of the day, and this can have a dramatic effect on the overall look of the shot.

The Magic Hour

If you are shooting scenic shots, be they of a natural scene or of a city, try to shoot during one of the magic hours. The *magic hour* is the hour just after sunrise or just before sunset. There's a wonderful warm quality to light at this time of day. In addition, you don't have to contend with harsh shadows as long as the sun is behind you.

Death at High Noon

This is the least flattering time to shoot people because direct overhead lighting creates dark shadows on a person's face. Even if you turn the person so that the sunlight strikes them at an angle, part of his or her face will be dark and without detail because of the limited tonal range of video cameras. One solution is to use a reflector (a white card or Flexfill) to bounce light into the darkened area (Figure 12-33).

A better solution is to avoid high noon altogether and shoot in the morning or afternoon when the sun is lower in the sky. You might still need to use a reflector, but the shadows won't be as difficult to work with.

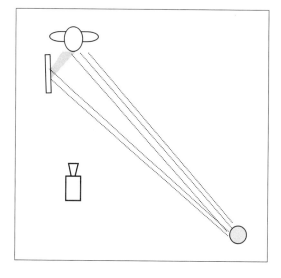

Figure 12-33.

When shooting outdoors, use a reflector to fill in shadows caused by the sun (acting as the key light).

The middle of the day is a good time to shoot if you want to emphasize edges and contrasts.

Sun Guns

If you are going to be doing a lot of outdoor shooting, you might want to rent a small, battery-operated light known as a *sun gun*. You use the sun gun as a fill light to soften the harsh shadows produced by sunlight. It can also be used as a back light to separate your subject from the background.

 Make sure you rent extra battery belts for the sun gun if you are going to be a long way from electrical power.

Cloudy Days

A fully overcast day gives you even lighting, which works well for interviews or scenes with people. There is a restful quality to shots captured on an overcast day.

But a partly cloudy day can wreak havoc with a production. You have to choose which lighting situation (cloudy or sunny) you want to use and then shoot only when that lighting situation occurs. You also have to be aware of how the background's appearance changes as the clouds come and go.

Tips for Indoor Lighting

With an indoor location, you are able to control the lighting to a much greater extent. Of course, it takes time to set up and adjust several lights, so you need to plan extra time in your production schedule for indoor locations.

The following are several examples of typical lighting situations. Your location will probably be different, but the techniques described apply to many scenarios.

Lighting for One Person (Interviews)

The simplest lighting setup that produces a textured image involves two lights: a key and a back light (Figure 12-34). This only works in sit-

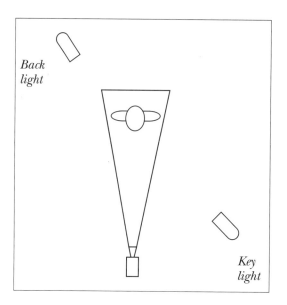

Figure 12-34.

When shooting a person with only two lights, use a key and back light. Move the key light closer to the camera to remove any unwanted shadows.

uations where the available light level is fairly high; otherwise, the background will be dark.

A shot where none of the background is visible is called a *limbo shot* because the person is not situated within a background, i.e., in limbo. This shot is accomplished with the two-light setup shown in Figure 12-34, with the exception that the key light is rotated a bit more to the side to decrease the amount of light that falls on the background.

The disadvantages of a two-light setup are that the unbalanced key light may cast harsh shadows on the subject, and that sometimes the background will be dark. To avoid these problems, you need to add a third light.

A typical three-light setup is shown in Figure 12-35. The fill light softens shadows on the person's face and helps illuminate the area behind the subject.

For most situations, these are all the lights you'll need to use. But if you have the time, adding a light to emphasize part of the background helps add depth to the shot. The most natural way to do this is to include a regular (or "practical") lamp in the shot and use a special 150- or 200-Watt photoflood bulb in it (Figure 12-36). A photoflood bulb is set to the proper tungsten balance. Normal lightbulbs will appear orange.

Figure 12-35.

The typical lighting setup with three lights. If the person is looking off camera, position the key light so that the person is looking toward the key light.

If the scene has a particularly deep background (more than 20 feet), a 200-Watt bulb won't throw off enough light. A clever cheat is to add a light (out of frame) that illuminates the background behind the practical lamp (Figure 12-37). This creates the illusion of a brighter lamp.

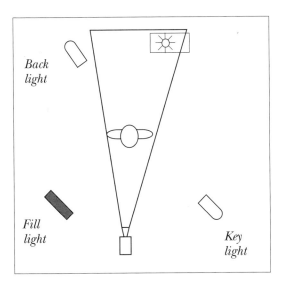

Figure 12-36.

Adding a lamp in the background helps add depth to a shot.

Figure 12-37.

If the background lamp is far away from the camera, it might not seem bright enough. You can augment the brightness of the lamp by pointing a light at the wall behind the lamp. This produces the illusion that the lamp is brighter.

 The intensity of a light decreases dramatically with distance (technically, as the square of the distance). This means that a light placed twice as far from the camera will seem one-fourth as bright.

If the background is plain—e.g., a flat wall—you can add artificial texture to it by throwing a diagonal slash of light across it (Figure 12-38). It often helps to add a gel to this light to create a colored slash of light.

To create a slash you need to use a *close-faced light,* one that comes with a *Fresnel lens.* This lens concentrates the light into a narrow beam.

Figure 12-38.

You can turn a blank wall into an interesting background by pointing a closed-face light (with a Fresnel lens) at the wall and narrowing the light's barn doors to create a slash.

Trying to produce a slash with a normal light adds a broad swath of color to the background, not a well-defined slash.

Lighting for Two People

Generally speaking, the more people you add to a scene, the more complicated the lighting setup becomes. A lot depends on the relative positions of the people (which way they are looking and how close they are together). Let's look at a fairly simple situation of two people standing near each other and at right angles.

The most complete way to light this scene is to use six lights: a key, a fill, and a back light for each person (Figure 12-39). You need to use close-faced lights; otherwise the key light for the first person might spill over into the fill of the other (which would cause unusual shadows and unnecessarily flat lighting).

If you don't want to set up six different lights, there are a number of other setups that provide adequate lighting. You can light the two of them as if they were one person, with one key, one fill, and one back

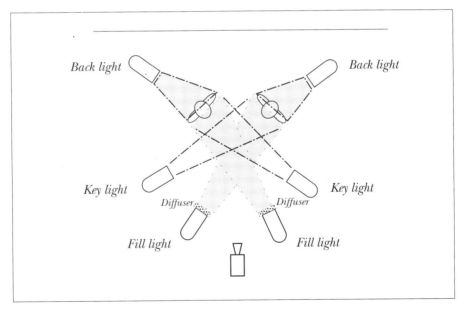

Figure 12-39. Lighting two people with six lights. Each person is lit with a key, a fill, and a back light. You might need to use close-faced lights to prevent one light from interfering with the others.

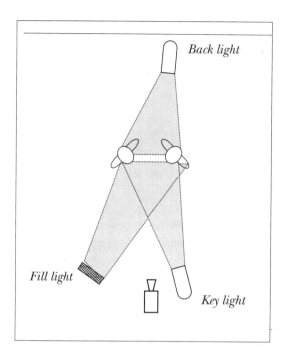

Figure 12-40.

Lighting two people with three lights. If you only have three lights to work with, treat the two people as one unit and light them accordingly with a key, a fill, and a back light. In this situation, the back light needs to be hung from the ceiling; otherwise its light stand will be visible in the shot.

light (Figure 12-40). This generally works better if the people turn a bit more toward the camera.

Another option is to have the back light for each person act as the fill light for the other (Figure 12-41). You may have to put a half scrim on each back light to decrease the intensity of the light falling on the people's shoulders. You then just need to light the background.

Adding another person to this scene makes for an even more complicated situation. Unless you want to spend hours lighting, you might want to think about lighting the entire room, which is discussed in the next section.

Lighting a Large Area

The quickest and easiest method for lighting a large area or an area where people are moving around a lot is to bounce a light, or lights, off the ceiling. This raises the overall brightness of the room. You can then add lights to brighten particular parts of the scene.

If the ceiling is high enough, you can simulate sunlight coming into the room by building a wall of lights (Figure 12-42). Depending on the

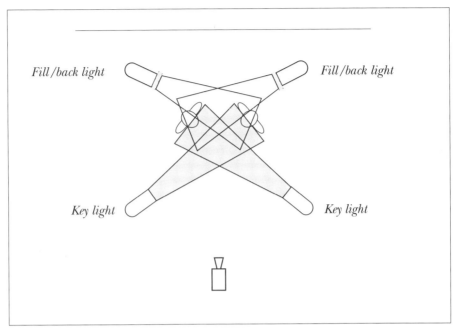

Figure 12-41.   Lighting two people with four lights. In this case, each back light serves as the fill light for the other person.

size of the room, you may need to pump in more than 5,000 Watts of light to create this effect.

Tips for Indoor/Outdoor Lighting

The color temperature of sunlight is so much hotter than indoor lighting that you can't mix the two without some modification. In addition, sunlight is much more intense than a typical light. So the direction of the sunlight with respect to the camera position will affect how you light an indoor/outdoor situation.

Sunlight as a Key Light

This is the least complicated way of using sunlight in a shot since it utilizes the sun's intensity to provide the main lighting for the shot. A typical setup is shown in Figure 12-43.

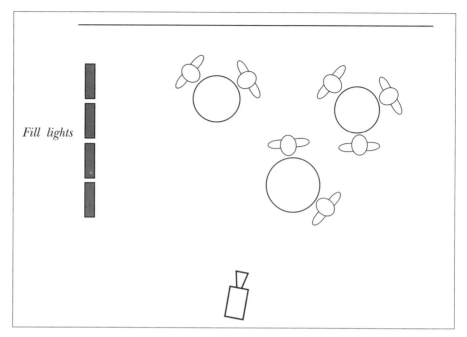

Figure 12-42. When you are shooting a large scene and don't have time to light each element independently, a quick solution is to create a wall of light with three or more large lights (2,000 Watts or more). The lights should be diffused to create soft, even lighting. They must be set high off the ground. This mimics diffuse sunlight coming through a bank of windows.

Because of the color temperature difference between tungsten lights and sunlight, you need to add blue gel to the fill and backlights. Otherwise, they will cast an orange light on the scene.

Sunlight as a Fill Light

Sometimes you will want to use sunlight as the fill because you want to include a certain part of a background in the shot (Figure 12-44). This requires a fairly powerful key light because the fill light (the sun) is so strong. The key has to be covered with a blue gel to match the color temperature of the sun, which makes matters worse because the gel reduces the intensity of the key light. It's not uncommon to use a 2,000-Watt key light in this type of situation.

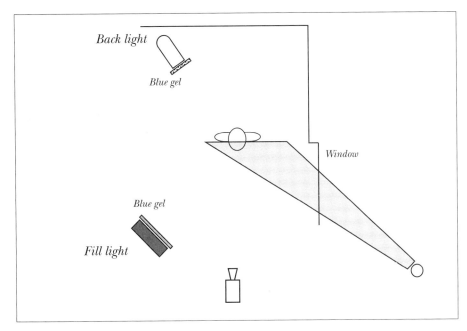

Figure 12-43.   When using the sun as a key light, add blue gels to the fill and back light to match the color temperature of sunlight.

An alternative is to use a light that produces light similar in color to sunlight. The best known of these lights is the HMI. Because you don't have to gel these lights, their effective intensity is much higher.

Sunlit Backgrounds

This is by far the most complicated situation. Sunlight is just too strong to overcome when it is lighting the background. For example, let's say you're shooting in an office that has two picture windows overlooking the New York skyline. That's a great background, so you decide to include it in the shot.

Instead of converting the indoor lights to match sunlight, you do the reverse: You cover the windows with a gel that decreases the brightness of the background and converts the color of the sunlight to match the interior lights. The gel used for this job, called ND-CC, comes in wide rolls of varying thicknesses (the thicker the gel, the less light that gets through). The trick is to apply the gel evenly on the windows, because ridges and bubbles reflect the key light and produce

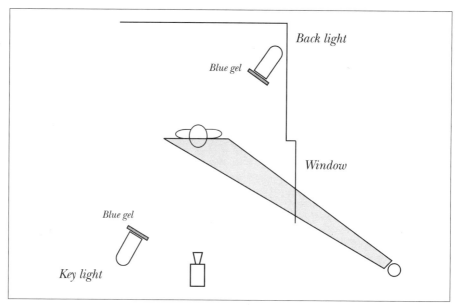

Figure 12-44. Using the sun as a fill light. Because sunlight is so strong, you probably have to use a very intense light (2,000 Watts or more) as the key light. The key and back light should be gelled with daylight blue gel to match the color of sunlight.

unwanted points of light in the background. The best way is to spray the windows with water and then smooth out the gel with a squeegee.

You then set up a key and a fill light in a typical configuration, but without blue gels (Figure 12-45). As you might guess, this is a lot of work. It had better be a pretty amazing background to go through all this trouble!

Other Situations

Even when sunlight does not play a major role in the shot, if it is present to any degree, it adds a bluish cast to certain objects in the shot. You won't see the bluish casts in the black-and-white viewfinder of the camera, which is why it helps to bring a color monitor along on your shoots. You can either try to eliminate the sources of sunlight (through open windows, half-closed blinds, etc.) or gel all your lights and reset the white balance for sunlight.

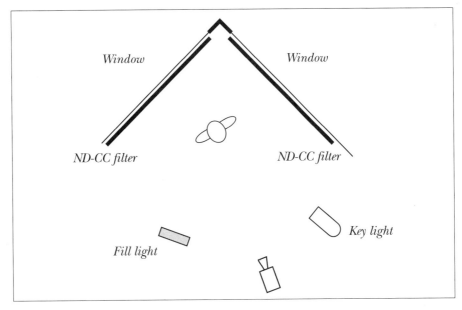

Figure 12-45.   If the shot has a sunlit background, you will not be able to overcome its brightness. Instead, you should cover the windows with a gel that decreases the brightness of the background.

Common Lighting Mistakes

The choice of a camera position and the lighting plan are invariably linked. Too often, people pick the shot first, then try to light the scene to make the shot work. The end result is often a well-composed shot that is poorly lit.

You can also run into trouble if you've overscheduled the shoot day and haven't left enough time to light properly. Here are a few general rules for how long it takes to set up lights under different lighting conditions:

- **Indoor/Outdoor:** at least an hour, more if the window area is particularly large

- **Indoor:** 30 minutes for a one-person setup, 45 minutes for a two-person setup, 60 minutes or more if you want to light the background

- **Outdoor:** 5 minutes or less, as long as you're not trying to shoot against a bright background

After a while, you'll develop your own sense of how long it takes you to set lights for particular situations.

The following are some common mistakes that are often caused by overscheduling.

Indoor Locations

- Failing to notice sunlight entering the scene
- Failing to make the subject stand out from the background (This is usually caused by the lack of a backlight but can also happen when the key light is set too low and lightens the background.)

Outdoor Locations

- Shooting the subject against a bright background
- Failing to remove harsh shadows with a reflector
- Causing a flare when direct sunlight hits the camera lens

Sound-Recording Basics

The main goal is to get the sounds you want and avoid the sounds you don't. It's better to get clean tracks of several sound elements in a scene and then go back and mix them in the editing, rather than to record them as one track in the field.

Types of Microphones

There is a wide variety of microphones, each suited for a specific task:

Camera mike: This is a fair mike for collecting background sound but fairly worthless for recording someone talking because it is just too far away from the person.

Lavalier or Tram mike: This is the standard microphone for recording interviews. It is clipped onto the person's clothes (usually a tie, lapel, or collar). It does a pretty good job and works for most situations. The disadvantage is that it can pick up the sound of clothes rustling if the person moves about in his or her chair.

Hypercardioid mike: This is the standard mike for recording dialog or people outside an interview setting. It is designed to capture sound from a small area around the front tip of the mike. It is often placed inside a wind screen. It can also be used to record interviews when it is hung from a boom above and slightly in front of the person's head.

Shotgun mike: This microphone is extremely directional, which makes it good for picking out sounds that are far away. You should not use this microphone indoors because it picks up echoes well. Use a hypercardioid mike instead.

Tips for Recording Sit-Down Interviews

The main concern in recording interviews is to make sure there aren't background noises that will pollute the audio. Besides air conditioning, machinery, telephones, and other devices, people talking nearby can be a problem. Don't be afraid to ask them to be quiet; you won't be recording for long.

At the end of the interview, you should record 30 seconds of silence. This isn't really silence but the *room tone*, a sample of the background sound of the location. This allows you to add natural-sounding pauses in the person's interview when you are editing.

Tips for Recording People On-the-Fly

If you are recording someone talking outside the controlled situation of a sit-down interview, it's a lot harder to control background sounds. Therefore, you should get the microphone as close to the speaker as possible. Work with the camera operator. If he or she is shooting a close-up of the person's face, you can move the microphone within a foot of the subject's mouth.

If you are going to be shooting one person in the middle of a group of people, you might want to rent a *wireless microphone*. The microphone is connected to a radio transmitter that is placed in the person's pocket. A separate unit, called the *receiver*, is operated by the sound recordist. It picks up the signal from the transmitter and then sends it to the tape deck.

Group Scenes

If you are shooting scripted scenes of a group of people, such as three people talking at a table, or people moving about in a room, use one or more hypercardioid mikes suspended from above. The mikes are either placed on extension arms called *booms*, which are supported by mike stands or are hung from the ceiling. The microphones are placed as close to the subjects as possible without being in the shot.

 Using a lightweight boom, you can hold a mike above the subjects with your hand, but it had better be a short shot. The microphone gets heavier when placed at the end of a long boom. A better option is to use a mike stand.

Natural Sound

Most people do not spend enough time getting good natural sounds. They are worried about the pictures, and as soon as they get them, they move to the next location. Take a few minutes to collect the particular background sounds from a location. It allows you to add texture to the audio track during editing.

You should be particularly aware of any actions in a shot that produce a sound, such as a door slam, a glass breaking, or a gun shot. Sometimes you won't be able to get the mike as close to the source of the sound as you would like because of the camera framing (you don't want the mike to be in the shot). In those situations, you should redo the action on a close shot, so you can move the mike closer and get better sound.

When recording general background sound, such as the sounds from a particular piece of machinery, a stream, or city traffic, point the microphone in different directions. Don't settle for any old sound, try to get the best possible.

Avoiding Common Sound-Recording Mistakes

Simply by paying attention to the sound being recorded, you can avoid many of the most common sound-recording mistakes. If you have a set of headphones, plug them into the output of the tape recorder. That way, you monitor what is actually being recorded, not a signal in between the microphone and the deck.

Wrap-Up

Video production is a craft that requires patience, attention to detail, and creativity. It's easy to be mediocre. It takes hard work to produce great pictures. You won't be an expert shooter on your first production, but if you keep trying to enhance your technique, the images you get will improve and that will lead to better movies.

CHAPTER 13

Working with Digital Video — Compression, Input, and Final Format

Video was never intended to be stored or manipulated in digital form. There's just too much data—too much to send from place to place inside your computer and too much to store on your hard disk or other storage device. That's why, until recently, the only place you'd find people working with digital video was in expensive video post-production facilities.

Cheaper memory, faster computers, and—most importantly—video compression have now made it possible for hundreds of thousands of people to create, edit, and display digital movies on their computers. Previous chapters discussed how to work with compressed video files. This chapter focuses on video compression itself and how it affects the process of converting video to digital files, and how compression affects playback from the final format (type of storage device) for your movie.

Managing the Data Deluge

A single frame of video is made up of 525 lines, although only 483 are used to create the image on the screen (the other lines are used for calibration purposes). Each line contains 720 pixels. When converted to a digital file, a single frame of video consists of 480 lines, each consisting of 640 pixels across. This amounts to a total of 307,200 pixels per frame.

To represent the color of an individual pixel in digital form accurately, you need 24 bits of information (8 bits each for red, green, and blue) for each pixel. This means that one frame of video requires 921,600 bytes. And that's just one frame. One second of video (30 frames) requires 27.6MB; one minute of video, 1.66 gigabytes (GB); a one-hour videotape, 99.5GB. Gets out of hand kind of quickly, doesn't it?

Fortunately, there are a number of ways to reduce this flood of data to a reasonable level:

- Reduce the size of the video window
- Reduce the number of frames of video that are displayed per second (*frame rate*)
- Apply some kind of image compression

Reducing the Size of the Video Window

Part of the reason why a frame of video requires so many bytes is that it consists of 307,200 pixels (640 × 480). By reducing the number of pixels, you immediately reduce the size of a video clip. Table 13-1 shows the effect of reducing the size of the video window for a 10-second video clip in 24-bit color. That's one reason why many digital videos measure 160 × 120 pixels. By squeezing the image into a smaller box, you reduce the file size by almost 16 times.

Table 13-1.   How Window Size Affects File Size

Window Size	Fraction of Total Screen	Number of Pixels	File Size (MB)
640 × 480	1	307,200	276.5
320 × 240	$1/4$	76,800	69.1
240 × 180	$1/7$	43,200	38.9
160 × 120	$1/16$	19,200	17.3

Reducing the Frame Rate

Normal video runs at 30 frames per second (fps). You can reduce the size of a file by simply showing every other frame (15 fps), every third frame (10 fps), or even fewer frames per second. The reduction in file size for an uncompressed video clip is directly proportional to the reduction in frame rate. Table 13-2 shows the relationship between frame rate and file size for a 10-second clip at 24-bit color in a 160 × 120 pixel window.

For most situations, 15 fps is sufficient to capture most of the motion in a clip. However, if there is a lot of action in a shot, you may need to use 30 fps; otherwise, the movement will occur in jumps.

Applying Image Compression

Image compression works by reducing the amount of information needed to represent an image on the screen. When low levels of compression are used it is nearly impossible to see the effect of compression. However, as more and more compression is applied, imperfections or *artifacts* show up in the video image. More and more compression, however, makes the size of a video file smaller and smaller. So there is a definite trade-off between the amount of compression and the quality of the video image:

High compression = low file size = low image quality

Medium compression = medium file size = medium image quality

Low compression = large file size = high image quality

Table 13-2.   How Frame Rate Affects File Size

Frame Rate (fps)	File Size (MB)
30	17.3
15	8.64
10	5.76
5	2.88

The overall goal is to set the compression as high as possible (to reduce file size) and maintain an acceptable level of image quality. There are two basic techniques of image compression: spatial compression and temporal compression. *Spatial compression* decreases the amount of information required for a single image or frame of video. *Temporal compression* compares two frames of video and stores only the differences between the frames.

Generally speaking, if a clip contains large areas of similar colors, you can use higher compression settings. For example, a person standing against a solid-color wall retains good quality under high spatial compression. You should try several different settings for a particular clip or movie to determine the most appropriate setting (highest compression at acceptable quality). Because a movie generally consists of several clips, you should pick a quality setting that produces the best average result for all the clips.

 QuickTime for Windows supports multiple compressors within a movie, which allows you to use the most appropriate compressor for individual sections of the movie.

As mentioned, temporal compression works by comparing two frames and storing the differences between the frames. One frame is the reference, or *key*, frame; the other frame is called the *difference frame* (Figure 13-1). Key frames are stored as complete frames, whereas difference frames are stored only as the difference between them and the previous frame.

Key frame

Key frame

Figure 13-1.

Key frames are stored as complete frames. Difference frames hold only the differences between that frame and the previous key frame. When the differences between a frame and a key frame exceed 95 percent, a new key frame is stored.

For example, if you have a shot of a person walking in front of a solid-color wall towards the camera, the difference frames would contain only the image of the person, not the background (which remains the same). After a number of difference frames, the accumulated differences don't accurately reproduce an image, which then degrades the image quality. At that point, a new key frame is used and the process starts all over again.

Generally speaking, static camera shots that don't include a lot of movement can withstand a large amount of temporal compression. Shots with camera moves (tilts, zooms, or pans), such as the pan of the windsurfer, degrade quickly with increasing temporal compression.

Besides affecting the quality of the image, the frequency of key frames can strongly affect how a movie is played back on someone else's machine. Please see "Choosing the Final Format" later in this chapter.

Lossy vs. Lossless Compression

Some compression methods do not change the basic quality of the image during compression and decompression. This is called *lossless compression* because nothing is lost. Most compression programs that work with non-video files (such as ZipIt or PKZIP) use lossless compression because it those circumstances you don't want to lose any data.

The opposite of lossless is *lossy compression*, where data is lost or removed from an image or video clip during compression. At moderate levels of compression, you don't notice the data that is lost—that's the advantage. However, at some point as you increase the amount of compression, the image degrades noticeably. In addition, when a lossy compression scheme is used over and over on the same clip, minor changes can build up, leading to a noticeable effect. This can occur when you are compositing several effects or filters on the same clip.

The amount of degradation due to compression artifacts depends on the image. There a few general rules (mentioned earlier) but for the most part you have try a few different settings and see what works best for you.

In a funny way video compression is like the processing of orange juice. I'm a big fan of fresh-squeezed orange juice (the equivalent of raw video). But in a pinch, I don't mind mixing up a pitcher from frozen concentrate, if it has pulp. This is equivalent to low levels of compression—it's not as good as the original, but it's close. Next down on the list is orange juice from concentrate that doesn't have pulp. It's certainly not the same as the original, but in certain situations—such as it's all that the convenience store had at 3 a.m.—it will do. This is equivalent to medium video compression. Finally there's Tang—you know, the orange juice that went to the moon. The only thing orange about it is its color. In this twisted analogy, this is the same as video with high levels of compression—it looks like video, but not the video you're used to seeing.

Adjusting Compression Levels

You can set the amount of spatial and temporal compression in the Compression Options dialog box (from the Video menu in VidEdit). Clicking on the Details button enlarges the dialog box, as shown in Figure 13-2.

Figure 13-2. The enlarged Compression Options dialog box. You set the amount of spatial and temporal compression here.

The types of adjustments you can make depend on the compression method you are using. The following controls are available when using Video for Windows.

Different playback devices have specific maximum data transfer rates. Single speed CD-ROMs, for example, can only transfer data at a maximum rate of 150K per second. You should match the maximum data rate of your intended playback device by adjusting the data rate control. The compression method will then adjust the amount of compression to maintain that data rate.

The Key Frame control allows you to set how often a key frame is used for temporal compression. The more difference frames you use between key frames, the more temporal compression is applied. As mentioned above, this type of compression works best for static scenes.

The Compressor Settings control slider allows you to maintain high quality images at the expense of a lower frame rate. High compressor settings (greater than 50) will reduce the frame rate. Low compression settings will increase the frame rate (up to 30 frames per second) but reduce the image quality.

You will usually have to try several different combinations of settings before you come up with a combination that works for your material. Make sure to save an uncompressed version of your video file and save the new, compressed versions with different names. This will allow you to compare the compressed versions with the uncompressed version.

Balancing Frame Rate, Image Dimensions, and Compression

The previous sections have discussed several methods for reducing the size of video files. The following is a fairly technical discussion of how these various factors work together and how you can balance the factors to achieve your desired result.

As mentioned earlier, the key factors that influence file size are the frame rate, the image dimensions, and the amount of compression. First we'll look at calculating the size of an uncompressed clip. You can determine the size in bytes of the video portion of a movie exactly by using the equation below:

$$\text{File size (in bytes)} = D \times H \times V \times BP \times FR / 8$$

where
D = duration of the clip (in seconds)

H = horizontal length of the video image (in pixels)

V = vertical length of the video image (in pixels)

BP = bits per pixel (8, 16, or 24-bit color)

FR = frame rate (in frames per second)

 We divide the total by 8 to convert from bits to bytes.

For example, let's say you want to know what the file size would be for an uncompressed 30-second video clip with the following parameters:

15 frames per second

16-bit color

160 pixels by 120 pixels

Plugging these numbers into the equation yields:

$$\text{File size} = 30 \times 160 \times 120 \times 16 \times 15 / 8$$
$$= 17,280,000 \text{ bytes (or 17.3MB)}$$

Calculating the file size allows you to know whether you have enough space on your hard drive for the file, before you actually make the video capture.

Okay, now that we've captured the file, let's look at how compression fits in. Applying compression reduces the number of bits needed to represent each pixel (the "BP" term). Some people will actually talk about compression in terms of bits per pixel (as in, "with this compression scheme, only seven bits are required for each pixel"). Another way compression is evaluated is in terms of the compression ratio, which is the ratio of the file size of the compressed clip divided by the file size of the uncompressed image:

$$\text{Compression ratio} = \frac{\text{Compressed image (MB)}}{\text{Uncompressed image (MB)}}$$

For example, if the uncompressed image requires 10MB and the compressed image takes 1MB, then the compression ratio would be 1:10, or more simply 10 percent.

If you're working with compression ratios, then the file size equation is modified as shown:

$$\text{File size} = D \times H \times V \times BP \times FR \times CR \,/\, 8$$

where CR = compression ratio

 The compression ratio for a clip can be found by clicking on the Preview button in the Compression Options dialog box (see Figure 13-3).

Going back to our earlier example, let's say that we decide to use the Microsoft Video 1 compressor at a setting of 60, which yields an estimated compression ratio (in this example) of 40 percent. Plugging in the numbers again yields:

$$\text{File size} = 30 \times 160 \times 120 \times 16 \times 15 \times 0.4 \,/\, 8$$
$$= 6{,}912{,}000 \text{ bytes (or 6.9MB)}$$

Now, you might ask, Why bother to calculate the file size? Why don't we just set the amount of compression according the quality we want, apply the compression, and see how large the file is?

Well, in many situations you can do just that. But what if you're making a CD-ROM and you want to know how many minutes of video you can store on the disc? There is no simple answer. It depends on each one of the terms of the equation. For example, here are several answers to the question of how many minutes will fit on a typical CD-ROM (total practical storage is around 640MB).

Since we want to determine the total amount of video, we modify the equation slightly so that it reads:

$$\text{File size per minute} = H \times V \times BP \times FR \times CR \times 60 \,/\, 8$$

We added a factor of 60 to determine the file size per minute (as opposed to seconds). Once we know how much storage is required for each minute of digital video, we can divide that into the total amount of storage (600MB) to calculate the total number of minutes.

Figure 13-3. Clicking on the Preview button in the Compression Options dialog box (in VidEdit) reveals the compression ratio for that clip.

Answer #1—Training Videos

Let's say we're creating the CD-ROM as part of a training program. Visual quality isn't all that important and the image size can be small since we shot most of the material as close-ups. We choose a small image size, a low frame rate, 8-bit color, and a fair amount of compression (25 percent):

$$H = 120 \text{ pixels}$$
$$V = 90 \text{ pixels}$$
$$B = 8 \text{ bits/pixel}$$
$$FR = 10 \text{ frames/second}$$
$$CR = 0.25 \text{ (25 percent)}$$

Plugging this into the equation we get:

$$\text{File size/minute} = 120 \times 90 \times 8 \times 10 \times 0.25 \times 60 \ / \ 8$$
$$= 1{,}620{,}000 \text{ bytes (or 1.62MB)/minute}$$

We then divide this into the total amount of storage (600MB):

$$\text{Total time} = 600\text{MB} / (1.62\text{MB/min.})$$
$$= 370 \text{ minutes (roughly 6 hours)}$$

By making the image small with a low frame rate and a fair amount of compression, we can store slightly more than 6 hours of video on a single CD-ROM.

Answer #2—Consumer Title

This time visual quality is important—but we still want to store as much video as possible. We choose a medium image size, 24 bits/pixel, a moderate frame rate, and a moderate amount of compression:

H = 240 pixels

V = 180 pixels

B = 24 bits/pixel

FR = 15 frames/second

CR = 0.4 (40 percent)

Plugging these figures into the equation we get:

$$\text{File size/minute} = 240 \times 180 \times 24 \times 15 \times 0.4 \times 60 / 8$$
$$= 46{,}656{,}000 \text{ bytes (or 46.7MB)/minute}$$

$$\text{Total time} = 600\text{MB} / (46.7\text{MB/min.}) = 12.9 \text{ minutes}$$

We didn't change each factor very much—but combined they have a tremendous impact on the total amount of video (13 minutes vs. 370 minutes).

Answer #3—Consumer Title Revisited

Let's take the previous example and try to stuff a bit more video in. There are an almost infinite number of ways to do this, but the easiest way is to increase the amount of compression (from a compression ratio of 40 to 25 percent). All the other terms remain the same:

H = 240 pixels

V = 180 pixels

B = 24 bits/pixel

FR = 15 frames/second

CR = 0.25 (30 percent)

File size/minute = $240 \times 180 \times 24 \times 15 \times 0.25 \times 60 \, / \, 8$

= 29,160,000 bytes (or 29.2MB)/minute

Total time = 600MB / (29.2MB/min.) = 20.6 minutes

By increasing the compression (and lowering the quality a bit) we can squeeze in an additional seven minutes onto the disc.

 These calculations were based on the Microsoft Video 1 compressor. Most developers use the Cinepak compressor for CD-ROM applications because it yields higher-quality images at fairly high amounts of compression (ratios of 10 percent). However, because Cinepak uses a combination of temporal and spatial compression, the compression ratio shown in the preview window in Video for Windows isn't particularly accurate (since it only estimates spatial compression). In general, you can assume a compression ratio of between 10 and 15 percent when using the Cinepak compressor.

These are the types of calculations that CD-ROM developers do every day. It's all a matter of trade-offs. A little more compression here, a slightly larger image size there, a slower frame rate over here.

In the examples above we assumed that we would make the digital movies in the same way (size, compression, etc.). In reality, each movie can have its own set of parameters. This means you have a lot more flexibility, but at the price of more complexity.

Hardware Compression

So far we've been talking about software-only compression. To achieve high frame rates and large image dimensions, you need to use some kind of hardware compression. Hardware compression boards allow you to edit full-screen video and play it back in real time. But video clips compressed with a hardware board must be played back on a computer that has the same hardware board. Currently there are two main methods used for hardware compression: JPEG and MPEG.

JPEG Compression

JPEG is an acronym for the Joint Photographic Engineering Group, which developed the JPEG standards as a way of compressing still images. JPEG uses a sophisticated algorithm (called DCT, for discrete cosine transform) which performs high-quality spatial compression. Technically, JPEG is a lossy compressor, but at low levels of compression (20 percent) the compression artifacts are barely noticeable. However, at higher compression levels (5 percent), areas of high contrast are degraded. Typical areas of high contrast include titles. Nonetheless, a hardware JPEG compressor outperforms any software compressor in terms of frame rate, quality and image dimensions.

MPEG Compression

The Motion Picture Engineering Group (MPEG) developed the MPEG standard specifically for compressing moving images—video. It relies on a combination of spatial and temporal compression to achieve extremely high compression ratios (0.5 to 1 percent). As is typical of any compressor than uses temporal compression, MPEG works best for static video clips that do not contain a great deal of motion. More sophisticated MPEG schemes, such as DVI (from Intel), use a variety of computationally intense algorithms to achieve high compression (and high frame rates) for almost any type of video clip.

The drawback to MPEG compression is that to compress a video clip with MPEG requires an expensive MPEG encoder ($20,000 and up) and a lot of time. But once the video clip is encoded, all you need is an MPEG playback board and the video clip will play in real time. Another disadvantage with MPEG is that since it uses temporal compression, not every frame of video is easily accessible—an important part of video editing.

OK, it costs a lot to work with and it's not suitable for editing, so why would you want to use MPEG? For one simple, very important reason. At compression ratios of 0.5 to 1 percent, it is possible to display a full-screen (640×480 pixels), full-motion video clip from a double-speed CD-ROM. It also means that you can store up to 72 minutes of full-screen video on a single CD-ROM.

To sum up, JPEG is better for video editing, while MPEG is better for full-screen playback. So one strategy might be this: use JPEG to achieve high frames and image dimensions for capture and editing—making sure to use as little compression as possible to maintain image quality. Then convert the final program or set of clips to MPEG for distribution on CD-ROM.

Until recently there weren't any low-cost MPEG playback boards, so it was a moot point for most applications. However, Sigma Designs has recently come out with ReelMagic, which (for $500) provides MPEG support for PCs. If these boards sell well, expect to see a lot of CD-ROM developers using MPEG encoding, which will probably drive down the price for encoders.

Digitizing Your Clips

Digitizing video is no small task, given the immense data rates for video. So far we've been concerned with the size of the files needed for video clips, but the speed at which video information streams into a digitizing board is tremendous. Every second, another 27.6MB. Even if you are only capturing to a 160×120 pixel window, it's still 1.7MB per second.

To give you a perspective on what your computer and digitizing board are trying to do, let's look at what happens after you decide to capture a section of video:

- **Time = 0:** You click the mouse to start the digitizing process.

- **0 to 0.03 second:** Your finger has barely moved. Into your digitizing board and onto your CPU, 58,000 bytes have streamed—the equivalent of a 60-page document. Along the way, the full 720×525 pixel video screen was shrunk (through millions of calculations) to one-sixteenth its normal size.

- **0.03 to 0.06 second:** Your finger begins to move up. The first frame of data is on its way to your hard drive. The second frame, another 60-page document, has raced through the digitizing board and is on its way to the CPU.

- **0.06 to 0.1 second:** You finally released the mouse. In just one-tenth of a second, nearly 200,000 bytes coursed through the board and the CPU and onto your hard drive.

And how long was that segment you wanted to digitize?

Digitizing Video

When you digitize, one of your main concerns is achieving the highest possible frame rate. There are four major factors that affect how fast a frame rate you can get out of your digitizing board:

- **The capabilities of the board itself:** Various boards use different methods to convert an analog video signal into digital information.

- **The size of your capture window:** A 320×240 window requires four times as much data throughput as a 160×120 window.

- **The speed of your CPU:** A 33MHz 486 would be able to grab a 320×240 window at 15 fps, whereas a 25MHz 386 might only get 10 fps in a 160×120 window (with the same digitizing board).

- **The type and access time of your hard disk:** If your hard drive isn't fast enough to take all the digital data your CPU is creating, then the your frame rate will go down.

Achieving the Maximum Frame Rate

There are a few techniques and procedures you can follow that help you get the maximum frame rates possible for your particular system:

- Don't have any other programs running while you digitize video. These programs take up RAM and, in some cases, actually put a load on your CPU (which uses every clock cycle it can for digitizing).

- Turn off any utilities that might put a load on the CPU (such as screen savers).

- If you have a lot of RAM (more than 8MB), try recording directly to RAM. This is faster than recording to your hard drive.

- If you are recording to a hard drive, partition your disk and defragment the partition regularly. If the drive has to go looking for space, then it can't be writing to the disk. An even better solution is to have a dedicated hard drive just for recording video clips.

- Use a fast hard drive that has a sustained data transfer rate of at least 2MB per second. If you intend on capturing long sequences of video, you should get a drive specifically designed for that purpose.

Maximizing the Image Quality

Achieving a high frame rate is only part of the battle. You also need to get good quality images. Most digitizing boards come with a variety of color and image controls that can improve image quality:

- **Hue:** This is similar to the tint control on your television set. It is generally used to overcome any artifacts (image imperfections) caused by the video deck.

- **Saturation:** This is similar to the color control on a television set. The normal setting usually works best. However, if you are digitizing from a VHS tape that is a copy of a copy, you might want to reduce the saturation slightly.

- **Brightness:** This increases or decreases the overall brightness of the video image. You can use this control to lighten a dark image, but this will also turn black areas in an image gray. In this case, you should also increase the contrast to compensate. This control, however, won't decrease the brightness of an entirely white region of an image (see the discussion on white level in the next list).

- **Contrast:** It's generally a good idea to use a medium- to high-contrast setting when digitizing. This increases the *tonal range* of the image (the range between brightest and darkest pixels), thus yielding a more detailed picture. A good tonal range also improves image quality during compression.

In addition to the basic image controls just listed, some digitizing boards offer the following:

- **Black level:** This controls the blackness of the dark areas of an image. It can be used in conjunction with the brightness control to lighten a dark image. To set the proper black level, increase it slowly until you start to lose details in the dark regions of the image. Then back off a bit until the details reappear. The proper black level improves image compression by removing noise from the video signal.

- **White level:** This controls the whiteness of the bright areas of an image. It should be used in place of the brightness control for darkening an overly bright image.

Balancing Frame Rate and Image Size

Each hardware configuration (CPU, capture board, and hard drive) has it own maximum capture data rate. The following is a technical discussion of how you can balance frame rate and image size for a particular hardware configuration. There is a very direct relationship between the capture data rate, frame rate, and image size, which can be expressed in the following equation:

$$\text{Max. capture data rate (bytes/sec)} = H \times V \times FR \times Q$$

where H = horizontal dimension

V = vertical dimension

FR = frame rate

Q = a combination of factors relating to color settings, CPU speed, capture board characteristics, and hard-disk data transfer rate.

In practical terms, Q is fixed by your system. You don't need to calculate it. The main thing to realize is that an increase in image size requires a proportional decrease in frame rate, and vice versa. For example, if on your system you are able to capture a 240 × 180 pixel image at 15 frames per second and you increase the image size to 320 × 240, you will only be able to capture eight frames per second.

Since Q doesn't change (it's still the same hardware), you can use the following equation to calculate the new frame rate:

$$FR_2 = H_1 \times V_1 \times FR_1 / (H_2 \times V_2)$$

where the subscript 1 represents the values for one set of parameters and the subscript 2 stands for the second set of parameters. Going back to our example, the equation looks like this:

$$FR_2 = 240 \times 180 \times 15 / (320 \times 240) = 8.4 \text{ frames/sec.}$$

The reason that the frame rate is decreased by roughly a factor of 2 (8.4 vs. 15) for a seemingly small increase in image dimension is that the total number of pixels (the area of the image) has increased by a factor of 2 (76,800 vs. 43,200 pixels). So when you think about expanding the size of the image, remember that since you have to increase both the horizontal and vertical dimensions (to maintain the proper aspect ratio), the net effect will be a significant reduction in frame rate.

Digitizing Audio

Compared to video, digitizing audio is fairly easy. Some digitizing boards come with an audio capture capability built in; with other boards you need to use a separate audio digitizer, such as the Sound Blaster Pro.

Digitizing audio involves two steps: setting the audio level controls and choosing the level of audio resolution.

Setting the Audio Levels

Your goal is to produce digital audio with as little distortion as possible. Most digitizing boards and devices allow you to listen to the digitized audio sound before actually recording it (audio play-through). There are two basic types of distorted audio: clipped and muffled. *Clipped audio* sounds harsh, with a lot of crackle and hiss. *Muffled audio* sounds, well, muffled.

Avoiding Clipped Audio   Clipping occurs when the audio is digitized at too high a volume. This can occur because the audio output from the video or audio deck is too high or because the digitizer volume control is set too high.

If your audio or video deck has an output volume meter, the audio volume should be set so that it falls within the middle range of the meter (near the 0 db level). If the volume is much higher than that, reduce the volume to the proper level.

If you still have distortion, reduce the volume setting on the digitizing board.

The reason for adjusting the output volume on your deck first is that it is nearly impossible to remove distortion once it's been added. Therefore, you should always start at the beginning of the data path and remove distortion when it is introduced, not later.

Avoiding Muffled Audio   Muffled audio occurs when the audio is digitized at too low a volume. Again, this can be caused by either the output of the video or audio deck or by the digitizing board. The procedure for correcting this problem is the same as with clipping, except that you are looking for audio volumes that are too low (far below the 0 db level).

Setting the Audio Resolution

Two parameters affect the quality of the digitized audio and the size of the audio file: bit depth and sampling rate. These are analogous to color depth and frame rate for digitizing video.

Setting the Audio Bit Depth   The standard bit depth for most audio boards is 8-bit audio. There are, however, several devices that can produce 16-bit audio, which yields superior sound compared to 8-bit audio. If possible, use a board that supports 16-bit audio. The file sizes for your audio clips are twice as large, but the improved quality is worth it.

Setting the Audio Sampling Rate   The sampling rate determines how often an analog audio signal is cut up to make a digital audio clip. Higher sampling rates yield better quality. Most digitizing devices allow you to digitize at either 8 kHz, 11 kHz, or 22 kHz (i.e., 8,000, 11,000, or 22,000 samples per second). Whenever possible, you should digitize at 22 kHz to maximize audio quality. You can always reduce the sampling rate when you compress the file later.

There is, however, a direct trade-off between sampling rate and file size. A clip digitized at 22 kHz takes up twice as much room on your hard drive as the same clip digitized at 11 kHz. Sampling at 22 kHz also increases the data rate through the digitizing board, which can reduce the maximum frame rate for the video capture.

Evaluating Digitizers

There is a dizzying array of capture boards out on the market (with new boards on the way). For the purposes of this book, we'll separate them into three categories: *Getting Started*, *On Your Way*, and *Pushing the Envelope*.

Getting Started

If you haven't worked with video before and just want to experiment with video on your PC, then you should look at the low-cost options. Low-end boards are generally used to capture small-sized windows at rates up to 15 frames per second (depending on your computer). You may also need to use another board to capture sound. At the time of this writing (early 1994), the following boards fit in the Getting Started group:

Video Blaster—Creative Labs (list price: $499)

VideoSpigot for Windows—Creative Labs ($399)

WinMovie—Sigma Designs ($299)

Win/TV—Hauppauge Computer Works ($495)

Pro MovieStudio—Media Vision ($449)

Video Clipper—CEI ($499)

 Phone numbers and addresses of video board manufacturers can be found in Appendix B.

On Your Way

If you're working an a CD-ROM application, you should consider a mid-range board that allows you to capture larger-sized windows (320 × 240 pixels) at a reasonable frame rate (15 frames per second). These boards typically utilize some kind of hardware compression assistance (but not JPEG) to achieve the desired frame rates. The boards also usually include audio capture capabilities. The prices vary but you can expect to spend around $1,000 for a board in this group. Possible choices include:

Bravado/16—Truevision ($1,295)

VideoSurge—AITech ($995)

ISVR—Intel ($600)

Many board manufacturers advertise their low- and medium-range boards as capturing 640×480 images and capturing 30 frames per second. What they don't tell you is that you can't do both at the same time (i.e., 640×480 at 30 frames per second). You can capture a 160×120 image at 30 frames per second or a 640×480 at 2 frames per second. Only high-end boards, which typically use hardware JPEG compression, are capable of full-screen (640×480), full-motion (30 frames per second) captures.

Pushing the Envelope

There are a number of boards that use sophisticated compression schemes, usually hardware JPEG, to achieve full-frame, full-motion capture and playback. Because hardware JPEG compression occurs in real time, these boards greatly improve your editing efficiency (you spend less time waiting). Some boards in this category also include video encoders, which allow you to record digital video files onto videotape. This is very handy feature when working with clients that don't have sophisticated computer systems.

 These boards often require specialized hard drives to achieve maximum performance, so make sure to ask your dealer for the recommended system hardware before you buy the board. At least then you'll know the total cost of using a particular board.

This area of digital video is changing very rapidly so the list below may be outdated shortly after you read this:

Video Wizard—CEI ($1,995)

Win/TV Studio—Hauppauge Computer Works ($995)

M&M Pro—Omnicomp Graphics ($2,195)

Marvel—Matrox ($995)

 These boards include a wide variety of options that may not be reflected in the prices listed above. Contact the manufacturer for a full (and current) list of features and prices.

Caution   Many manufacturers tout the software packages that are bundled with their boards. Don't buy a piece of hardware for the software that comes with it. Get the board that best meets your needs. You can always buy the software you need later on. That's better than having to put out another large chunk of money for a new board because your board doesn't meet your demands.

Choosing the Final Storage Format

You've made your movie and now it's time to put it in a form that others can see and use. The best storage format for your particular movie depends on the size of the movie (or movies), the size of your audience, the probable delivery platform (playback device), and cost. Your basic choices are floppy disk, hard disk, removable media (magnetic or optical), and CD-ROM.

Storing on Floppy Disks

This option only works for small movies (less than 10 seconds), slightly longer movies (less than 30 seconds) that are heavily compressed, and animations. To reduce the file size, you can reduce the frame rate and reduce the quality setting on the compressor.

The advantage of this option, of course, is that every PC can read a floppy disk so it's a good format for video postcards and other short clips. The end user should copy the movie onto his or her hard drive before playing it.

Storing on a Hard Disk

If you are going to be displaying the movie on a dedicated machine, as in an information kiosk, then you can simply store the movie on your hard drive. Be sure to defragment your hard disk (or your partition) before you make the final movie so that the movie is stored as one uninterrupted string of data.

If possible, you should try to use a fast hard drive to play back the movie—one that is capable of transferring data at least 2MB per second. This helps eliminate any stutters or pauses while the movie plays.

Storing and Distributing on Removable Media

If the intended audience is likely to have a large hard drive and the capability of using removable media such as a SyQuest removable hard drive or a Sony floptical drive, then distributing on these formats might make sense.

You can store as much as 44, 88, or 105MB on a removable hard drive (depending on the format). You're better off using a 44MB removable drive because it can be read by an 88MB drive, but not vice versa.

You should use a limited amount of temporal compression. Different machines (486 vs. 386) play the movie back at different rates. More frequent key frames make it easier for the CPU to display a smooth sequence of frames.

Neither of these devices (floptical or removable hard drives) should be used for playback. The data transfer rates are usually much slower than a hard drive's. The intended users should be instructed to copy the video files to their hard drives before playing the movies.

Storing on CD-ROMs

If you intend to distribute your movies to a large number of people (more than 100), then you should consider producing a CD-ROM. A single CD can hold roughly 600MB of information—more than enough for most digital video applications. In addition, the cost of producing a hundred CDs works out to a couple of dollars per CD—not that much more expensive than a floppy disk. However, there are two main disadvantages with storing and distributing movies on a CD-ROM: seek time and data transfer rate.

CD Seek Time

Seek time is the amount of time it takes a CD player to find a particular file or portion of data on the disc. Depending on the CD player (some are faster than others), the average seek time is somewhere between 100 and 500 milliseconds (0.1 to 0.5 seconds). If you are distributing a collection of stand-alone movies, then a long seek time won't matter that much. But if your video files are part of an interactive application, then half a second can seem like an incredibly long period of time.

CD Data Transfer Rate

Once the CD player finds a particular video file, the quickest it can read the data off the disc is 150K per second for a single-speed drive or 300K per second for the newer double-speed drives. This is roughly half the data transfer rate of an average hard drive and one-twelfth the rate of a fast hard drive. This means that for your movies to play off a CD-ROM smoothly—that is, without pauses or huge jumps in the video—the data transfer rate (video and audio) can't exceed the maximum data rate of your CD. For a number of technical reasons, the maximum, practical data transfer rate from a CD-ROM is less than the maximum, about 90K per second for a single speed drive and 240K for a double-speed drive.

 Many developers are designing their products to run on double-speed drives to take advantage of the faster data rate. The products will run on single-speed drives but the frame rates of the video clips will be much less.

As mentioned in the technical discussions of compression earlier in this chapter, the actual data transfer rate required to play a movie accurately (at its set frame rate) is determined by a number of different parameters, including frame rate, window size, compression level, color-bit level, and the method of storage on the CD for the video and audio data. The simplest way to make sure your movie will play accurately is to set the maximum frame rate (in the Compression Options dialog box) to 90K per second for single-speed CD-ROMs and 240K per second for double-speed CD-ROMs, and use the Cinepak compressor.

Wrap-Up

Digital video on a PC would not be possible without image compression. It not only reduces the file sizes of digital video, but it also reduces the amount of data transferred between your computer and hard drive. The correct amount of compression varies from clip to clip and depends on the final format (storage device) for your movie. In general, you should try to digitize with little or no compression so that you are working with the highest-quality video clips in your editing program. You can then apply compression when the edited movie is finished. At some point, however, there is a trade-off between the level of quality you desire and the size of your hard disk(s). A good option is to use a removable drive, which allows you to add storage easily.

CHAPTER 14

Video and Interactive Multimedia

Digital video opens up almost unlimited possibilities for the use of video in interactive multimedia. In the past, multimedia developers who wanted to include video in their presentations had to produce a videodisc and use a videodisc player to play the video. Now with Video for Windows or QuickTime for Windows, developers can incorporate digital video without the time and expense of using videodiscs.

The field of interactive multimedia is huge and getting larger all the time. A thorough treatment of the topic is beyond the scope of a single chapter—it requires a whole book. Instead, this chapter discusses how video can be used within a multimedia presentation, examines some of the basic issues in interactive design, and offers a number of examples of the use of video in interactive programs.

What Is Interactive Multimedia?

First, let's get our terms straight. A *multimedia presentation* incorporates sounds and images (still images, text, animation, or video); so television is multimedia and so is a slide show put to music. *Interactive multimedia* involves the use of a computer, which allows the user to affect or control the presentation. The interaction between the user and the program transforms the experience from a passive one (such as television) to an active one, which can be more engaging and enriching.

Examples of Interactive Multimedia

In the past decade, thousands of interactive multimedia presentations or programs have been created. The presentations themselves differ widely; practically the only thing they have in common is that they are interactive. The following sections give brief descriptions of a few basic interactive presentations. They are intended to give you a sense of what interactive multimedia can do. By no means do they cover the complete spectrum of what is possible.

Example 1: A Business Presentation

The marketing manager for company XYZ has to talk at a large trade show. Two years ago, she produced a set of slides for a similar conference. But this time, she produced an interactive presentation that includes the following:

- An animation of the XYZ company logo
- An animated outline for her talk
- Various animations, text screens, and graphics describing the company's product
- Testimonials from customers (on video)
- A closing animation

At the conference, she controls the pace of the presentation by clicking the mouse to move to the next section. She has already prepared several additional short programs in anticipation of likely questions. In response to particular questions, she calls up the appropriate "answer" by clicking on an on-screen button.

Example 2: Patient Information

Hospital ABC cares for a predominantly older population. As such, it has a tremendous need to educate patients about chronic illnesses that affect senior citizens, such as heart disease, cancer, high blood pressure, and diabetes. In the past, it produced patient information videotapes for each of these subject areas.

The hospital's public services director decides to use interactive technologies to supplement the videotapes. He supervises the production of several public information kiosks that sit in the waiting areas of the hospital's large clinics. The kiosks include basic information about various conditions and diseases. Patients can learn more about any particular condition (symptoms, possible treatments, complications) that interests them. They can also view short patient case studies (on video) that offer much of the same information in a more personal format.

Example 3: Educational Products

The Educational Film Group, a video production company specializing in educational materials, has decided to produce interactive products based on its nature and science documentaries. The company re-edits its videos to produce 15 three-minute segments. It then incorporates these video segments into a text- and graphics-based interactive program. The students can read about a particular subject, see a graphic that describes it further, or view a video segment in which leading experts talk about the subject.

Why Use Video?

The examples just described all use video segments in some way, either to add credibility (business example); present information in a more personal way (hospital example); or tell short, encapsulated stories (educational example). These are all good reasons for using video within an interactive presentation. But as discussed in Chapter 13, there are drawbacks to using video:

- Digital video uses up a tremendous amount of memory on your hard drive. You can use CD-ROMs, but the access time is slower, which causes distracting delays in an interactive presentation.

- Most applications coming from a CD-ROM can only use small image dimensions (160×120 pixels to 320×240 pixels), which limits the amount of visual detail that can be shown in the video.

- Although video is not as expensive to produce as it once was, it is still expensive compared to other media (still images, graphics, text, etc.).

 Because of the current limitations of digital video, some interactive programs still use videodiscs. Videodiscs, which store video in analog form, can provide full-screen, full-motion video for less than digital video systems. This situation, however, is changing rapidly, and many people feel that videodiscs will no longer be an attractive option by late 1994.

Because of these drawbacks, you should have a good reason for using video in place of other media. Some justifiable reasons for incorporating video include the following:

- It is a personal form of communication. People like to see other people. We are used to hearing and seeing people talk to us (even if it is through the medium of video). You should make sure that your video has good production values (i.e., camerawork, lighting, sound, and editing).

- Video is particularly good for demonstrating procedures in training or educational projects because it shows how something moves over time.

- A visual story is a powerful means for delivering information with context. You not only can provide the details of a subject or situation but also can show how these details relate to larger issues, be they business, education, or personal.

- Using video adds a touch of novelty to your productions that can provide a competitive advantage. This novelty will wear off within a few years, but the early adopters can take advantage of this window to establish their reputations.

Designing Interactive Multimedia

There are countless ways to use video in an interactive program, but the best results will be achieved if you focus on what you are trying to accomplish with the program (and how video fits into that goal). Some of the questions you might want to consider are:

- Will the users be expected to make a lot of choices about what to see next?
- How often will users have to make a choice?
- Are you trying to deliver a specific set of details (as in training)?
- Will users be able to explore the material freely without a particular goal?
- Will video segments be short—for example, 10- to 20-second footnotes to other material?
- Will video segments be longer segments that form the core of the program?
- What is the amount of time a person is likely to spend using the program?
- How familiar is the average user likely to be with computers?

These are the types of issues interactive designers have to address when developing an interactive program. One way of approaching these issues is to evaluate the program in two ways: how much interactivity is required and how will information be organized (the conceptual layout).

Level of Interactivity

Interactive multimedia differs from television and other passive media in that the user controls the flow of the program. The extent to which the user controls the program, the *level of interactivity*, however, can vary from program to program. And this can affect how often the user is expected to interact.

Spectrum of Interactivity

A simple, yet revealing measure of interactivity is the number of interactions per minute.

With television, your only choice is to watch or not to watch. And if you skip to another channel, you will have missed something when you come back. With a taped program, you gain a bit more interactivity (you can replay a section or skip past the commercials), but most of the time you are just watching, not making any choices.

Interactions per minute: less than 1

Higher up on the spectrum of interactivity would be business presentations; for example, the business example discussed earlier. Here, the presenter controls the flow and pace of the presentation, moving from one segment to the next. Depending on the length of each segment, the presenter might make 10 to 20 choices for a 10-minute presentation.

Interactions per minute: 1–2

Information kiosks offer a bit more interactivity. Here you are trying to present a large amount of information to the user. The user doesn't need—or want—to see all the information. Therefore, a well-designed kiosk allows him or her to find any particular piece of information quickly. Depending on how long it takes the user to find and then absorb a particular piece of information (an *info bite*), the number of decisions, or interactions, the user has to make for a single, five-minute session might range from 20 to 50.

Interactions per minute: 4–10

Interactive programs for training and educational purposes can vary widely in their interactivity. If you are providing a lot of disconnected information (encyclopedic information), then the length of an info bite might be fairly short. But if you are presenting detailed information about particular subjects, the user might spend a long time (1–3 minutes) in the same area. Within each area, however, you can allow the user to control the flow of information.

Interactions per minute: 5–15

At the high end of the interactivity spectrum are computer games, the original interactive multimedia programs. *Pong* included images and sounds. A typical shoot-'em-up game can involve more than 100 interactions per minute. A more sedate game, such as a simulation game like *SimCity 2000*, might still require 10 interactions per minute. Even an educational game—such as *Where in the World Is Carmen San*

Diego?—involves at least 30 interactions per case, which last for about five minutes each.

Interactions per minute: 6–100

The levels of interactivity for various programs are shown graphically in Figure 14-1.

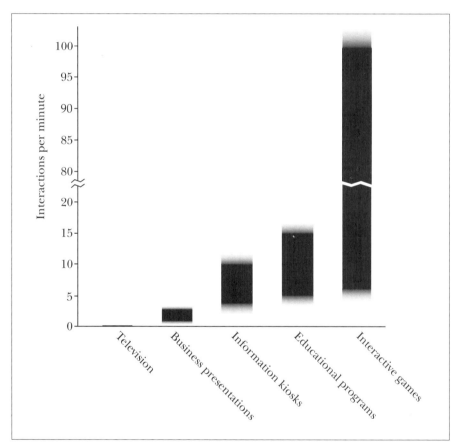

Figure 14-1.   Multimedia programs differ in the amount of interaction they require of the user. Games demand a lot of interaction, whereas business presentations require very little. (This chart is based on a presentation by Trip Hawkins at the January 1992 meeting of the International Interactive Communications Society in San Francisco.)

A general trend that seems to exist in this culture is that younger people tend to enjoy higher levels of interactivity than older people. Whether this is the result of exposure to fast-paced editing on television (MTV and elsewhere) or the prevalence of computer games, you should consider this trend when designing for your particular audience.

Video and Interactivity

Now what does all this have to do with video? Well, in most cases video is noninteractive: you generally watch a video clip from beginning to end. If you stop and pause in the middle of a clip and then start it again from the same point, it can be difficult to pick up the flow of the segment immediately, even if the pause is brief.

Because a video segment will generally be seen in one large block, you need to consider the length of your video segments in light of the level of interactivity. If you are designing a business presentation in which there are long periods without any interaction (low interactivity), then a fairly long (two-minute) video segment will seem natural. The same-length video segment will seem exceedingly long in the middle of a highly interactive game.

This doesn't mean that all the info bites within an interactive program have to be the same length. There is something to be said for providing a sense of pacing within an interactive program. But you need to consider the mix of your info bites and have a reason for making some longer than others. You should also make the user aware of the differences.

Choosing a Conceptual Layout

There are many different ways of organizing and compiling information. For example, consider the difference between an encyclopedia and a book on a particular topic. Even if you pull out of the encyclopedia all the parts related to the book's topic, the information is still organized alphabetically. On the other hand, the book organizes the subject material in a clear and understandable way (if it is written well), often at the expense of leaving out a lot of material.

In addition, there can be different strategies for searching for a particular subject or piece of information. For example, a table of contents and an index both allow the reader to find a particular topic.

One offers an outline-oriented approach (the table of contents), whereas the other is a strictly alphabetical list of subjects and key words.

With interactive multimedia, the organization and the search strategy are intimately linked. It is unlikely that the user will start at the beginning (if it is even defined that way) and go straight through to the end. Instead, the user will navigate through the information space along the pathways created by the interactive designer.

 Although we've been talking about organizing and finding information, we could just as easily be talking about parts of an interactive game.

This is like creating trails within a wilderness area for others to use. What parts of the wilderness do you want them to see (the waterfall, a beaver's nest, a lake, etc.)? How many paths do you want to create? Do you want there to be several key paths so that everyone sees the same things? Or do you want a myriad of paths so that each person ends up taking his or her own route?

This analogy ultimately breaks down because, with interactive multimedia, you are not limited to three dimensions as in the real world. The information space you create can have as many or as few dimensions as you like. Going back to the wilderness analogy, you could allow the person to jump immediately from one part of the wilderness to another, without having to walk the usual path between the two points.

The terms *conceptual layout* or *conceptual architecture* are often used to describe how an information space is organized and what types of pathways are used. A number of standard conceptual architectures have already been developed for interactive multimedia projects.

Types of Conceptual Architectures

Creating the conceptual architecture is often the first step in developing an interactive project. It lays an overall framework that is tied to the goals of the project. The following architectures differ widely in the types of user experience they allow.

 The figures for the various architectures are inherently inaccurate because they are two-dimensional representations of what are, in reality, three- (or more) dimensional information spaces.

Multibranched Tree Architecture   This allows the user to navigate to any particular piece of information (info bite) quickly (Figure 14-2). In some ways, it is like a layered table of contents. This architecture is often used for public information kiosks and training programs where a typical user is interested in only one particular part of the program and wants to find it quickly.

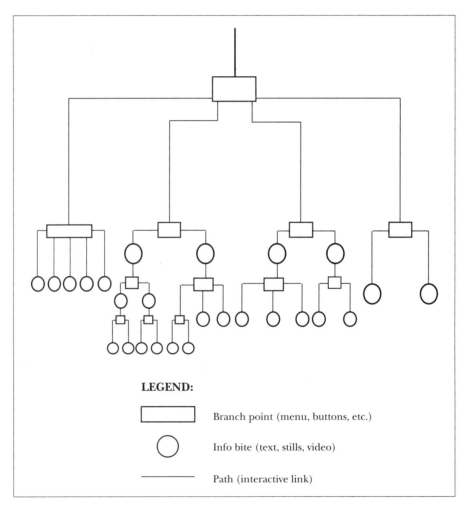

LEGEND:

Branch point (menu, buttons, etc.)

Info bite (text, stills, video)

Path (interactive link)

Figure 14-2.   The multibranched tree structure allows the user to retrieve any particular piece of information quickly. Many public information kiosks use this type of architecture.

Cross-Linked Architecture Here the user can move to any element from any other one (Figure 14-3). This architecture is useful when the amount of information isn't particularly large and ease of use is important. Marketing presentations often use this type of architecture because they will be used by a wide range of people with varying levels of computer sophistication and familiarity.

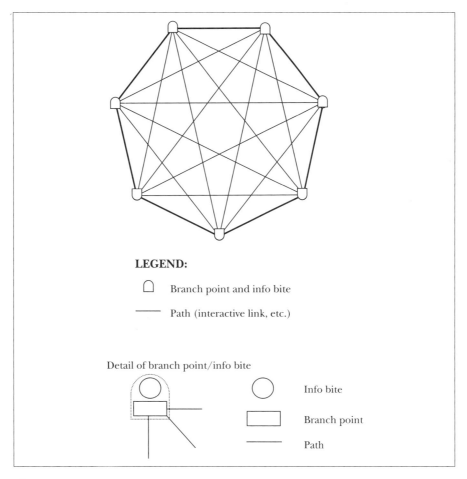

LEGEND:

⌂   Branch point and info bite

——   Path (interactive link, etc.)

Detail of branch point/info bite

○   Info bite

▭   Branch point

——   Path

Figure 14-3.   A cross-linked architecture allows the user to move easily between different parts of the interactive program. Generally used for programs that do not contain a lot of information.

Open-Exploration Architecture   This is similar to a cross-linked or branched-tree architecture that is extended to three dimensions (Figure 14-4). The user can jump from any info bite to a number of other info bites, either within the same general area (the same plane) or in a remote part of the architecture. An example of this architecture would be an online thesaurus.

The advantage of this architecture is that it allows the user to make complex connections between different pieces of information.

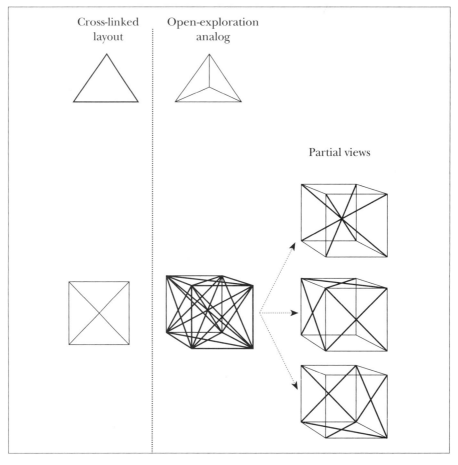

Figure 14-4.   The open-exploration architecture gives users the maximum amount of freedom in exploring the interactive program. An online thesaurus uses this type of architecture, as do many educational programs.

However, a key concern with this type of architecture is making sure the user knows where he or she is within the program (i.e., within the multi-dimensional information space). This type of architecture is often used for certain types of educational projects where the emphasis is on exploration as opposed to structured learning.

Linear-with-Branches Architecture In contrast to the previous architectures, this leads the user along a particular path (Figure 14-5). The user can gain additional information along the way, but the overall direction is set.

This type of architecture can be used to convert standard, linear, educational material into interactive presentations. The branches can contain video, animation, or additional text material that supports the main pathway.

LEGEND:

☐ Branch point

○ Info bite

— Path

Figure 14-5. A linear path with branches moves the user along a particular direction, while allowing the user to take side trips to explore various topics.

Multiple-Pathways Architecture   This also leads the user in a distinct direction. But instead of a single path, the user can travel—or be sent—along any one of many pathways. One example of this type of architecture is a tutorial that automatically offers additional information to those who need it (Figure 14-6). An example of where the user chooses the pathway is a program on history in which the user can view different perspectives of the same event (Figure 14-7).

 The conceptual architecture need not be visible to the user. You can create a metaphor that ties into the physical world or a fictionalized world. The user then interacts with the metaphor, not the architecture itself. This involves issues of interface design that are closely linked with the conceptual architecture.

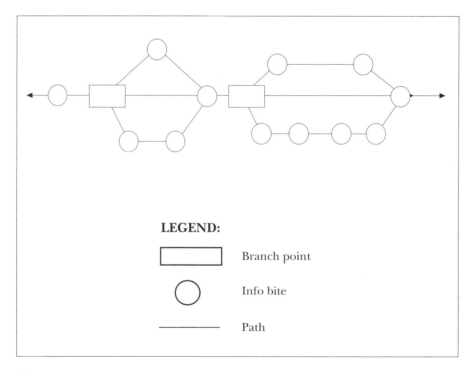

LEGEND:

Branch point

Info bite

Path

Figure 14-6.   Multiple pathways allow the user to take one of several parallel paths through particular parts of the program. A tutorial program that allows users to choose the speed at which they learn particular concepts is an example of a program that uses this type of architecture.

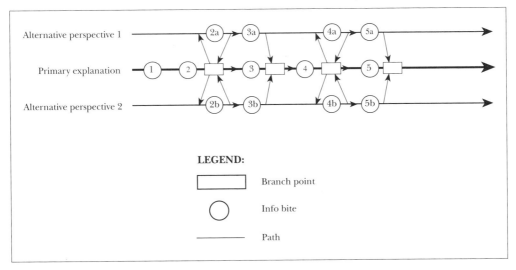

Figure 14-7.   A second type of the multiple-pathways architecture sets up several parallel paths that run the length of the program. At various points in the program, the user can choose to switch pathways or stay on the current one. An educational program that provides alternative perspectives of an historical event is a good example of this type of architecture.

Building upon the Conceptual Architecture

You may have noticed that the previous discussion barely mentioned which types of media would be used. That's because a conceptual architecture is only a blueprint for the project, not what the user will actually see. Depending on your particular project and your design constraints (amount of memory, type of computer, etc.), you can use whichever medium works best at a specific point in the program.

The mix of media you choose to use usually affects the conceptual architecture to some degree; in which case you need to modify the structure to suit the media. The advantage of starting with the conceptual architecture first is that it helps you determine the goals of your program and keeps you focused on your objectives.

Working Video into the Conceptual Architecture

Now, once again, what does all this discussion about conceptual architecture have to do with video? Again, the answer is that video is primarily a linear medium. Therefore, it can be used as an info bite in a linear portion of a conceptual architecture, or at the end of a branch. But it is difficult to include it as a branch point; if the user has to think about making a choice, then he or she is not concentrating on the video.

Advantages and Disadvantages of Various Media

When deciding which type of media (video, stills, animation, sound, text, etc.) to use in a specific part of a program, you should perform a kind of cost-benefit analysis: What am I gaining by using this medium, and can this topic be covered in another, less expensive way? The expense involves both the cost of producing or acquiring the material and the amount of memory it requires.

If you have an extremely large budget and unlimited hard disk memory, then you don't need to weigh these issues. But for those of us who feel these constraints, deciding which elements of the production are displayed in which media becomes a zero-sum game. Ultimately, you run out of memory (on your hard disk or CD-ROM), run out of money, or both. The following is a review of the various media and their respective benefits and drawbacks. See Table 14-1 for a comprehensive view of the various media.

Video

The benefits of using video are that it is a personal form of communication, it can show emotion and motion better than most other media, and it can add a touch of novelty to your program (at least for a while). Unfortunately, digital video requires an enormous amount of memory, many times more than any other medium (in terms of bytes per second). In addition, it is expensive to produce. And until hardware compression and decompression become cheaper, it won't be practical to present full-screen, full-motion video clips. Therefore, unless you plan to store your video segments on videodisc (which is not digital video), you should use video only when it adds something that cannot be achieved with other media (motion and emotion as mentioned before).

Table 14-1.   **Advantages and Disadvantages of Different Media and Their Approximate Storage Requirements**

Media Type	Storage (K/sec)	Advantages	Disadvantages
Video	$\approx 350^1$	Realistic, personal; conveys motion and emotion	Memory hog, expensive to produce
Stills	$\approx 15^2$	Realistic; can convey emotion	Static, moderate memory requirement
Animation	$\approx 170^3$	Displays certain types of information better than other media	Can be a memory hog, can be expensive to produce
Audio	$\approx 22^4$	Creates a more complex experience; music affects mood and tone	Moderate memory requirement
Text	0.033^5	Descriptive; cost per byte extremely low	Static, nongraphical

[1] 160×120 image dimensions, 24-bit color, 30 fps, compression ratio of 20 percent
[2] 320×240 image dimensions, 24-bit color, compression ratio of 20 percent, user views still for 3 seconds
[3] 160×120 image dimensions, 24-bit color, 30 fps, compression ratio of 10 percent
[4] 22 kHz sampling rate, 8-bit sample size, no compression
[5] Reading speed 400 words/minute, 5 characters/word, 1 byte/character

Still Images

Still photographs can provide a sense of realism, as video does, but without the same memory requirements. When used with an engaging soundtrack, still images can sometimes be more powerful than video because people look more deeply at the images, rather than allowing the moving images of video to wash over them.

The drawbacks to using stills are that they are static, and they cannot convey movement or the passage of time (although a series of stills can provide some). Another minor drawback is that even a still image requires a fair amount of memory (as much as a megabyte). You can reduce the memory requirements by decreasing the size of the image and/or using an image-compression scheme, such as JPEG.

Animation

It's difficult to evaluate a typical animation because there isn't one. Simple 2-D animations don't require much memory and can be produced inexpensively. Complex 3-D animations can cost thousands of dollars per second and require as much and sometimes more memory than video. However, there are certain concepts, particularly those dealing with science, that cannot be covered adequately by any other medium. If you intend to use such segments, be prepared to use a fair portion of your resources (memory and money) on these animations.

Sound

Nearly all interactive multimedia projects include some kind of sound. So it's not a question of whether or not to use sound; it's a matter of what kind of sound to use.

Audio feedback for an interaction, such as a beep when the user clicks a button on the screen, is an essential part of a good user interface. It helps connect the user with the program. And don't settle for simple sounds (like a beep); try using exotic sounds and sound effects, such as bird chirps, various musical instruments (triangle, tubular bell, flute, etc.), rasps, scraping sounds, and champagne corks. Get creative!

Music can dramatically improve an interactive program. Even short, five-second, musical cues enhance the user's experience. A typical use of musical cues is to introduce a new segment or make a transition to another part of the program. If you are going to be using a lot of music, you might want to consider using MIDI audio, which is stored as a score of notes and then recreated live during the presentation.

Digitized audio of speech or music can require a lot of memory, not as much as video but a large amount nonetheless—around 10MB per minute for CD-quality sound (stereo), about 2.5MB per minute for 8-bit, 22 kHz-quality audio.

Text

Last, there's humble old text. If you're going to be presenting a lot of detailed information, there's no better medium. It's cheap, easy to produce, and gets the point across.

Exploring the Possibilities

Perhaps the greatest impact of digital video is that it allows thousands more people to experiment in the intriguing and rich field of interactive multimedia. Sure, the video windows are small. But when compared to text or a still photograph, a digital video clip can provide a much deeper experience for the user. What will be produced? Who knows. What new forms of interactive multimedia will emerge? The possibilities are just now being explored.

This section offers some examples intended to demonstrate how video can be used to enhance interactive presentations. This review is not meant as a definitive list. It's provided with the hope that it will encourage you to go beyond what is presented here.

Scientific Communication

Scientific communication often includes still images that are snapshots of dynamic phenomena; for example, a graphic of how the earth's climate may change as global temperatures rise. With digital video, you can present a much richer picture of the dynamics of the system.

Technical Information

The program would start with an animation showing one prediction of how the climate might change over the next 20 years. This animation would include an explanation from the presenter (in voice-over). Following this short introduction, the user would be able to see additional information about the animation, such as:

- A technical paper about global climate change
- The technical details of how animation was created
- References to pertinent literature
- A summary of the technical paper written for the layperson

The program would also allow the user to replay the animation, forward or backward, at several different speeds.

Multiple Case Studies

A more comprehensive program would offer, in addition to the features just mentioned, several predictions based on differing basic assumptions for the climate model. By viewing the different cases, the user would be able to see the effect of various parameters and assumptions on the model's predictions.

Medical Information

With new medical discoveries and advances occurring nearly every day, it's almost impossible for patients (and doctors) to stay current with the latest information. Interactive programs can help manage this flood of data by giving people the information they need in a form they can use.

Patient Information Kiosk

The program would provide information on a number of different conditions (such as heart disease, cancer, and alcoholism). The users could choose to see a variety of different types of information about their condition. They could read about typical symptoms and possible treatments. They could also view case studies, in video segments, of real patients undergoing the procedure.

By using the kiosk, patients would be able to learn about the general issues regarding their condition. This would allow them to spend more time talking with the doctor about their particular situation.

Medical Procedures

One of the fastest-growing areas of medicine involves the use of sophisticated procedures. An interactive program could not only provide detailed explanations of a procedure but also include video segments showing the procedure itself. A more comprehensive version of the program could show the same procedure from several different camera angles. It could also present examples of typical problems that arise during the procedure. This program could be used in conjunction with a training course.

Educational Programs

The possibilities in the field of education are deep and profound. Interactive technologies could allow students to learn about particular topics in greater and richer detail. They could also offer a number of different methods for learning, which would be better geared to the different ways that people actually learn. Rather than replace the invaluable contribution of a teacher, these programs could shift education from a system of mass production to more intimate learning.

Intelligent Tutors

These programs would analyze a student's responses and modify the learning program to meet the student's needs. The student would be able to choose from a selection of tutors that would appear in a video segment and provide help. The selection of tutors could include people of different races, ages, and backgrounds.

New Perspectives on Social Studies

History and social studies have often been taught from one perspective—the one supported by the status quo. With interactive programs, you could allow students to review several different perspectives of the same issue, event, or period of time and come to their own conclusions. A set of uncontested facts would be presented and then the various perspectives on them could be viewed; for example:

- Views from Israelis and Arabs about the Mideast conflict
- Solutions from police and civil libertarians for reducing drug abuse
- Arguments for and against abortion
- Perspectives from Native Americans and early settlers about the expansion of white people across the continent

Business Uses

How a company manages its information is becoming as important as how it produces its products. Interactive programs can facilitate business communication in a number of important areas.

Training

According to some reports, the amount of in-house training done by companies equals the sum total of public education in this country on a yearly basis. Interactive programs could be used to tailor the training materials to the specific needs of individual workers. The program could also provide on-screen help in the form of helpers, or guides, who would offer encouragement and advice. The helper segments would be video segments of actors portraying different types of characters. The worker would be able to call on whichever character he or she preferred. Based on the situation, the program might also include the following:

- Humorous comments from the helper to create a more friendly and relaxed atmosphere

- Video segments showing how to use a particular piece of equipment or a software program

- Simulations of complex machinery or software programs that allow the worker to learn by trial and error

- Self-paced tests, which could be used for wage increases based on merit and skill

Marketing

The potential uses of interactive multimedia for marketing are too numerous to count. Here are some examples of existing programs.

Point-of-Sale Kiosks   These interactive programs give potential buyers a detailed look at a company's product. They often include flashy animations and customer testimonials.

Promotional Materials   Several companies have produced CD-ROMs that demonstrate and explain the company's services. They often include examples of recent projects.

Interactive Résumés (Personal Marketing)   An interactive résumé not only presents information about your background and talents but also indirectly demonstrates your use of interactive multimedia.

Wrap-Up

This chapter has barely touched upon the exciting possibilities in the field of interactive multimedia. The arrival of digital video has opened the door to new means of communication—not just with video, but with rich combinations of text, audio, video, and animation all interwoven in interactive programs. In such fast-moving times as these, it's often difficult to see how much things are really changing. But someday people may look back and say, "You mean they once made computers that only worked with words and numbers?"

PART IV

APPENDIXES

The following section is a resource guide for you to learn more about digital video, software, and hardware products. Appendix A is an annotated bibliography of books and magazines that provides additional insights on the topics covered in this book. Appendix B lists the addresses and phone numbers of companies that offer digital video products.

APPENDIX A

Suggested Reading

Books

Ambron, Sueann, and Hooper, Kristina, Eds. *Interactive Multimedia.* Redmond, WA: Microsoft Press, 1984. One of the first thorough treatments of interactive multimedia, this book still provides a lot of insight into the challenge of producing interactive programs. Discusses numerous case studies. Examination of technology issues is dated.

Anderson, Carol J., and Veljkov, Mark D. *Creating Interactive Multimedia.* Glenview, IL: Scott Foresman and Company, 1990. A clear overview of the process of producing an interactive multimedia program. Discusses the importance of including various experts in your production team.

Arijon, Daniel. *Grammar of the Film Language.* Los Angeles: Silman-James Press, 1976. A thorough explanation of editing theory. Chapters 3–7 provide detailed descriptions of how to shoot and edit common situations. Extensively illustrated with somewhat-sexist diagrams.

Dmytryk, Edward. *On Film Editing.* Boston: Focal Press, 1984. An entertaining and informative description of the film editing process. As both an editor and a director of numerous Hollywood films, Dmytryk gives an insider's view of the art of editing. Provides a good framework for people entering the editing craft.

Laurel, Brenda. *The Art of Human-Computer Interface Design.* Addison-Wesley Publishing Company, 1990. Although this book focuses solely on computer interface issues for Macintosh developers, the case studies provide great insights to the difficulty of producing intuitive, interactive interfaces.

Millerson, Gerald. *Lighting for Video*, 3d edition. Boston: Focal Press, 1991. An exhaustive compendium of lighting techniques for studio and remote locations. Clear explanations make it a good primer. There's even something for experienced video directors.

Millerson, Gerald. *Video Camera Techniques.* Boston: Focal Press, 1989. A comprehensive guide to the essentials of working with a video camera. Includes an extensive review of camera techniques and suggestions for common problem situations.

Reisz, Karel, and Millar, Gavin. *The Technique of Film Editing*, 2d Edition. Boston: Focal Press, 1991. The definitive book on film editing. Provides both a solid underpinning of editing theory and explanations of editing techniques. Includes an intriguing account of the history of film editing from its beginnings at the turn of the century. An essential book for anyone seriously interested in film or video editing.

Rubin, Michael. *Nonlinear.* Gainesville, FL: Triad Publishing Company, 1991. A complete but somewhat technical overview of nonlinear editing. Rubin, a multiformat editor (film, offline, and online videotape), has been an active player in the development of nonlinear editing systems. Contains an interesting historical review of the advent of videotape editing and nonlinear editing.

Speed, Austin H. *Desktop Video.* New York: Harcourt Brace Jovanovich, 1988. A practical layperson's guide to video production and analog editing. Discussion of technical issues somewhat dated.

Vaughan, Tay. *Multimedia*, Making It Work. New York: Osborne/McGraw-Hill, 1993. The complete guide to making multimedia productions. Extensive coverage of all aspects of multimedia including audio, video, text, graphics, and animation.

Magazines

Digital Video World
TechMedia Publishing, an IDG Company
80 Elm St.,
Peterborough, NH 03458
800-441-4403

Started in 1993, this magazine is a must-read for anyone wanting to stay in touch with the latest developments. Covers all platforms (PC, Mac, Amiga) with clear articles from industry experts.

New Media Magazine
Hypermedia Inc.,
901 Mariner's Island Boulevard, Suite 365
San Mateo, CA 94404
415-573-5170

Although this magazine is not devoted strictly to digital video, it does provide a good overview of what's happening in interactive multimedia. Coverage tends to focus more on products than techniques or analysis.

APPENDIX B

Company Information

Adobe Systems, Inc.
1585 Charleston Road,
P.O. Box 7900
Mountain View, CA 94039-7900
415-961-4400

AITech
47971 Fremont Blvd.
Fremont, CA 94538
800-882-8184

Apple Computer, Inc.
20525 Mariani Avenue
Cupertino, CA 95014
408-996-1010

Creative Labs
1901 McCarthy Blvd.
Milpitas, CA 95035
800-998-5227

Digital Vision
270 Bridge Street
Dedham, MA 02026
617-329-5400

Hauppauge Computer Works
91 Cabor Court
Hauppauge, NY 11788
516-434-1600

HSC Software
1661 Lincoln Blvd., Suite 101
Santa Monica, CA 90404
310-392-8441

Intel Corporation
2200 Mission College Blvd.
Santa Clara, CA 95054-1537
800-538-3373

Matrox
1055 St. Regis Blvd.
Dorval, Quebec
Canada H9P 2T4
514-685-2853

Media Vision
3185 Laurelview Court
Fremont, CA 94538
510-770-8600

Microsoft Corporation
One Microsoft Way
Redmond, WA 98052
206-882-8080

Omnicomp Graphics
1734 West Sam Houston Parkway North
Houston, TX 77043
713-464-2990

Sigma Designs
47900 Bayside Parkway
Fremont, CA 94538
510-770-0100

TouchVision Systems
1800 Winnemac Avenue
Chicago, IL 60640
312-989-2160

TrueVision
7340 Shadeland Station
Indianapolis, IN 46256
317-841-0332

GLOSSARY

A

A/B roll A type of video editing in which two inputs are merged through a special effect such as a wipe or dissolve. Used most often in analog editing.

Address track timecode A type of timecode that is laid down while a shot is being recorded. See *timecode.*

All-digital editing A method of editing a full-screen, full-motion video segment in digital form on a computer.

Authoring systems Applications programs that allow you to create, or author, interactive multimedia programs.

Auto-iris A common camera feature that automatically adjusts the lens iris to maintain proper exposure for a shot.

Available light The existing light in a scene. In outdoor locations, the sun; in indoor locations, the everyday lighting for the scene.

B

Barn doors A metal frame attached to a light consisting of four flaps that block parts of the light beam.

Back light A light placed behind a subject. Often used to create a rim of light around the edge of a subject, which helps the subject stand out from the background. Also known as a *rim light.*

Blue screening A video production technique in which the main subject is shot against a dark blue screen. The screen is then made transparent during editing. A standard technique for incorporating video footage with animation. See *chroma blue.*

Boom mike A microphone that is hung from a long pole, called a boom, over a subject.

Branch point In an interactive multimedia program, a part of the program that allows the user to make a choice.

Bump up The process of transferring video from one tape format to a higher quality one, as in "bumping-up from Hi-8 tape to Beta SP."

C

Camera move A shot where the camera framing changes. See *pan, tilt,* and *zoom.*

Chroma blue A blue color of a specific hue, saturation, and intensity used for superimposing a person or object over animation or another video shot.

Clip A segment of digital video.

Clip music Generic or background music, usually available on a compact disk, that does not require prior permission. Also called *needle-drop.*

Clipping A type of audio distortion caused by too much volume.

Close shot A camera framing that focuses on a particular object or person, extending from a several inches above the person's head to the top of their shirt.

Close-faced light A light that is covered by a Fresnel lens. Produces a concentrated beam of light.

Close-up   A camera framing that focuses tightly on a particular object or person, usually extending from the top of the person's hair to just under his or her chin.

Codec   Short for a "compression/decompression" technique. Can be a piece of hardware equipment or a software program.

Color temperature   A measure of a light's color based on the temperature of the light-emitting element.

Compositing   An editing technique in which individual elements are added to a video clip one at a time.

Compression   The process of reducing the amount of information required to store an image or a segment of digital video. See *lossy* and *lossless*.

Conceptual architecture   A blueprint for an interactive multimedia program. Specifies how a user will access different parts of the program. Also known as a conceptual layout.

Constant-effect filter   In Adobe Premiere, filters that produce dynamic effects, but the level of the effects do not change over the course of a clip.

Continuity   A style of editing that attempts to create the illusion of reality by making people's motions and positions seem accurate and plausible. During production, the process of making sure that an actor's position or appearance does not change from take to take. See *mixed format* and *montage*.

Crane shot   A shot that is taken from a camera platform at the end of a crane. Generally used to follow upward motion or to provide a different vantage point on a scene.

Cross-fade   An audio editing technique used to blend two audio clips at a transition. The first audio clip is faded out while the second audio clip is faded in.

Crossing over the line   The act of crossing the line of interest in a scene, which switches the positions of the subjects on the screen. See *line of interest.*

Cut   1. (*n*) A portion of a digital video clip as defined by an In and Out point. 2. (*n*) A simple edit where one video clip follows another without a special effect. 3. (*v*) To perform a simple edit.

Cutaway   A shot taken from a different camera angle or with a different camera framing than the main camera shot. See *master shot.*

Cutting   Performing a simple edit as in "cutting from shot 1 to shot 2."

D

Decompression   The process of creating a viewable digital image or video clip based on a compressed file. See *compression.*

Depth of field   The range of distances where a subject is seen in focus.

Dialog cutting   A type of editing involving human speech.

Difference frame   In temporal compression, a frame that is stored as the difference between it and the previous key frame. See *key frame.*

Diffuser   A translucent material placed in front of a light to convert hard light to soft light. Can also be used to reduce the intensity of a light.

Digitize   To convert an analog signal, such as video or audio, into a digital format.

Dolly shot   A shot taken from a moving camera. The camera and tripod are placed on a moving platform called a dolly.

Drop-frame timecode   A type of timecode used in online editing systems for final video segments. It follows real (clock) time by dropping two frames every minute. See *non–drop-frame timecode.*

Dropout   A black spot or spots in a video image caused by imperfections in the videotape.

Dub   1. (*n*) A copy of a videotape. 2. (*v*) To make a copy of a videotape.

Dynamic filter   In Adobe Premiere, a filter whose effect changes over the course of a clip.

Dynamic tracking   A device used in online editing systems that allows you to play a videotape at frame rates other than 30 frames per second.

E

Edit controller   An analog editing device that controls two or more videotape machines to produce edits.

Edited master   In analog editing, the original version of an edited video segment or program.

Encoder   A device that converts an RGB (red, blue, green) signal into an NTSC signal. Used for recording digital video clips onto videotape.

Establishing shot   A shot that depicts the main elements of a scene and the background. Most often a long or full shot used at the beginning of a scene.

F

Fade control   In Adobe Premiere, an audio control that allows you to adjust the volume or level of an audio clip.

Fade in   To increase the level of an audio clip from zero to an audible level.

Fade out   To decrease the level of an audio clip until it cannot be heard.

Field   One half of an interlaced frame of video. The odd field is made up of lines 1, 3, 5, etc.; the even field consists of lines 2, 4, 6, etc.

Finger   In Adobe Premiere, a hand-shaped cursor used to adjust an audio or motion handle.

Fix list   A list of jump cuts or other problem edits to be fixed during the final edit.

Foley   An audio special effects technique in which you try to create a set of footsteps that match a person's steps in a video clip.

Frame rate   The number of video frames displayed per second. Videotape is played at a constant 30 frames per second. Digital video frame rates range from 1 to 30 fps.

Frame   A single image of a continuous video segment. In analog video, a frame lasts $1/30$ second.

Framing   The image inside the viewfinder of a camera. Also known as the camera framing.

Freeze frame   A still frame created from a segment of video. Often used in special effect transitions.

Fresnel lens   A lens placed over certain types of lights to create a concentrated beam of light.

Full shot   A shot that shows a person's entire body.

G

Gel   A piece of transparent, colored plastic placed over a light to alter the color of the light.

H

Hand held   A camera technique in which the camera is placed on the camera operator's shoulder or carried in his or her hands (as opposed to being set on a tripod).

Handle   In Adobe Premiere, a point created along the audio fade control line to alter the level of an audio clip. Handles are also used in Premiere's motion feature.

I

In point   The beginning of a cut. Also known as the In.

In synch   A situation in which the audio and video are matched in time.

Incremental progression   In Adobe Premiere, a technique of changing the effect of a filter over time in a stepwise fashion.

Info bite   In an interactive multimedia program, a unit of information that is absorbed in a continuous period of time. See *branch point*.

Information space   A multi-dimensional space consisting of particular pieces of information and the links between them.

Interactive multimedia   A presentation consisting of images and sounds that is controlled by the user.

Intercut   An editing technique in which shots from two different cameras are interwoven. The material from each camera can be of the same scene, or different scenes.

Interlaced video   An analog video signal consisting of alternating odd and even fields.

J

Jump cut   An edit in which a person or an object seems to move abruptly or in an unnatural motion.

K

Key frame In temporal compression, a frame that is stored as an entire image.

Key light The main source of light in a scene. It is usually the strongest of the three common types of lights: key, fill, and back lights.

L

Layer To add a new element on top of a video image. Often used in conjunction with compositing, as in to layer another element during compositing.

Level The volume of an audio clip or source.

Level of interactivity In an interactive program, the average amount of interaction required of the user per unit of time.

Limbo shot A shot in which there is no visible background. Usually created by moving the key and fill lights to either side of the subject so that they don't illuminate the background.

Line of interest An imaginary line that runs through the central elements in a scene. Once you have determined a line of interest for a scene, you must keep the camera on one side of the line or else the main subjects will switch positions in the shot.

Log 1. (*n*) A list of the positions and content of video shots within a videotape. 2. (*v*) To write down the position and content of video shots within a videotape.

Long shot A camera framing that shows the overall layout of a scene. Is often used to establish a scene and its main elements. Also called a wide shot.

Loop In audio editing, to repeat a section of audio—for example, to repeat the sound of a police siren several times.

Lossless   A type of image compression in which there is no loss of image quality after decompression.

Lossy   The opposite of lossless compression—image quality is decreased through compression and decompression.

M

Master shot   A shot showing a major part or all of a particular scene, action, or procedure. Provides the main view of an action or scene.

Match length   When matching an event in a video clip with a particular sound in the audio track, the amount of time from the last edit to the video event.

Medium shot   In most general terms, a camera framing between a full shot and a close shot, usually extending from about a foot over a person's head to just above his or her waist.

Mix down   In audio editing, the process of adjusting the levels of several audio sources or clips to achieve the optimum balance.

Mixed format   A style of editing that combines impressionistic images with text, graphics, and often narration. Often used for commercials and music videos. See *continuity* and *montage*.

Montage   A style of editing in which there is no attempt to create the illusion of reality. Emphasis is placed on the impressionistic and emotional value of images and the juxtaposition of the images.

Multimedia   A presentation consisting of images and sounds. See *interactive multimedia*.

N

Nat sound   Short for "natural sound." The sound naturally occurring in a scene, also known as wild sound.

Needle-drop   Music that can be used in video segment or multimedia presentation without prior approval. When contained on a compact disc, it is often called clip music. See *clip music.*

Neutral shot   In continuity editing, a shot directed along the line of interest of a scene. It is used to establish a new line of interest.

Non–drop-frame timecode   A numbering system that assigns a unique number to each frame of video in the format *hours:minutes:seconds:frames*. Because video runs at 59.997 frames per second, non-drop–frame timecode is not exactly the same as clock time. See *drop-frame timecode.*

Non-interlaced   The standard form of images on a computer. The monitor displays the image by drawing one line after another from top to bottom on the screen. See *interlaced.*

O

Odd field   One of the two fields making up a single frame of video. Consists of all the odd-numbered lines in an image.

Online   A sophisticated editing system used to create the final version of a video segment. Usually includes frame-accurate video decks that are controlled by an edit controller, and a switcher that allows the editor to mix two video sources.

Open up   To increase the aperture of a camera lens, which increases the overall brightness of a shot.

Out point   The end of a cut. Also known as the Out.

Overlapping   In Adobe Premiere, a situation in which two video or audio clips are located on different tracks but share the same part of a timeline. Video overlaps are used to create special effects. Audio overlaps are used to cross-fade the audio between two clips.

P

Pad In audio editing, the amount of time between when a person starts talking and the In point of the clip, or the time from when a person stops talking and the Out point of the clip. Usually between five and seven frames long.

Pan A camera move in which the camera moves from side to side.

Panning The act of making a camera pan.

Paper cut A rough outline of a video segment created on paper. Usually the second step, after logging, in preparing to edit a video segment.

Pass In compositing, one step in the process of adding elements to a video clip. The addition of each new element results in a pass.

Pixels Short for "picture element." One of the small dots on a computer screen that make up an image. A standard 13-inch computer screen consists of 307,200 pixels (640 columns by 480 rows).

Progressive effect filters Filters whose effect can be changed over the course of a video clip.

R

Rack focus A camera technique in which the focus is changed during the shot. Used to shift the viewer's attention from a foreground element to a background element in a scene (or vice versa).

Raw video Uncompressed digital video.

Receiver In audio recording, a device that receives a signal from a wireless microphone.

Record deck In analog editing, a video deck that records video signals provided by source decks.

Refresh The process of redrawing an image on a computer monitor. Many monitors refresh the screen 60 times a second.

Reverse shot A shot showing a subject from the opposite angle. In an interview situation, a shot showing the interviewer.

Rim light A light that produces a rim of light around the edge of a subject. Also known as a *back light*.

Room tone The natural ambience of an interior location.

Rough assembly The initial rough edit of a video segment. Sometimes called a rough cut.

Rule of thirds A standard method of composing a shot in which the screen is divided into thirds and the central element is placed along one of these divisions.

S

Scratch narration A rough, preliminary narration used while editing the rough cut. It is usually recorded in the edit room during editing.

Scrim A wire screen placed over a light to reduce the light's intensity without affecting its color.

Scrubbing In Adobe Premiere, a technique for previewing an edit by moving the mouse along the time ruler.

Seek time The amount of time it takes a CD-ROM player to find a particular piece of data on a CD-ROM disc.

Simple dissolve In Adobe Premiere, a technique for fading a filter in or out by dissolving between the filtered cut and an unfiltered copy.

Sound bite A short video and audio segment of a person talking. Usually lasts between 5 and 30 seconds.

Source deck   In analog editing, a video deck that provides a video signal for editing. See *record deck*.

Special effects   There are two types of special effects: video and audio. Video special effects are used to create transitions between two adjoining video cuts. Audio special effects are additional sounds, either natural or produced, used to enrich a soundtrack.

Split screen   A visual effect in which two video images appear in different halves of the screen—most often side by side.

Static filters   In Adobe Premiere, filters whose effect does not change over the course of a clip.

Stop down   To reduce the aperture of a camera lens, which decreases the overall brightness of a shot.

Storyboards   Rough sketches depicting an edited scene. Used during pre-production to determine how a scene will be shot.

Stretch pointer   In Adobe Premiere, a cursor consisting of two vertical lines and arrows pointing outwards, used to change the duration of a cut.

Sun gun   A small portable light often used in outdoor locations as a fill light.

Super   1. (*n*) An image that is placed over a video image. Part of the overlaid image is transparent. 2. (*v*) To place one image over a video image and make part of the overlaid image transparent.

Switcher   In analog editing, a device that combines two input video signals into a single output signal. Often includes the capability to combine the input video signals in a number of ways, such as with a dissolve or wipe.

Synch   Short for "synchronize." To adjust the timing of an audio and video clip so that the audio matches the action in the video.

T

Take   One of several repeated shots of a particular action or scene.

Talking head   A person talking in a shot.

Three-quarter shot   A standard camera framing for an interview in which three-quarters of the person's face is seen.

Tilting   A camera move in which the camera is tilted up or down.

Timecode   A numbering system that assigns a unique number to each frame of a videotape using the format *hours:minutes:seconds:frames*. See *drop-frame* and *non–drop-frame timecode*.

Timecode generator   A device used to add timecode to a videotape.

Time ruler   In Adobe Premiere, a timeline at the top of the Construction window that indicates the position of clips in the final video segment.

Time unit selector   In Adobe Premiere, a control that allows you to adjust the resolution of the time ruler.

Treatment   A statement of the goals and purpose of a video segment. Often the first step in producing a video piece.

Two-Shot   A shot containing two people, often used to separate two people within a larger group.

V

Vérité   A production technique, often used in documentaries, in which the action is shot as it happens and no attempt is made to control or affect the action.

Video capture board   A device that converts an analog video signal into digital information. Often consists of a circuit board that is placed inside a computer.

VITC   Vertical interval timecode. A type of timecode that is placed in a particular part of the video signal (the vertical interval).

Voice-over   An audio clip of someone talking that is used without the video portion.

W

Walking shot   A shot in which the camera operator walks with the camera during the shot.

Waveform   A representation of an audio signal or clip. Indicates the volume of the clip over time.

Window dub   A copy of a timecoded videotape that displays the timecode in a window laid over the video image.

Wireless microphone   A microphone that does not require a wire between the microphone and the recording device.

Work area   In Adobe Premiere, a portion of the Construction window. It is the part shown during a preview.

Z

Zoom   A camera move in which the camera framing becomes larger or smaller, as in "to zoom out from a close shot to a medium shot."

INDEX

Other Prima Computer Books

Available Now!

1-2-3 for Windows: The Visual Learning Guide	$19.95
WINDOWS Magazine Presents: Access from the Ground Up	$19.95
Adventures in Windows	$14.95
CompuServe Information Manager for Windows:	
The Complete Membership Kit & Handbook (with two 3 ½" disks)	$29.95
CorelDRAW! 4 Revealed!	$24.95
Create Wealth with Quicken	$19.95
WINDOWS Magazine Presents: Encyclopedia for Windows	$29.95
Excel 4 for Windows: The Visual Learning Guide	$19.95
Excel 5 for Windows: The Visual Learning Guide	$19.95
Free Electronic Networks	$24.95
WINDOWS Magazine Presents:	
Freelance Graphics for Windows: The Art of Presentation	$27.95
Harvard Graphics for Windows: The Art of Presentation	$27.95
Improv 2.1 Revealed! (with 3 ½" disk)	$27.95
Lotus Notes 3 Revealed!	$24.95
Microsoft Works for Windows By Example	$24.95
PageMaker 5 for Windows: Everything You Need to Know	$19.95
Quicken 3 for Windows: The Visual Learning Guide	$19.95
Smalltalk Programming for Windows (with 3 ½" disk)	$39.95
Superbase Revealed!	$29.95
Windows 3.1: The Visual Learning Guide	$19.95
Windows for Teens	$14.95
Word for Windows 2: The Visual Learning Guide	$19.95
Word for Windows 2 Desktop Publishing By Example	$24.95
Word for Windows 6: The Visual Learning Guide	$19.95
WordPerfect 5.1 for Windows Desktop Publishing By Example	$24.95
WordPerfect 6 for Windows: The Visual Learning Guide	$19.95
Your FoxPro for Windows Consultant (with 3 ½" disk)	$39.95

To order by phone with Visa or MasterCard, call (916) 786-0426, Mon.–Fri., 9–4 Pacific Standard Time.

To order by mail fill out the information below and send with your remittance to: Prima Publishing, P.O. Box 1260, Rocklin, CA 95677-1260.

Quantity	Title	Unit Price	Total
_____	_____	_____	_____
_____	_____	_____	_____
_____	_____	_____	_____
_____	_____	_____	_____
_____	_____	_____	_____

Subtotal _____

7.25% Sales Tax (CA only) _____

Shipping* _____

Total _____

Name _____

Street Address _____

City _____ State____ ZIP _____

Visa/MC# _____ Exp. _____

Signature _____

* $4.00 shipping charge for the first book and 50¢ for each additional book.